THE
ELEPHANTS
IN MY
BACKYARD

a memoir

RAJIV SURENDRA

RANDOM HOUSE CANADA

PUBLISHED BY RANDOM HOUSE CANADA

www.penguinrandomhouse.ca

Random House Canada and colophon are registered trademarks.

Library and Archives Canada Cataloguing in Publication

Surendra, Rajiv, 1989–, author
The elephants in my backyard / Rajiv Surendra.

Issued in print and electronic formats.

ISBN 978-0-345-81680-1
eBook ISBN 978-0-345-81682-5

1. Surendra, Rajiv, 1989–. 2. Motion picture actors and actresses—
Canada—Biography. I. Title.

PN1998.3.S87A3 2016   791.4302'80922   C2016-904542-0

Text design by Nancy Singer
Jacket design by Leah Springate
Interior and jacket illustrations by Rajiv Surendra
Jacket photography by James Tse

Printed and bound in the United States of America

10 9 8 7 6 5 4 3 2 1

Penguin
Random House
RANDOM HOUSE CANADA

TO

SETH ROLAND BAIRD,

EDITOR AND CHIEF AND CHIEF EDITOR,

ICH SAGE AUCH DANKE.

"Every life is in many days, day after day. We walk through ourselves, meeting robbers, ghosts, giants, old men, young men, wives, widows, brothers-in-love. But always, meeting ourselves."

— James Joyce,
Ulysses

1.

W HEN I WAS a kid, my parents would dress my two sisters and
me in traditional Indian garb and cart us off to the Hindu temple in Richmond Hill, where portly bare-chested Brahmin priests in
white loincloths chanted sacred Sanskrit prayers in front of huge granite idols. The stone gods were brilliantly dressed in bright red, yellow,
purple, and green silks, flower garlands, and jewelry encrusted with
precious gems. I was in heaven. Brass bells ringing loudly, ancient fire
rituals, and hundreds of other Tamil people packed into the temple,
each vying for a glimpse of the idol. Looking up at the smiling face
of Vishnu, who would give me whatever I asked for if I prayed hard
enough, was something that filled my little two-year-old heart with im-
mense joy.

My religious fervor wasn't restricted to just Hinduism. My Irish
aunt Brigid (my uncle had scandalously married outside the Tamil
race) took me to Catholic Mass with her on Sundays, and here was
yet another story, another house of God soliciting my devotion. A bit
more gruesome, with blood dripping from the wounds of this white
man hanging on a cross, but still otherworldly. It didn't matter that I
couldn't understand a word of Latin, or that I wasn't allowed to go up
with Aunty Bridgy to get that little piece of Communion bread and sip

of wine—she'd always sneak back a piece of the wafer for me, whispering that this was where I belonged.

One Sunday, Aunty Bridgy assured me it was okay that we were missing Mass—the Holy Mother had appeared to a farmer in a small town three hours away from Toronto, instructing him to gather the flock, for she would come again for those who believed. So there we were in the car, driving for ages along a lone country road, with the hopes that she (excuse me, *She*) would show herself to us. We joined hundreds of others who had staked out a claim with their picnic blankets and folding chairs in the farmer's field on that sunny fall afternoon. We never did see Mary, but Aunty Bridgy assured me that She was there, in all our hearts. Frankly, just between you and me, I would have preferred to have actually seen what color robe the Blessed Virgin had chosen to wear that day.

Being encouraged to have faith in something that was so incredibly fantastical was fuel for my wild imagination, especially as I got older and it started becoming clear that I wasn't really allowed to live my life in the story-filled world I loved. Ma would throw open my bedroom door on school nights and catch me in the act of jumping off my bed, dressed up as a Greek warrior, practicing my sword-fighting drills, or ceremonially draping a towel over my head and shoulders, a lone Bedouin preparing to cross the Sahara—then she'd reprimand me for neglecting my math homework. But I couldn't help myself, and I continued to find ways of blurring the lines between the fictitious realm in which I wanted to live, and the real one I was born into.

Our house backed onto a huge valley that bordered the Toronto Zoo, and in the evenings I'd hear elephants, lions, and wolves through my bedroom window. I was twelve when I was overcome with the need to play zookeeper myself and build a chicken coop in my backyard. My dad loved the idea, but there was much protesting from Ma. We already had a pet, she said, our little shih tzu named Meesha. Which I had to share with my sisters, I argued; I wanted chickens for myself. "They smell, child," Ma insisted impatiently, "and they make noise. And I doubt it very much that we are allowed to have chickens in the backyard."

I heaved the giant telephone directory onto the kitchen table one afternoon, looked up the number for the city zoning office, and eventually ended up speaking to a woman who sounded like she was fed up with the mundane questions she had to answer all day.

"No," she grunted, "you're in a residential zone. No animals of a barnyard nature can be legally kept in your area." We lived in Scarborough, the most eastern suburb of Toronto, in an urban subdivision where the houses were only twenty feet apart. There was a pause, and then she continued, "But . . . we won't know about it unless one of your neighbors complains."

"Does that mean I can keep them, if they don't bother the neighbors?!" I asked excitedly.

"We won't *know about it*," she repeated, louder this time, " . . . unless your *neighbors complain!*"

Ma finally caved and I filled my coop with Araucana hens—a South American breed that lay beautiful blue- and green-shelled eggs. The backyard, laden with the trumpeting of elephants, the occasional roar from a lion, and finally, the soothing sound of six little hens clucking away became my own little kingdom. I was mayor of Chickentown, keeping a watchful eye on my flock and breaking apart petty squabbles as the hens established their pecking order. Giddy with excitement, I'd wake up every morning at five and rush down to the backyard to greet my hennies as they emerged from their brooding house, bleary-eyed. They'd move lethargically and let out long, drawn-out squawks. I'd echo back their noises while I filled up their feeding trough and replenished their water. A handful of kitchen scraps never failed to send them into an instant flurry, rummaging fervently through bits of cabbage, carrot skins, and apple cores.

At thirteen, I took my love of quiet, nostalgic domestic practices, like tending to livestock, to the next level when I began volunteering at Black Creek Pioneer Village—a historic site just north of Toronto, where a collection of buildings from the 1800s depicted life in a typical rural Ontario village in the nineteenth century. Twice a month, I'd change into my pioneer costume and apprentice with the blacksmith, the cabinetmaker, the baker, or the weaver.

I first went to Pioneer Village on a school trip in second grade, during a mandatory unit on pioneers. My classmates and I were sitting on the pine floor of the farmer's log cabin as the tour guide warned our class not to touch anything and then started her spiel, but I couldn't hear her—I was completely in awe of the huge squared pine logs that made up the walls and ceiling, the fieldstone fireplace, the flaking red paint on the harvest table and the gnarly wooden bowl that sat on it. Everything here was two hundred years old, yet I felt so at home.

I was always more at peace in my imaginary worlds than beneath the actual roof I lived under. Things weren't always pleasant growing up.

I must have been about three years old when my big sister and I were drawing on the concrete walls of our basement with sticks of chalk one evening. A door slammed loudly, jolting us out of our coloring daze, and we turned to face each other, fearing we were about to be caught in the act. Ma was running down the stairs, still dressed in her office clothes—a knee-length blue-and-white dress and sheer, black pantyhose.

"Come. Come here, baby!" Ma called to me, smiling. There was something disturbing about her smile though; her lips were quivering as she extended her arms toward me, her fingers frantically gesturing for me to run into her grasp. There was the usual sweetness in Ma's voice but she was panting heavily. I dropped my chalk as she scooped me up and gently rested my head on the thick shoulder pad of her dress. I inhaled Ma's scent—a soothing mix of fresh laundry and Avon lipstick. Another door slammed, closer this time, and suddenly we could hear my dad's slurred shouting, booming down from the top of the stairs.

"Come, darling, quickly," Ma whispered to my sister, taking her by the hand while looking over her shoulder. I lifted my head to follow her gaze and caught sight of my dad, running at us with a butcher knife. He continued to yell as he stumbled forward, shirtless, his legs pulling his faded green cotton sarong taut with each stride, his bald head and his flat nose glistening with sweat under the lone lightbulb that hung from a wire in our unfinished basement.

Just hours before, he had been feeding us a dinner of rice and chicken curry, while Ma was still at work. Now, his bloodshot eyes were bulging out of his head as he lunged toward us. My eyes fell to my sister below, scurrying alongside Ma as my head bobbed up and down while we ran up the stairs to the main floor. My dad wasn't far behind and he lifted the knife high into the air as he chased us from room to room, continuing to yell at the top of his lungs, a deafening, growling sound full of fury. Ma was managing to stay ahead of him, until he cornered us in the study room—the tiny side room off the main hall where a lone desk stood beside a big, gray melamine pantry cupboard that held Ma's excess cooking ingredients—large glass jars of spices, sugar, rice, red lentils, and packets of plastic-wrapped tamarind.

Ma pushed my face into her shoulder while she shouted out frantically, her voice breaking. I could hear her crying as she barked back at my dad. There was a brief moment of silence. I jerked my head up to catch my dad on the floor with the knife beside him and Ma opening the other door of the study room—the one that led to our garage. The garage happened to be open to the street and there was still some light out on that summer evening—Ma scurried down the three plywood steps into the dim garage and the spring-loaded door slammed shut behind us. She was putting me down when the door flung back open with my yelling dad silhouetted in its frame, knife in tow.

"Run, children!" Ma shouted, crying while darting her eyes between us and my dad. "Run outside!"

"No, Ma, *nooooooo* . . ." I bawled, grabbing on to the hem of her thin dress just as my dad pressed the large, white, square button for the garage door. The creaking mechanics came alive with the heavy sound of rattling metal and the garage started getting darker as the paneled wooden door descended.

"Run, baby, go!" Ma pushed me away from her and I took my sister's hand, running with her. We made it outside and turned to face Ma but she was still inside. I can clearly remember standing on the pink concrete pavers of our driveway watching in complete horror as that huge door moved down in front of us.

I stopped breathing and started gasping for air, not knowing whether I would ever see Ma again. And there, behind us, in the street on that humid summer evening, the neighbor kids were playing basketball and laughing cheerfully.

There was only about a foot of space left before Ma finally rolled out of the darkness and onto the driveway. She brushed herself off, stood up quickly and then readjusted her dress, turning her head to see whether the neighbors were watching. I looked up at her—two wavy black lines ran down her cheeks and circled her fuchsia-colored lips. Her mouth was still quivering as she smiled down at me. She looked up toward the sky and blinked her eyes repeatedly, running both her index fingers along her lower eyelids and partially smearing the wavy black lines on her face. And then she picked me back up and took my sister's hand.

It took a few years for me to realize that my dad had a problem—

one that was linked to the glass bottles he'd bring home in a paper bag every few days and swiftly escort down to a corner in our basement.

While I eventually grew out of my religious obsessions, Ma continued to turn in solace to the elephant-headed god, Ganesha, Lord Overcomer of Obstacles. I'd sometimes spot her praying to the idols in the linen closet that had been converted into a mini shrine, her eyes pursed shut and her hands pushed together in prayer. I wondered what she was asking for.

I had developed my own ways of coping.

Escaping to the worlds in my head became so appealing to me I eventually began thinking about making it a real part of my life.

Ma wasn't supportive or enthusiastic about me pursuing yet another distraction from school, but when I landed my first official audition at twelve years old, I begged her to drive me downtown. She didn't say much as she reluctantly maneuvered our giant white Buick along narrow one-way streets, making our way into the heart of the city.

"Don't be nervous, darling," Ma uttered finally, as she led the way up a steep flight of creaky wooden stairs to the casting office. There was a warmth in her tone that surprised me, and I sensed that her impatience with my outlandish endeavors might be fading away.

The audition was for an episode of a spooky kids TV series called "Goosebumps," based on the novels by R. L. Stein. I have absolutely no recollection of what happened during the actual audition. What I do remember is that I went home and immediately checked the answering machine, disappointed that there was no call. The next day I was fidgety in school, dying to return home in the hopes that there was a message from my agent, Clibby. I took matters into my own hands, and began calling her every couple of days, only to hear that she didn't know yet. And then eventually I called and asked, yet again, "Have you heard back, Clibby? Did I get the part?"

"No, kid, you didn't. And if you had, I would have called you, okay? You can't call me after every audition, okay?" It took a couple of years before I could go to an audition, give it my best try, and then forget about it.

I knew I needed a teacher, a coach, who could help me look at my work in a constructive way.

Marcia was well-known in the circle of young Toronto actors; she taught regular auditioning workshops and was hired by major television shows as their on-set acting coach. She was also a veteran character actress in her fifties, with dozens of small roles on television shows, movies, and commercials. I would see her on TV regularly, while flipping through the channels—playing the role of a sweet-natured grandmother in a weekly movie or touting the noteworthy traits of a special denture grip in a popular commercial.

I started bi-weekly private coaching classes with Marcia when I was fifteen—I'd get on the bus after school and travel in the direction opposite home, heading out of the suburbs into the city proper, to a slightly sketchy part of the downtown core.

There was a turning point in my meetings with Marcia. She had given me a scene from a movie in which a boy is sitting on the bedside of his dying father. It was meaty stuff to work with—letting go, last words, tears . . . high drama. I had memorized my lines before arriving at Marcia's house and was ready to give it my best try. The scene took place in a hospital room, so Marcia pulled a chair next to the sofa, where she lay down to play the father, and we both cleared our throats, took our places, and began the scene. Marcia had the first line, "Where's your mother, dear?"

"She just stepped out to make a call, Dad; she'll be back soon," I said.

Marcia's eyes and mine were locked together; a beam of orangish light from the setting sun was streaming in through her window. She was staring deep into my eyes as I said my line and then she squinted a bit, looked away, and looked back at me before she said, "You know, dear, I remember how horrible it was when my father passed away."

"I'm sorry, Marcia," I said.

She looked confused. "What do you mean?"

"I'm sorry—about your father," I clarified.

"Oh, no, dear, that was in the script."

I had been waiting for her to say her line, "You know, dear, I remember how horrible it was when my father passed away." I had *memorized* it! I knew it was coming! But when Marcia looked me in the eyes, and then *looked away*, I thought, "Oh she's going to tell me something *real*." As she spoke about the horribleness of her father's death, I felt for her, and reacted. We both laughed about the misunderstanding, but I had learned a valuable acting lesson; when Marcia said her lines, she *was* telling me something real. What she was saying was so true that I forgot what I was doing—which was pretending. Marcia wasn't pretending; she wasn't reciting lines she had memorized; she was living them.

On the long bus and subway ride home that night, I mentally put together my Oscar speech:

"I used to think that *love* was the greatest gift that a person could share with someone else," I'd begin, holding my precious golden statue at waist level. "But it's not . . . because love is fleeting."

The rose-colored rims of Meryl's tired but all-knowing eyes would meet mine from the front row where she'd be sitting. "*Where is he going with this,*" they'd say.

"*Knowledge* is the greatest gift you can give another person," I'd continue. "To *teach* someone something—to give someone else a skill that they can carry with them for the rest of their life, long after the two of you have parted—*that* is the most valuable thing a human can give another." Meryl would nod wisely, in agreement. I would have to remember to catch up with her later at the *Vanity Fair* party, and subtly quote a famous line from one of her movies. "Sabu, dis' is a chief. You-are-not-a-chief!"

My acting endeavors were put on a brief hiatus when I was sixteen. It wasn't related at all to the continuing trauma at home, my dad still drinking and picking fights with Ma on a regular basis. No, this was something that caught me completely off guard—my agent died. Poor Clibby had a heart attack, leaving me orphaned in the acting world, scrambling for representation. I found a new agent in the form of a Daddy Warbucks figure named Gerry.

I jumped for joy when I landed my first acting job in a local kids' TV show. We put on comedic sketches and reenacted bastardized versions of famous movie scenes. Once, I had to wear a diaper for a skit called "Days of Blunder," in which my costar and I raced each other on tricycles. The costumes weren't exactly made to measure, and when my left testicle fell out during the first take, I panicked. But we just cut the camera and I discreetly tucked in the fugitive genital before continuing. Everything would be okay; it was safe. Here, the beginning, middle, and end of the story were plotted out beforehand—all I had to do was dive right in, completely committing to the prescribed set of parameters. Done. To me, this was the ultimate escape, and I was being paid to do it. There were no surprises in this scripted world where the highs and lows of life had neatly been laid out on paper.

When the audition for *Mean Girls* came up, I was sent in to read for the part of the gay kid, Damian. I delivered what I felt was a decent audition. I didn't hear back from the casting director for a few weeks, so I assumed that I was out of the running. *Maybe I was too nervous? Maybe my performance wasn't as strong as I thought and I was playing it too safe. Or Maybe I just wasn't gay enough? Maybe I should have cocked my hip and fluttered my eyes a little more?*

Then Gerry called and told me they wanted to see me for another part, a rapping mathlete named Kevin Gnapoor. I did my best to memorize the incredibly long rap contained in the eight pages of my audition script. At the audition, the waiting room was full of Chinese guys and I wondered if the role was meant to be Chinese and they were simply "trying out" the character as Indian by asking me to read for it. Regardless, I was thrilled to be reading for a role that was atypical to the ones I usually tried out for. As a young, skinny, brown actor in Toronto, nine out of ten auditions that came my way were for terrorists, assistant terrorists, or techies working in call centers in India. The character descriptions for these roles were always the same—"gangly, awkward, with a bad haircut"—but the probability of landing the job was high, as there were essentially only three of us brown guys who showed up to every one of these auditions. Between Ishan, Ali, and me, one of us would be bobbling our heads slyly and planting a bomb in the next episode of whatever crime drama was shooting in the city that month. I longed for the day when I'd be auditioning for an epic character of *Lawrence of Arabia* or *Out of Africa* proportions, the chances of which seemed pretty bleak at the time, when the only lead role I had gone up for by then had been in *Harold and Kumar*, with the audition scene entailing trimming my pubic hair into the shape of Osama Bin Laden's beard. Mm-hmm, yeah. This is why I was pleasantly surprised when I was asked to audition for the role of a gangsta math enthusiast. Despite the fact that I was terrible at math and had to drop out of calculus because I was failing miserably, high schools in Scarborough had no shortage of brown guys who walked with swagger as their baggy Enyce jeans slumped down past their asses, revealing their underwear—and although these chameleons put on the airs of complete thugs, there were many of them who got straight As in their math and science classes. I knew the mindset of this type like the back of my hand.

The casting assistant walked out and called "Rajiv Surendra" and as I followed her into the room where the casting director and camera guy were waiting, I desperately hoped that I wouldn't forget any of the rhyming couplets of the rap. But that didn't happen. I kept screwing up the lines and they'd restart and give me another try. And after four tries, I conceded to the casting director that I wasn't going to get it, but that I had given it my best shot. I left the room rolling my eyes.

A week later, I was caught completely off guard when I was invited to a callback where I'd be auditioning with the director and executive producer in the room.

I arrived at the casting office and the waiting room was empty. As I took a seat, a pretty brunette came out of the washroom nearby and joined me on the long bench I was sitting on. She smiled and extended her hand, "I'm Rachel."

"I'm Rajiv," I said, shaking her hand. "What part are you reading for?"

"The bitch, Regina George," she said, raising her eyebrows.

She sure doesn't seem like the "bitch" type, I thought to myself. *Maybe she's just a really good actress.*

The casting assistant emerged and asked me to follow her into the room.

"Good luck," the brunette whispered.

The walk down the corridor to the auditioning room felt like I was being escorted along the yellow brick road to meet the Great and Powerful Wizard of Oz. The assistant opened the door and stepped in, bidding me to enter behind her. There I was, being invited to cross the threshold between my real and imaginary worlds, and now it was no longer a childhood habit or a game in the basement . . . now it was officially a very big deal. I stepped in, and the assistant closed the door behind me.

"Everyone, this is Rajiv. Rajiv, this is Mark," she said, extending her hand toward the man seated in front of me, "our director. And this is Jill, who's producing." The smartly dressed woman seated behind Mark gave me a tiny wave. Behind both of them was the casting director I already knew. I was nervous, but in a good way.

I did a couple of the scenes assigned, and Mark chuckled. "Nice, I like this," he said, and then proceeded to give me directions, tweaking minor details. When it came time for me to do the rap, in a tiny moment of clarity, I reminded myself that I wasn't *pretending* to be a rapping mathlete—I *was* one. Cloaked with pure confidence, I let it rip, effervescent lyrics bubbling out of my mouth. Mark's guttural, baritone laugh filled the room and egged my rapper ego further. I threw my arms into the air and swaggered from one side of the room to the other, increasing the volume of my voice in competition with the growing laughter.

I had fully transformed into the rapping mathlete. The words on the page had become my own, and for those few moments, the world of the script was the only one I knew.

It paid off. I got the part.

2.

DAMN, *JESUS CHRIST had a great body*—I thought, as his smooth, naked torso appeared on the giant screen in front of me, lighting up the small dark room with his illuminated flesh. The beginnings of a six-pack were clearly visible, his upper abs following the curves of his rib cage, defined just enough to bring you to the conclusion that this guy knew how to eat well—fish mostly, in all probability. His obliques provided the Adonis belt, aka "sex lines," that led one's eyes downward toward the slightest hint of a happy trail. With his arms raised, his lack of armpit hair gave way to an unobstructed view of his thick lat muscles, which extended to a girth that placed him in the category of an *athletic physique* (defined by the clothing industry as a man whose chest measures eight inches or more than his waist). His shoulders were built *just* enough to entail an inward curve at their bases, where they met his biceps and triceps, which also bulged out *not too much*, but were long and sinewy. Don't even get me started on his chest, the epitome of what every pair of pecs should strive to become; these weren't bulging man-boobies, but taut and square at their corners, like thin but firm pillows, leading upward and outward from the perfect cleft they formed between his clavicle and the base of his sternum. Who, I wondered, might have laid their head on those pec-pillows? His legs followed the template of his torso—lean, long, and tight quads with calf muscles that were *ever so slightly* verging on emaciated.

It was my first week of classes at the University of Toronto and I was majoring in art history and classics—a combination that entailed quite a bit of overlap; my courses in the classics arena dealt with ancient Rome and Greece, whose cultures formed the foundation of Western art. This particular course was called "The Image of Christ" and was full of rich, young, white girls who spent the class mostly twisting their long tresses in their fingers and sipping from Starbucks cups while the instructor babbled on about the reed and birch twigs in the painting, blah, blah, blah. She never once referred to his hard nipples.

I was slightly surprised that my first realization of the ideal male form, and my appreciation for it, were conjured up by this *Ecce Homo*, but perhaps it had something to do with the fact that within a few weeks I would be ripping my shirt off as the cameras were rolling on the set of the first major motion picture that I had been cast in. My body, although much darker, paled in comparison to the one in front of me. I was ninety-six pounds of skin and bones with a visible rib cage that left little to the imagination. So far, no one involved in the movie had actually seen what was under my shirt—not the director, the casting director, or even my agent, for that matter. I had visions of being on set and ripping my shirt open, followed by the director yelling, "*Cut*! Oh my God, what is this, a charity commercial for starving orphans from the Third World? We can't work with *that*—he has the body of a ten-year-old barely surviving a famine!"

School was only a short walk away from set, as most of the scenes were filmed in the center of the city, with a few actually shot on the university campus itself. The commute from home to school, however, was long, and required two treacherous hours of a bus and subway combination.

Certain members of the crew were highly skeptical of how *Mean Girls* would fare in theaters—particularly the hairstylist, a buxom blonde in her forties who I suspected rode with the Hells Angels on her days off. I was patiently sitting in the hair and makeup trailer early one morning while she pulled a dangerously hot flat iron through my curly hair, straightening it as smoke dissipated from my scalp. Fascinated to learn that she had been in the "biz" for years and had worked on some pretty big movies, I asked for her informed opinion of how she thought this movie would fare. She popped the giant bubble of gum she was blowing. "Please . . ." she sneered, "it's starring Lindsay Lohan, and it's called *Mean Girls*; it's goin' straight to DVD, babe."

My heart sank a little. I knew she was probably right; most of the small movies that my Canadian actor friends were in never saw the light of day. Still, I was over the moon to be a part of an official Paramount Pictures production, even though it was tricky juggling my first year of university with the movie's shooting schedule. Call times were often early (five a.m.) and I ended up missing quite a few classes to be on set. It didn't bother me—I welcomed any excuse to cut class in the name of a higher, worthier form of self-education.

Even back in elementary school, I can remember waking up lethargically and dreading leaving the house—I would much rather have stayed at home and focused on the things that I actually wanted to learn about, perfecting the flour-to-water ratio of my papier-mâché paste, strategically rearranging the carnivorous Venus fly traps and pitcher plants in my terrarium, or helping Ma prepare the ingredients for her daily Tamil cooking, scraping coconuts using a hand-cranked tool from Sri Lanka that resembled a medieval torture device. To Ma, however, who had childhood dreams of becoming a doctor but never ended up going to college, her children would only be considered fully educated if they had impressive degrees to hang on the living room wall. It's not that I found school difficult or that I was opposed to reading . . . I loved to read, just not what I was *forced* to read. Throughout high school, textbooks for geography, history, and French were regularly set aside for books like *Ornamental Pen Designs and Flourishes*, *Setting Up Your Chicken Coop*, and *The Art of Water-Gilding: A Practical Manual.*

I tried my best to read my biology textbook in between takes on set, even though it was excruciatingly tough to focus on mitochondria while Regina George and the Plastics were flailing their arms and hopping around in red vinyl skirts on the stage in front of me.

Despite my previous flibbertigibbet approach to school, I was bound and determined to change my ways and excel academically—a goal that was perhaps fueled by the astronomical costs of my tuition. But fate had something else in store for me that year. And it all started at the snack table on the set of *Mean Girls*.

Three of us were standing side by side, each preparing our own bagels—the cameraman, Lindsay Lohan, and me. The cameraman had his bagel in the toaster while Lindsay and I waited for our turns. Lindsay was ripping the insides out of her sliced bagel. I stood watching for a few moments before I could contain myself no longer, asking out of pure bewilderment, "What are you doing?"

"It's less bagel . . ." she explained casually.

"Why don't you just . . ." I thought out loud, "eat *half* the bagel?" She stopped only for a moment and stared down at the crumpled shell she was holding. "Whatever . . ." she muttered, continuing where she had left off.

Silence ensued and then the cameraman, in his fifties and wearing a khaki vest with too many pockets, turned to me as I put my bagel in the toaster.

"Humph," he puffed, eyeing me with a sly smile, ". . . you're in the book I just finished." I hadn't spent much time with him and didn't quite know what to make of his declaration.

"Huh?" I responded.

"Have you read *Life of Pi*?" he asked.

I knew of the book—its cover had become a repeated sight on the subway during my long commute downtown every day, but I had no idea of what the book was actually about.

"No, not yet," I answered.

"You've gotta read it, bud. It's a book about you," he said matter-of-factly as he headed off, biting into his bagel.

Later that day, I was nodding off as I desperately struggled to get through the week's assigned readings for school. Defeated, I put down my biology textbook during our lunch break and walked to the Manulife Centre at the corner of Bloor and Bay—the shopping complex that housed a cinema, a food court, and a three-story bookstore. Bustling office workers scurried around me as I pulled open the heavy glass door and headed to the second floor, where I found the fiction section and began scanning the books penned by authors with the last name starting with M. There it was, Yann Martel's *Life of Pi*. The carpet under my shoes was soft and cushiony as my index finger pressed the top of the book, tipping it on its corner and wedging it free from the others. I surveyed the cover—a whimsical drawing of a tiger's face above blue waves with fish jumping out of the water. A tattooed forty-something guy wearing a polyester blue vest rang me up and I put the book in my worn leather satchel, heading back to the set.

I spent the next two days reading the book on all my breaks, in between scenes and during camera setups. Occasionally the camera man would pass by and ask excitedly, "What do you think?" My steadfast response was always that I wasn't finished yet, and that he'd be the first to know, then I'd dive right back into reading.

How exactly did he know that this book was about me, that I was *in* this story?

The book is about Pi, a sixteen-year-old son of a zookeeper who leaves India with his family, headed for Canada. The family sells all their animals to North American zoos and is traveling in a cargo ship with their menagerie when disaster strikes, and the ship sinks. Pi ends up on a life raft in the middle of the ocean, along with a hyena, an orangutan, and a Bengal tiger. The bulk of the story is Pi's saga of crossing the Pacific as a castaway, and surviving, with the tiger in tow, the whole way.

What drew me into the book was the description of the main character early on—a young Indian boy named Pi. He was Tamil and grew up in the South Indian town of Pondicherry, one of the few places in India colonized by the French. I was also Tamil, with parents who were from Sri Lanka (Ceylon being its former name, before the British gave it independence—it's the name that my parents, aunts, and uncles still use), and I grew up with mandatory French classes through elementary and high school. Note: For those of you who are wondering what Tamil means, I should probably clarify; Tamil is both a language and an ethnicity. The Tamil people are a type of Indian (*not* the *Pocahontas* kind, that's North *American* . . . duh) native to both South India and Sri Lanka.

Pi was fascinated with religion and took to practicing multiple faiths as a child.

He grew up as the son of a zookeeper, and the family lived in the zoo itself. The sights and sounds of all kinds of wild and exotic animals were commonplace to him, just as they were to me. Here was another boy with elephants in his backyard.

Pi leaves India and ends up in Toronto, more specifically, the suburb of Scarborough, where we lived. He becomes a student at the University of Toronto and belongs to St. Michael's College—where I happened to be enrolled. Pi was five foot five, thin-framed, with a coffee-colored complexion. Need I say more? This was bat-shit crazy.

Lights and cameras were being set up in the gymnasium of the abandoned high school that we were using as our set and I was sitting alone in an empty storage room when I reached the last page of the book. As if on cue, the cameraman's head appeared from around the corner. "Are you done?" he asked quietly. I nodded. "What did you think?" his voice was almost a whisper. I was at a loss for words. I recall a simple shrug. I don't think I knew *what* to think at the time—the book, in some creepy strange way, was a story about a guy just like me, who embarks on an unintentional journey that magnifies every element of who he was, and puts those qualities to the test through the struggle of survival. What was I supposed to make of this?

The production arranged to have one of the drivers take me home after filming that night, which was now actually the wee hours of the morning. It was early November, but light snow was already falling. Winter had arrived in Toronto. I pushed aside formality and climbed into the passenger seat up front, my breath clearly visible in the cold night air. The driver was a grandfather type, wearing a thick wool coat and a tuque that covered most of his white hair; I guessed he was maybe in his seventies.

"How long have you been doing this?" I asked.

"Oh . . . a long time," he answered with a sigh. "More than fifty years."

Half a decade of driving actors around Toronto—I was intrigued by the things this man must have seen and heard over the years.

"What's one of the memories that sticks out the most?"

"Oh . . . I dunno . . ." the driver pondered with his head cocked to one side as he rubbed his short white beard. Snow was accumulating on the windshield and he flicked on the wipers, ". . . let's see now . . ." He was quiet for a bit, then he smiled.

"I was driving Elizabeth Taylor back to the King Eddie one night"—that was local speak for the King Edward Hotel, fancy-schmancy Toronto accommodations—"around the time she was having an affair with Richard Burton," he continued. "I could see that a large crowd had gathered, expecting her. As we got closer to the hotel, I asked her over my shoulder if she wanted me to take her around to the rear entrance. She leaned forward, put her hand on the back of my seat, and daintily said, 'Oh *no*, darling, *this* is what it's all about.'" The driver and I laughed heartily.

Getting ready for bed, I cracked the window to let in some cold air. Meesha climbed into her little basket that sat at the foot of my bed, and as I pulled down the covers, I marveled at the nature of a story. What was seemingly over and done with, dead and forgotten, was still alive. The driver had his story, Elizabeth Taylor had hers, and now I had a version of it for myself—all related to that one night decades ago when she was in Toronto. It was a consoling thought at the closing of a long day, which ended with the sound of wolves from the zoo through my open window.

3.

I HAD STOPPED BREATHING. Then I gasped. A choke—then a cough. Finally, I shouted out loud. All the colored immigrant faces on the 86A TTC bus, headed from the Toronto Zoo to the subway station, turned around to face me accusingly for disturbing their quiet morning commute. There, on the newspaper in my lap, was the cause of the harshest cry of amazement that had ever been uttered by my lips (an expletive assembled by a friend of a friend, Derek LaJeunesse): "Jesus, Mary-humping, mother fucking Christ!!!"

Life of Pi was to be made into a film that summer. And, *of course*, the only notable brown director in Hollywood was attached—M. Night Shyamalan, of *The Sixth Sense* fame. *This* was the part that I had longed for, the role that defied all of Hollywood's conventional stereotypes— the title character *actually* being a skinny, little, brown kid, for fuck's sake. *"Tamil . . . five foot five, with a coffee-colored-complexion."* Ishan and Ali could have all the terrorist (and assistant terrorist) roles; I would gladly consent. Because finally, *finally*, this was the role of a lifetime—the stuff that legendary movies were made of—filming on location in India, but not modern India, *vintage* India. This was a world I had grown up hearing about; at family gatherings, where the house would be filled with my thirty cousins and dozens of aunts and uncles,

I was usually at the dinner table with the adults, listening intently as they reminisced about life in *Ceylon*, where falling asleep to the smell of mangos ripening under the bed was one of life's little pleasures.

And now, that world was going to be revived, reincarnated, and brought to the big screen with grandeur. There would be monkeys, tigers, and elephants on set—elephants; do you hear me?! *Elephants!*

I would be quietly ushered into the wardrobe office where the costume lady, a British seamstress by the name of Evelyn, would take my measurements for the one shirt that she'd be making for my entire life-raft voyage, the bulk of the film. "Linen, or cotton?" she would ask, as she circled the yellow tape measure around my waist. I would give her a long and detailed explanation about my own experiences painstakingly creating linen cloth by hand from the flax plant. Later, Evelyn would marvel at me noticing the French seams in the shirt she had so lovingly made—"*French seam*, how do *you* know what that is?" she'd ask softly, eyeing me over her tortoiseshell-rimmed spectacles pushed down to the tip of her nose. "Oh, come now, Evelyn! My mom might have worked at a bank her whole life, but on weekends and evenings, she ran her own company making curtains since I was two years old. That three-piece suit I wore to the press conference last week? I made it, completely by hand. Mwaa-haa-haa," I'd laugh. "Mwaa-ha-ha-ha," she'd laugh.

A grand orchestral score would accompany the movie. I would be asked to participate in some way, as M. Night (or rather, *Shyamalan-Anna*, as I'd be calling him, *Anna* being the Tamil term of endearment for "older brother," pronounced "Un-na") would have found out by that point that I had a penchant for classical South Indian Carnatic singing. He'd come up with the brilliant idea of me warbling the improvisational scales of the Kalyani ragam for the opening sequences to the movie. "*Thamby*," he'd say (Tamil for "little brother"), "that was great, but can you try it again? Just linger a little longer on that sad, melancholic note . . ."

Ma would probably want to wear a sari to the Oscars—typical. I would have to find some way to tell her politely that it was far too predictable that she'd wear Indian garb, so it would serve her well to pick something else, something that would complement her jet-black, shoulder-length, ringlet curls. Something nice. After all, Ma continued to struggle so much in her marriage to my dad—maybe this would be an occasion for her to feel like it was all worth it in the end. What the hell, let's splurge! We would fly to Paris and make an appointment with one of the couture houses, Givenchy or Chanel, something classic. I would have to speak French, I guessed, and then translate to Ma in English. Since we'd already be in Paris, it'd probably be a good idea to take Ma's traditional South Indian gold *padakam* necklace to Cartier (the one she's had since she was eight). The clamshell-shaped pendant is fitted with artificial emeralds; this would be a suitable time to have all those removed and refitted with genuine gemstones—it could be the one *nod* to traditional attire—*yeah, that'll be okay, Ma wearing her padakam necklace,* she'd like that. And it really would be in the best hands at Cartier; after all, they were the ones who made the turban ornament with that insanely huge emerald for the maharajah of Kapurthala, Jagajit Singh, in the 1920s.

"What's your favorite sound?" I would be asked at the end of my interview for *Inside the Actor's Studio.*

"The wind blowing through the trees, James," I'd answer, and Mr. Lipton would nod knowingly, wisely, as he blinked slowly and then proceed to ask, "Your favorite curse word?"

Despite being exhausted and drained, I would have to find some way of squeezing in a quick dinner afterward with Jay Z (his request)—should I use the line, *"Can I get a . . ."* every time the waiter came by?

Better not; that would be tacky. But should I use my normal way of speaking while conversing with him, or should I try to sound a little black? Do I say, "What do you think . . ." or "Whatchu think?" Do I call him, "Mr. Z," "Jay," or use the more endearing *"Nigga"*?

Excuse me! *"Excuse me,* can ya move, please? Ya block dee way," said the Trinidadian lady sitting next to me on the bus, who was now standing up and leaning on the red-cushioned seats, her huge purse in hand as everyone else filed out and headed into the subway station to take the train downtown.

This was really happening. All daydreaming aside, this role was going to be up for grabs. My mind was in overdrive and I was twitching with excitement. The prospect of landing this part was almost too good to be true—who could *possibly* be more perfect for this role in every aspect, physically, mentally, and ethnically?

My classes on Thursday ended early, so I got home, took the dog out, and then hopped on my bike and pedaled to the zoo. I only had half an hour before they closed, but luckily the ride was mostly downhill, so it didn't take me very long to make my way through the turnstiles. I wandered around for a bit, taking in the sights and sounds at the end of the day, reveling in the fact that just like Pi, I felt completely at home in this zoo; I had been coming here since I was three. A peacock crossed my path, his huge fan of plumage quivering in the breeze as he turned about, displaying his glory.

I headed back to the entrance. A girl in her late teens was working behind the front desk and I hesitatingly asked if I could speak to the person who was in charge of the tigers. She seemed slightly caught off guard and I could tell she was mulling through the potential downsides of helping me out. She sighed slightly, mumbled into her walkie-talkie, and told me to have a seat on a nearby bench.

Within a few minutes, a golf cart driven by a short, redheaded man in his fifties made its way over to me. The man introduced himself as Ollie, curator of mammals, and he spoke with just the slightest hint of an Irish lilt. I opened my mouth to reply and verbally vomited all over him, telling him about *Mean Girls*, *Life of Pi*, and my uncanny resemblance to the Indian boy who grew up in a zoo. He listened patiently, with one hand resting on the steering wheel of his golf cart. He was wearing khakis and a sage green parka embroidered with a small, white "Toronto Zoo" on the breast pocket. His blue eyes looked tired, framed with red eyelashes and eyebrows, but they seemed to be entertained as I listed Pi's companions being an orangutan, a zebra, a hyena, and, for most of his journey, a Bengal tiger. I felt it was a long shot, but I asked him anyway if he could take me into the tiger enclosure.

"I think I could imagine the scenario in my head but . . . right now, it still seems fictional . . ." And then I realized why I was there: "I'd really like to make it real for myself; it would be amazing to know what it feels like to stand face to face with an actual tiger." He didn't hesitate at all, and gave me a wink as he told me to hop in beside him.

"Really?" I was shocked that it had actually worked.

"Yeah, come along." He motioned with his head for me to climb in. "Your timin's perfect, actually. Not many visitors left, and it's feeding time."

I held on to the metal bar to steady myself as we drove along the main asphalt pathways and cried out to Ollie when I caught an unexpected glimpse of my house, far off in the distance, across the Rouge Valley.

"Let's stop here first," he said, turning the cart onto a dirt path that meandered through a heavily wooded area and ended at the back of a nondescript concrete building. I was full of excitement as we made our way over to a giant metal door, where he swiped a keycard into a slot and then pulled the door open.

My heart leapt. He had brought me to the holding area of the orang-utan enclosure—the part of the building that the public never saw, the prep room of sorts, filled with transparent Rubbermaid containers that held blankets, towels, food, and various other supplies. It was warm and humid, and smelled earthy, like peat moss. A mother orangutan and her baby were sitting on a ledge eating raw spinach out of a plastic bag. A wall of iron bars was all that separated us from the animals, and Ollie walked me closer.

"The mum's called Puppe, and her daughter's named Sekali. Just don't touch them. They're highly susceptible to gettin' sick."

Silently, I stood just a few inches apart from these incredible animals. Puppe gingerly picked leaves of spinach out of the bag and put them into her mouth. She turned and slowly looked up at me from where she was seated. Her shiny, brown eyes were so humanlike I teared up and had to hold myself back from reaching out and touching a tuft of her long, bright, reddish-brown hair that was sticking out onto my side of the iron bars, just a short reach away from my hand. This orangutan seemed to exude the very essence of peace. I was overwhelmed with the wonder of what exactly made our two worlds so mind-bogglingly different. The baby sat cradled in Puppe's left arm and helped itself to spinach—soon, the bag was empty. The keeper, a girl in her twenties with a long ponytail, stepped up beside me.

"Are you done, Puppe?" she asked casually, as if she was talking to an old friend. "Okay? Give me the bag."

The mommy orangutan gently scrunched the empty bag into her palm and squeezed it through the space between two iron bars. Then, pursing her lips and sighing slightly, she gave it one slow and final poke with her index finger before it fell to our feet.

I waved goodbye to Puppe and her baby as we left the building. They didn't wave back. *Bitches.* I thought we were friends.

The sun was setting as Ollie drove the cart over to the Siberian tiger enclosure. The zoo didn't have Bengal tigers, he explained, but these Siberians were the closest thing—being only slightly bigger.

The tiger enclosure was a big concrete room, divided up into sections by walls of iron bars and, as we entered, the first thing that hit me was the sharp smell of cat piss—tiger pee, to be more precise—an intensely strong ammonialike smell that wasn't offensive.

There was an intricate series of doors and gates, also made of iron bars, that we made our way through, closing one before opening another—safety precautions, Ollie mentioned in passing. Finally, I stood at the center of the room, standing with the empty tiger enclosure right in front of me. The giant cat was still outdoors, but I could see him pacing by the square-shaped entrance that was blocked with iron gates. The keeper in there, a middle-aged woman, greeted us with a brief smile as she cut open sealed bags that contained raw meat, putting them into a bowl that was then placed into the enclosure.

Ollie narrated what was happening. "She's gotta double-check that the enclosures are locked securely after putting down the food, and then she'll let Tongua in."

A jittery nervousness came over me as the heavy clanking of metal on metal reverberated out into the space, the keeper's gloved hands rapidly running through the course of pushing and pulling various bolts and levers.

"She's ready for him now," Ollie said quietly, standing behind me, leaning against the wall of iron bars with his arms crossed.

I tried to remain calm, but I could feel my legs shaking a little as the keeper pulled on a rope, lifting the outer iron gates and allowing the huge tiger to enter. He gracefully bounded in, heading straight for his bowl of food. My eyes were drawn to the tufts of fluffy white fur that stuck up from behind his ears as his head was in his food bowl. Everything in the room gravitated to the tiger, like we were all planets and he was the sun. He was so regal-looking, his jowls edged with more downy white fur that softly framed his head, like delicate lace, seemingly incongruous to his other imposing traits. His face was enormous; his meaty tongue was of massive proportions; even the thickness of his long, white, waxy whiskers announced the sheer size and power of this creature.

"If he turns around and raises his tail," Ollie warned from the corner where he was standing, "step back—they spray occasionally, to mark their territory."

Tongua remained crouched down low over his bowl in a stance that was threateningly tense—his shoulders raised and his thick tail, over a meter long, low to the ground—he looked as if he was ready to pounce at any moment. I cautiously crouched down, trying to get a closer look at his face. His ears were perked and he kept raising his head and looking up at me menacingly between mouthfuls of food with his huge, golden eyes, at the center of which were round, black pupils that would expand and contract quickly, noticeably. Every now and then, he'd lick his mouth and then spread his lips open, hissing at me and showing his huge teeth.

The keeper opened the lid of a trash can to throw away the empty bags that had held the raw meat, shuffling plastic, when—*wham!* Tongua jumped up and *bammed* his paw, the size of a dinner plate, onto the bars in front of me, letting out an insanely loud, guttural *snarl*.

"*Aaaaahhh!*" I shouted out, jumping up. The deep snarl had reverberated through my body. The sound was not quite a roar, as I might have expected, but a combination of both a groan and a woof that was sickeningly intimidating.

"Tongua's a little protective of his food," Ollie chuckled. "Don't mind him."

I was still trembling slightly as we headed out of the concrete building and back into the golf cart.

"Come back whenever you'd like," Ollie offered with a smile, turning to face me as he started the motor. "And I do hope you get that part."

He dropped me off at the front gate, which was now closed, and the security guard let me out. I rode my bike home in the dark, wrapping my scarf around my face as a defense against the cold wind.

Richard Parker, the tiger in Pi's story, was now a solid, tangible character in my own world. *What else can I do?* I wondered, as I lifted my bum off the bicycle seat and put more leg power into pushing myself uphill. *I really could get this part.*

I didn't quite know where to start looking for information about the movie being made, but I figured that going back to the book might be a good place to start. I typed "Yann Martel" into the search bar on Yahoo. com's homepage. And then I started digging. "Stalker" is such a harsh term. How about we use "enthusiast" or "wooer"?

Yann Martel was surprisingly easy to locate (he just happened to be doing a writer's residency at the Saskatoon Public Library), and before I knew it, we were deep in conversation on the phone, I gushing about my similarities with Pi, and he relaying that he had been corresponding with M. Night Shyamalan. I was elated when he spoke encouragingly of my prospects and very generously offered to send me the email he had sent to the director, which contained suggestions for how the book might be best adapted to the big screen.

The ten-page email to Shyamalan was a treasure trove of information, not so much related to the process of making a film, but more an inside look into the author's view of his own work—identifying iconic symbols and key points of the book, and stating what was merely anecdotal. I felt like a detective with the most substantial piece of evidence in front of me, ready to get my hands dirty and crack some kind of code. Yann's email detailed what parts of the novel could potentially be cut out for the film and what he felt was essential. India and many things Indian were discussed at length. When it came to the role of Pi, he passionately described components of what made up the character and stated " . . . we'll of course have to find some brilliant young actor . . ."

I shared so many similarities with the character Yann had created, but I didn't know how to swim. I didn't even know how to float, and Pi is a great swimmer. And being cast adrift for 227 days was also something I couldn't relate to, at all. And then I realized that the main thing I had assumed we did share, our Indianness, was in fact only a superficial similarity; sure, our skin was the same color and we ate the same ethnic foods (Ma makes the best Tamil food), but Yann's notes to M. Night showed me that I could only *imagine* what Indian life was like—it still wasn't *real* to me, as it was to my parents, aunts, and uncles. Yann referred to India repeatedly, having spent six months there doing research, and his description of the country's culture, people, and psyche seemed so impressively accurate; there were many parts of the novel that reminded me of the scenes painted in my imagination by my parents, of their childhoods in Ceylon—a world where astrological charts determined the pairings of young brides and grooms in Hindu households, where fishermen, propped up on stilts at the seashore, caught fish by the moonlight, and where the heavy lifting on tea plantations was done by elephants . . . *elephants*, do you hear me?!

Back on the set of *Mean Girls*, I relayed my new *Life of Pi* discovery to Daniel Franzese and Lizzy Caplan (who were playing Damian and Janis). Lizzy took me by the arm, walked me to the executive producer, and then declared, "We need your help!" "We," she said. Was I slowly acquiring an army of support behind me? The producer, who happened to know Shyamalan, happily agreed to send him a package of my material; my headshot, résumé.

I was new at this game and still unfamiliar with the inner workings of Hollywood protocol. Thus far, I hadn't really discussed business with anyone of authority on set. There was definitely an unspoken code of propriety here, and I had witnessed the boundaries being crossed a couple of times. While shooting one of the final scenes in the film, Tina Fey had quietly given me direction about saying a line she had written. The line was "I feel that . . ." and she pulled me aside to tell me that the emphasis was to be placed on "I" rather than "feel." I think we had both forgotten that she was wearing a lapel microphone and that the director could hear her, because he made a beeline over to me and, in a slightly reprimanding tone, told me that *like he had said earlier,* he wanted the emphasis on "feel." Tina and I exchanged glances of "eek" and "oops."

Another time, I was shooting a classroom scene with Tina, and we were waiting quietly between takes when I noticed one of the extras who was playing a mathlete (a very socially awkward, pimply kid) creepily staring at Tina's face with his mouth slightly ajar. Uncomfortably close to each other, the three of us were standing on our marks (small pieces of tape on the ground indicating our positions for the shot), stuck there while technical adjustments were being made to lights and lenses. She must have felt him staring, because she turned to face him briefly and gave him a little smile. All of a sudden, he blurted out, "How'd you get that?" running his index finger along the side of his face, referencing the scar she had on her cheek. She didn't miss a beat and politely but firmly chided, "It's none of your business. You should know not to ask people questions like that."

"Oh, sorry," he wheezed out.

"Don't worry about it," she consented with a smile.

I looked away, pretending to be distracted, embarrassed for this kid, and wanting no part of the awkward interaction. My experiences of working on a real, bona fide Hollywood production were teaching me that there was no handbook on how to navigate through this world, and if I was going to seek the help of key players in the industry, it would need to be made clear to them that I deserved their assistance.

Mean Girls was released in theaters in April of 2004 and debuted at number one at the box office that weekend. I envisioned the blonde hairdresser on a Harley somewhere, rolling her eyes when she found out, her large breasts heaving and falling as the bike bounced over bumps in the road.

I took a huge posse of my cousins to the theater on opening night, and found it oddly bizarre to see my own face blown up twenty times its normal size on the big screen. There it was, the manifestation of a goal I had fantasized about—I can remember casually telling Ma once that if I were ever in a movie, I'd take all my cousins to go see it together. It was an emboldening feeling, sitting in the theater of Scarborough Town Centre and munching on popcorn while the crowd around me laughed in all the right places. Success. People seemed amused by the antics of the rapping mathlete. I had already seen the movie a few times, so I guess I zoned out and began to wonder if this was just the beginning of something much bigger. My face popped up on the screen once again. Why *shouldn't* I be Pi? I can do this. I'll *make* it happen.

My first year of university was coming to a close, and the more I thought about the *Pi* movie, the more I realized that school would always be there, but there would only be a small window of opportunity *to even attempt* to seize this part. This was a once-in-a-lifetime chance. I found myself standing dangerously close to the edge of a cliff. Far below me was an incredible abyss with no end in sight. I could turn back and safely return to where I had come from, or I could throw caution to the wind, lift my arms up into the air . . . and jump. When the time came to audition for the role of Pi, I wanted to walk into the casting agent's office and know that I wasn't just acting—I wanted to go in there knowing that I had *become* Pi, that I had the experiences, feelings, and history that the character had.

Just like Tongua, the tiger at the zoo, there were elements of Yann Martel's fictional tale that actually existed out there in the real world. All I had to do to encounter them on a tangible level was seek them out. My instincts told me that I needed to throw every bit of myself into landing the role of Pi. At the registrar's office on the university campus, a few weeks before my classes were over, I inquired about pulling out of school and signed the necessary paperwork, making it official that I wouldn't be returning in September. And then I called the travel agent my parents used and booked a one-way ticket to India.

From: yann_martel1963@yahoo.com
To: rajivsca@yahoo.ca
Subject: RE: hello-from-t.o.
Date: Wed, 19 May 2004 03:42:50

Dear Rajiv,

Thank you for your letter. Your penmanship is worthy of the 16th century.

There are three big zoos in the south of India that I visited. The best is in Mysore, Karnataka. The one I spent the most time in is in Trivandrum, in Kerala. And there's one just south of Madras, so that would be the one closest to Pondicherry, though it was the least appealing of the three.

Congratulations on Mean Girls. That's a big movie. When I have a moment, I'll go see it.

Good luck in India. Take your time. Poke around. Open yourself. It's an amazing place.

Stay well.

Yours,

Yann

4.

I WAS GREETED WITH the wild chaos, disorder, and craziness in which India seemed to function perfectly well. My first major challenge: I had to cross the street.

Having just arrived in Pondicherry, the air, thick with moisture and heat, exuded a kind of primeval energy that had a strangely calming effect on me. Even the light seemed different here. I was fueled by a sense of adventure, my feet now planted in a completely new world.

For a few weeks prior to my arrival, I had been corresponding with the principal of Petit Séminaire, the very *real* boy's school that the *fictional* Pi attended. After explaining to him why I wanted to learn how to walk, talk, and behave like a local boy, and that I hoped to absorb as much of life in Pondicherry as possible, he granted me permission to sit at the back of an eleventh grade classroom for a few weeks, observing the boys who went to school there. He had read *Life of Pi* and told me that the school was happy to help me with my quest. He even offered me accommodations on the premises, but suggested that I would be more comfortable at a nearby hotel and graciously took the initiative of booking my room for me.

I checked into the Hotel Surguru and then ventured out, walking down the main road to Petit Séminaire. *Yes!* The first destination on my Pi checklist in India—a real building with a real history that I could physically become a part of. There it was, in front of me but across the street, which was a discombobulated mess of motorbikes, rickshaws, bicycles, and cows—*Bam! Boom! Thaka-thom!*—an immediate assault on my senses with rich smells, new sounds, and people everywhere. It was all moving, around, about, up the street, and down. I felt as though I was being pulled into it, like I wasn't allowed to just stand there, being overwhelmed and scared, but forced to move, move somewhere, out of someone's way or into someone else's, to just walk, walk and become a part of it. There weren't any actual lanes of traffic as far as I could tell, and everything just seemed to weave in and out of itself, all higgledy-piggledy. No traffic lights or crosswalks. I surveyed my immediate surroundings—a crumbling side-walk and two sari-clad, nose-pierced old ladies sitting nearby on a straw mat selling five different types of bananas. One of the ladies adjusted the thick bun of hair on her head and yelled at me, telling me in Tamil that I needed to taste her bananas. But I had bigger issues to deal with—I was beginning to wonder whether people simply never crossed the streets in India when I noticed a woman in a teal-colored sari just step in front of oncoming traffic and make her way across. Amazingly, everything seemed to weave around her as she kept her eyes on the other side of the street and sauntered through.

I took a deep breath and followed her lead, stepping into the road. The traffic just made its way around me as I held my steadfast gaze straight ahead on the iron gates of Petit Séminaire. *Good, good, you got this.* I was feeling the vibe, already starting to fit in with the locals. *You look like one of them—they'll never know you're faking it—just keep walking, casually, keep your head up, squint your eyes, like the rest of them, gently swing your arms as you walk; yeah, yeah, you got this.* And then I made a grave error—I looked to my left and registered that a kid on a huge, black bicycle was headed right for me. And then I stopped walking, instinctively, to let him pass. Big, big mistake. The boy screeched to a halt, bouncing down from the seat of his bike—causing a rickshaw that was just slightly behind him to crash into him. The pedal of his bike was somehow caught on the side of the rickshaw and the lady seated in the back started yelling at the boy in Tamil, who piped up and was yelling back at her. I interjected, waving my hands as I tried my best to tell them, in very broken Tamil, that I was to blame—"*No*, no, me mistake make, no him!"—but it was of no use; they hardly looked my way. With *all* the traffic stopped around me, I guiltily used the opportunity to slip away to the entrance of the school, where a cow chewing on some mango leaves eyed me suspiciously.

Stupid, stupid me. I felt like a dumb tourist. *How, when I couldn't even make it across the street, could I think that I was worthy of playing a young, authentic Tamil kid?* It was a very good lesson to learn early on. If I was to fit in, I would have to do so by observing and adapting to a new way of behavior, however foreign it might seem to me.

Petit Séminaire was an expansive complex of loggias that opened onto a huge central courtyard built in the nineteenth century, and as I left the noisy street and entered the school, I heard faint shouting— short, high-pitched, little yelps. As I got closer to the principal's office, the whimpers got louder and were separated by a thwacking sound. I turned the corner to the principal's office, and saw a Tamil man, dressed in a long, white Catholic priest's cassock, standing in front of a kneeling boy, about twelve years old. The priest, using his bare hand, was beating the kid on his back . . . *whack*—squeal . . . *whack*—squeal . . . I froze in horror.

After he was finished, the priest and the boy exchanged a few quiet words in Tamil, then the boy turned around and walked out, wiping tears away from his face. I made a mental note to be a good boy while I was here.

The priest looked at me curiously. I nervously spoke in English and told him who I was, that I had been in contact with the principal, and was to check in with him when I arrived. He left the room and returned with another Tamil man, also dressed in a priest's cassock.

The principal's name was Father Antonisamy and he was a Tamil Catholic priest. Although I hardly spoke Tamil, I grew up hearing my parents speak it and could understand it almost fluently. I knew that the principal's very title and name was a sort of religious oxymoron. "Father Antony" was wham-bam in-your-face Roman Catholic, but *Sami* (also *Swami*) was the colloquial Tamil word for God, and the *traditional* Tamil reference to God—way before Jesus arrived in India—would have been a reference to a *Hindu* god. Hinduism is one of the oldest religions in existence that is still being practiced—and the Tamils are associated with its origins. Somewhere along the line, some Roman Catholic missionaries in South India convinced a handful of ever-obliging, welcoming Tamils to do away with their prostrations before stone idols dressed in silk and gold, and trust in a more inconspicuous form of worship. They happily consented, but with the one clause they hold on to just a teeny-weeny bit of their heritage, for tradition's sake—and *this* was the "samy" suffix of the principal's name.

Oddly enough, I was in a similar position to Father Antonisamy, a kind of oxymoron with regards to my own identity. In Canada, I grudgingly identified as being Tamil—when I was asked in Toronto where I "was from," the question always implied deciphering my ethnicity. The sassy response was that I was simply "Canadian," but when pushed, I would consent to saying, "Sri Lankan" or "Tamil." My cousins and I usually did everything we could to shy away from having to admit that we were Tamil to people, who might mistakenly associate our identity with the FOBs (Fresh off the Boat) that filled the suburbs with their backward ways, hacking and hoarking up their winter boogers while seated on the bus or strolling to the corner store in their sarongs. We would make fun of how Tamil immigrants, recently arriving in Toronto, would pronounce certain words—"app-ra-kate" (appreciate) was a big one—and we'd point and roll our eyes embarrassingly at the behavior ingrained in these people from the land in which they were raised.

That land was now where I had traveled to, and here in Pondicherry, I saw myself, for the first time, in another light—an unflattering one. I too was in a sort of nowhere place with regards to a firm cultural identity. No, I could not confidently say that I was only Canadian. And now, in India, I felt completely unworthy of calling myself Tamil when I couldn't even speak the language or cross the damn street. What was I? Where was I from? It was kind of a traumatic realization so far away from home . . . or was it even really home? I was here to learn of the ways that I had previously balked at, and with humility I hoped that I would not be treated in the same manner that I had so snobbishly displayed toward these people on my turf. The behavior, gestures, and accents that I had once dismissed as being crude, uneducated, and completely beneath me were now the jewels that I had come to India to find, the vital elements of becoming Pi. Now I was the one with a desperate need to assimilate.

Father Antonisamy led me into his small wood-paneled office and gestured for me to sit on the other side of his desk. I was wearing jeans and a polo shirt (which was now soaked with perspiration), and was speaking to him as an equal, but thinking of Ma, I began to worry that I hadn't been deferential enough. In her reminiscences of her childhood, Ma had always referred to her teachers with much reverence—they were treated like gods.

Father Antonisamy was a lot more reserved than I had imagined for the position he held at the school, and as we conversed, we were regularly interrupted by his servant, Samandam (about fifty, barefoot, bald, and clad in a pale blue polyester shirt and pants set), who would enter the room, speak in hushed tones while remaining in a permanent position of bowing, and then exit the room without turning his back to us. Whatever the dynamic was between the principal and me, Father Antonisamy might have been making a bold effort to treat me as an equal, because after telling me that I could start attending classes at the school the following day, he mentioned that he had a good friend who owned a restaurant by the ocean and asked me to have dinner with him that night. I wanted to say yes right away, but started second-guessing myself, wondering whether he was just being polite and debating whether I was obliged to say, as my older relatives always did when offered something, "No, I wouldn't want to be a bother . . ." It was a Tamil thing, for sure, so I just hemmed a little, audibly, "Uhhhhh . . . heh . . . hmm . . ." and then accepted humbly, "only if it wouldn't be too much trouble."

The vestibule outside Father Antonisamy's office was quiet and empty as I waited for him later that evening. He told me to meet him at eight, and I was a little early. I was curiously poking around the two-hundred-year-old building when the deafening caws of crows drew me to the open courtyard. There were hundreds of crows in the huge trees that anchored the corners of the tropical garden. Darkness hid the details, but everything was softly lit with a blue hue from the moon, nearly full in the indigo sky above. *I have entered the book*, I thought. Just a few months ago *Life of Pi* was an inch and a half of pages that I could hold in one hand, and now I was standing in the middle of a setting that I could see, smell, and touch. *I am here.*

Father Antonisamy walked up quietly from behind, without me noticing, and explained that the crows sought refuge there because it was one of the few quiet, secluded places in the middle of town.

In his long cassock, he seemed to float about like a sort of angelic being, but now he was dressed in plain clothes, and seeing him in trousers brought him down to earth, to my level.

46

We walked out to the front of the school where Samandam was waiting for us with a car, and as we were driven to the restaurant, Father Antonisamy turned to me with a concerned look on his face. "Now, Surendra," he said (I wasn't sure why exactly he continued to use my last name—maybe it was another local formality that I was unfamiliar with), "I am told you were in an accident in the street earlier today? Are you all right?"

How did *he* know about that? Perhaps he really was all-seeing, all-knowing.

Dinner was traditional Tamil food, the delicious comfort food that I had grown up with—fluffy basmati rice and a huge spread of vegetable curries—lentils, aubergines, tomatoes with cucumber and green beans with shredded coconut. This was followed by a very traditional dessert—fruit salad. It was something Ma had often made for us during the summer, when fresh mangoes were in season at the Tamil grocery stores in Scarborough. As she cut up the fruit, her eyes would glaze over while she rambled on about her father taking her to some thatched roof café near the ocean in Ceylon where the fruit salad was divine. We'd eat the concoction she was trying to emulate in Scarborough, but it never really lived up to the hype of her reminiscing. Then I tried the fruit salad in Pondicherry and was floored—everything was local, ripe, and seasonal. Plain fruit, chopped up and served in a glass goblet, had never tasted so good, and it blew my mind.

Father Antonisamy's friend, who ran the restaurant, came out at the end of our meal and seemed very excited to be hosting a foreigner. He was introduced as Mr. Venu, and was a former schoolteacher who had moved on to become a successful businessman. "Surendra is my esteemed Canadian guest," Father Antonisamy said, introducing me. "It is my mission to ensure that he never forgets his time in Pondicherry."

Mr. Venu enthusiastically waved his hands about, and made it a point to tell me that he had been trying, to no avail, to get Father Antonisamy to eat in his restaurant for the previous two years—and that I should be very honored that the principal had ventured off school grounds on my behalf. "Yes," I agreed; it was an honor. Then he brought out his head cook, puffed out his chest, and proudly told us that it was the man's wedding night, but he forced him to come in to cook because it was such a joyous occasion to have us at the restaurant. Now I was ashamed.

The cook bowed deeply, bobbled his head, and then scurried off—I assumed he was frantic to head back to his big night, which had been put on pause while he slaved away stirring curries bubbling in red clay pots to make our dinner.

Next, Mr. Venu opened a bag he was holding and pulled out a silk shawl, which he draped over my shoulders; then he and Father Antonisamy clapped while nodding their heads, telling me that this was the traditional welcome in South India.

Back at the hotel, sleep hit me like a brick in the face.

I dream that night: *It's the middle of the night in our house in Scarborough, dark and quiet—only the light from the upstairs bathroom is on. My sisters and I hold on to the railing of the banister upstairs, peering down to the floor below. Dad is talking quietly to someone, a stranger we don't recognize. Something about Ma and a heart attack. We strain to hear what they're saying. Somehow the three of us know—Ma has died. I can't breathe—I fall to my knees, losing all control of holding my body upright. When I argued fiercely with her, usually over something stupid, she'd shake her head and say through tears, "When I'm gone, you'll be sorry. One day, you'll know what it's like not to have a mother." Yeah, whatever, Ma, I would think. The feeling is unbearable. Her smiling face comes to mind, then her laugh—to be seen and heard never again. I am frozen, numb;*

I want to move, but it's impossible—everything is dark, dad is talking about funeral arrangements. Poor Ma . . . No, no, this can't be happening . . . I can't breathe . . .

I woke up and caught my breath—I wiped away the stream of tears that had soaked my face. *That's what it will feel like.* I shuddered. Ma was right—I'll be sorry. Never before had I dreamed something that was so very real. Holy Mary—I'm never yelling at her again.

Was India to blame for my crazy dream, this ancient land of mysticism, sages, and soothsayers? I picked up the box of the anti-malaria pills that were sitting on my bedside table. They had been prescribed by my doctor, to be taken two weeks prior to travel and then regularly throughout the trip. Mefloquine. Sure enough, in the fine print under "side effects," there it was—*vivid dreams.*

When my dad and Ma were fighting, when things got really bad and he'd threaten to kill her, she'd do her best to remain defiant, countering every one of his insults with a stronger volley. The matches always seemed to end in the same place, though. "If I die," Ma would yell, in one of her last attempts to reason with this madman, before her voice would break and she'd be fighting back tears, "God help these children . . ." And as my sisters and I listened from upstairs, that falter in her voice was the moment of real fear for us, because it was the first indication of potentially being defeated by my dad. The first glimpse of reality of life without Ma—and the scariest part of it all, this feeling of being completely and utterly lost. She was the glue that kept our lives together. She cooked, cleaned, paid the bills, washed our clothes and put them away, worked two jobs, and attended every parent-teacher meeting. She'd pack our lunches for school every morning, and every night before we'd go to sleep, without fail, she would kiss my forehead while whispering, "I love you, *kanna.* God bless you."

In that hotel room in Pondicherry that night, I recalled a dusty corner of our basement in Scarborough where a framed black-and-white picture sat forgotten on the floor—Ma at nineteen, wearing a white sari and playing the veena—a big, South Indian plucked instrument. But it dawned on me that I was so far removed from the early life of the girl who was playing that veena. The Ma I had always known was a woman who wore super-high heels, maintained a trim figure and exuded a Beyoncé-esque elegance. Now I realized that Ma was a vestige of a different world. She had come from this ancient land of saris, monkey-infested temples, astrologers, and palm readers—a world of arranged marriages and curries cooked in clay pots over wood fires, a culture in which women never, ever cut their hair. To Ma, an elephant wasn't a zoo animal or an exotic creature on a postage stamp—it was a work animal, one that walked with a heavy gait on the dirt road in front of her childhood home, on its way to a ten-hour shift of clearing the fields.

Ma had assimilated to a life in the West, but I guess I had taken for granted that my roots, my cultural heritage, were stored in a beautiful, little four foot ten, ninety-pound hard drive of sorts, and that was Ma. I could not bear to lose her.

This revelation felt like a gift, provided at just the right time. *Here you are in India; go out there and become Tamil for yourself.* The bustling town around me was filled with all the necessary components—Indian families, colorful marketplaces, and ancient stone temples, engaged in all manners of Indianness; all I had to do was cross the street.

From: yann_martel1963@yahoo.com

To: rajivsca@yahoo.ca

Subject: RE: Mohammed comes to the mountain . . .

Date: Sun, 13 Feb 2005 06:37:56

Dear Rajiv,

May your travels continue, across oceans and into mountains, and especially, into remote corners of your imagination.

Glad to hear Pondicherry is still standing. A wonderful place, alive despite the decay, like all of India.

Yours,

Yann

5.

THERE WERE ABOUT THIRTY boisterous Indian boys in the classroom, all sixteen years old and dressed in their school uniforms—crisp white dress shirts, gray trousers, and slate blue ties. Their eyes were all on me as I made my way to the back of the room and I stared right back at them. I looked just like them, except I was wearing blue jeans and a Madras plaid shirt, and yet they looked at me mystified. My shirt was plastered to my back with sweat, but despite the overwhelming heat and humidity, I was enthralled to be here—the Mecca of my research—a Pondicherry classroom full of all the subtle nuances I hoped to take down and emulate as Pi.

Two boys were wobbling their heads in characteristic Indian fashion. I began rummaging through my bag for my pen and notebook, eager to take down these first observations, when the whole room suddenly went completely silent. I was still searching for my Bic rubber-grip pen when . . .

"Haah! So, then, you are whom?" A short, squat teacher with huge thick-lensed glasses had appeared out of thin air, standing beside my bench—a Tamil man in his late fifties who was bald save for the two patches of hair over his ears. He also had two tiny patches of hair growing *out* of his ears.

The boys were scurrying into their places, taking their seats on the rows of benches in front of me. "Good morning, sir! God bless you," they all shouted out in unison, in English. The teacher impatiently waved his hand in their direction as the boys raised their arms together in a gesture of reverence and continued, "Praise the Lord!" I rolled my eyes in my head at the formality of the colonialism that still remained here—these boys were probably all mostly Hindu.

With a furrowed brow, the teacher smiled curiously and rocked back and forth on his heels a few times, waiting for my response. "I'm Rajiv."

A puzzled look came over his face and he leaned in, motioning for me to repeat my name. "Rajiv . . ." I said again tentatively, "Um, I'm here for some research. I have permission from Father Antonisamy to sit—"

He cut me off, "Your name, once more?"

I was baffled, and nervous. My plan to draw as little attention to myself as possible had very quickly turned on its head to bite me in the ass.

One of the boys seated on the bench in front of me must have recognized the problem, because he quickly rose up and chimed in, "*Raaa*jeeve, sir," rolling the R heavily and placing the emphasis on the RA.

"Ahhh! *Raaa*jeeve," echoed the teacher in his high-pitched, nasal voice, bobbling his head. The boys in front of me bobbled their heads, as well, pleased that we all now knew what my name was. I made eye contact with the boy who had stood up, giving him a smile of gratitude. He smiled back and as he sat back down, it dawned on me that I probably should have stood up to address the teacher.

I was always aware that my last name was not a real Tamil name, as my dad's true name was Nadarajah *Surendiran*. He once told me that there weren't enough boxes on the form at the immigration office when he first arrived in Canada, so he hastily had to omit a couple of letters to make it fit, but who knows whether that's even true—it's very likely he was telling me this story after spending the afternoon with his best friends, Jack, Jim, and Johnnie—Jack Daniels, Jim Beam, and Johnnie Walker, that is.

My first name was the part I thought was authentic, but in that classroom in Pondicherry, I discovered that I had lived my whole life pronouncing *my* own name incorrectly, like a big dum-dum. My parents followed an old Tamil tradition and never addressed me by name but instead called me *mahan*, the Tamil word for "son," or *kanna*, a term of endearment meaning "precious one," but also a nickname for the blue god, Krishna, who wears a peacock-feather crown. My way of saying my name was always a short *Rajiv*, no emphasis on any particular part of the name, just one very fast *Ruj-eve*, almost as if it were accented with French. I had never really thought about the origin or meaning of my Indian name. Perhaps it's because it wasn't one that solicited questioning in the English-speaking world, unlike a girl in my ninth grade math class, a new implant from Bangladesh, a shy, little thing named Jannatul. By eleventh grade, she had grown aware of the salacious implications of her name and made a conscious effort to be addressed as the much more subtle Jan. The only things I knew about my name were that Ma picked it only because she liked the sound of it—and that it was the name of the prime minister of India—a handsome, princely figure named Rajiv Gandhi—who was serving at the time of my birth. He met his untimely end when a woman greeting him at a public event bent down to touch his feet in the traditional form of respectful salutation, only to set off a bomb under her sari, killing herself while assassinating the prime minister and over twenty-five others—brutal.

There were no backs to the benches we were seated on, and after a couple of hours of sitting up straight and rigid, the entire class was slouching and twitching as the teacher lectured in a jumbled mix of English and a formal version of Tamil that was too florid for me to understand. I was jet-lagged and started nodding off, so I tried to keep my eyes open by taking note of my surroundings, surveying the details of the room—crumbling plaster walls with flaking baby blue paint, twenty-foot ceilings, an old ceiling fan whirring overhead. There was a small crucifix attached to the chalkboard. To my right was an arched window that opened onto the covered exterior corridor, providing a beautiful view of the courtyard. The windowsill seemed to be the designated holding area for dozens of strange, brightly colored bags made of woven plastic gimp. The wooden bench I was seated on was smooth and worn from years of use, with a dark and shiny patina. This classroom felt like sacred ground to me—it was a significant part of Pi's life and a major setting in the novel. The teacher made his way through the rows, checking homework, and I was jarred out of my daze when he violently smacked his ruler down on one boy's notebook and snapped, "The date, *idiot*—the date!"

It was still midmorning but the heat was intense, and just as I was beginning to marvel at the boys' ability to remain focused, the one who had said my name poked the boy beside him in the ribs with the end of his pencil, making him jerk and knock the underside of the desk with his knees. The teacher turned around from the blackboard and yelled out something in Tamil, pointing to the innocent boy who had been poked. He slipped off the bench and knelt on the floor, remaining upright. I recalled this form of chastising that Ma had enforced only a few times when we were small kids—it got uncomfortable really fast. What amazed me was that there was no arguing, no back and forth between the kids and the teacher—no "It wasn't me!" or "Whaaaaat?" This is not what would have transpired back in Toronto—I recalled an incident in eleventh grade English class when a student spat in the teacher's face after an argument about his final grade.

Class ended and we were dismissed for lunch. We were all filing out of the room when the boy who had said my name appeared beside me. "King of life," he said in heavily accented English, his voice prepubescent. "*Raj*, like *raja* or king, and *jeeve, jivan, jivatma*—Sanskrit for life, the soul. *Rajiv* . . . king of life." He was taller and thinner than I was and had a big grin on his face as he looked down at me with two huge black eyes. For the first time ever, my name meant something to me.

"I am Akash," he continued, "and if the king of life is not preoccupied for lunch break, you may sit with me and my classmates." I had the sudden urge to pull out my tape recorder. This was the accent that I was hoping to mimic—the realest form of it, a sixteen-year-old Pondicherry boy, a native Tamil speaker who was conversing in English.

Boys from every other classroom in the school were making the mass exodus to lunch, and the corridors became a sea of brown faces with shiny black hair. It took me by complete surprise when Akash reached down and swiftly took my palm in his, holding my hand as he led me through the crowd. Boys hold hands in India and it isn't romantic. I didn't want to appear ungrateful for his kindness; still, it was new to me and it took quite a lot of effort to not pull my hand away.

The corridor and the courtyard were quickly filling with boys, each one of them claiming their spot in a sort of human jigsaw puzzle. Akash was still holding my hand when we stopped at a shaded corner of the corridor, in front of three other boys from our classroom—Rohit, Deepak, and Karthik. Each of the boys was holding one of those colorful woven plastic gimp bags. I watched curiously as each boy pulled out a little towel, placed it on the stone floor in front of him, and then sat down, cross-legged. I joined them on the ground and then a mild interrogation began: "Where you are from?" asked Rohit. He was fair-skinned and blue-eyed, with North Indian features that were model-handsome—even though his nickname was "Nosey," because of his large, beak-shaped nose.

When I said Toronto, and then clarified by saying, Canada, Karthik quickly cut in, "*Tu parles Français?*" His eyes were droopy and his deep voice sounded eager.

I responded in French with, "Yes, of course," and he beamed.

Deepak, the alpha of the group, who sported a mustache and was taller and thicker than the others, shoved Karthik and filled me in about his obsession with learning French (a language that still had a presence in Pondicherry).

"Will you be attending classes here?" Akash asked. They didn't seem to have stars in their eyes when I spoke of Hollywood, and just bobbled their heads as I filled them in on *Life of Pi*, the movie, and my research plans.

Then Nosey leaned in and squeezed my upper arm with his fingers. "Big biceps, very nice," he noted, and the others followed suit, each taking turns to squeeze my arm. "Yes, very nice," echoed Karthik, then, "Quite firm," Akash said. (FYI: They were not "nice" or "big"—these observations were simply relative to emaciated Indian standards.)

"May I have a look at that fancy pen you were using?" asked Deepak. I pulled out my ordinary ballpoint and handed it to him. "Oohhhh . . ." he said, gently caressing the rubber shaft with his fingertips, ". . . so very soft! We are not having access to pens like this in India."

"Take it; I have another one," I offered. Then there was a flurry of arguing in Tamil, the other boys accusing him of a rude welcome to their new guest. "No, no," Deepak said, preciously handing the pen back to me, "I simply wished to inspect it."

The boys each reached into their gimp bags and brought out stainless-steel tiffin containers—these three-tiered lunch pails contained either rice and various vegetable curries, or other Tamil meals that were best eaten when assembled just before consumption. I had no lunch, but politely declined when they insisted that I share theirs. Another round of questions: Where was I staying? How did I get to school? Was there anything I needed? They finished eating, and after packing away their tiffin containers, Deepak whispered something to Akash and then leaned in and quietly said to me, "You come with us now . . ."

We stepped around the maze of seated boys, snuck out of the school's back gate, and as we made our way down a tiny, quiet side street, Akash explained what was happening. They were forbidden to leave the school grounds, but every now and then they snuck off to have some "fun."

"You like video games?" he asked slyly.

"Yeah, sure," I lied. I was never a video game kind of kid. Cleaning out my chicken coop or hand-pollinating the blossoms in my pumpkin patch were much more appealing.

We arrived at a tiny, old, and decrepit building with a roof made of woven palm leaves, and an adorable little kid, about seven years old, ran out to greet us. He was barefoot and wore red cotton shorts with white trim and a ragged T-shirt with Bart Simpson on it. He held out his hand and each of the boys handed him a five-rupee note (about seven American cents). The little boy had his eyes on me the whole time, and in a tiny, squeaky voice cried out in Tamil, "Who is this?" Deepak told him to "never mind," and pushed him aside, ducking and making his way through the tiny doorway into the dimly lit building. We all followed as the boy lingered nearby and imploringly continued in Tamil, "Who is this? Where is he from?" I turned to him and met his gaze. The other boys headed over to pinball machines and little video game booths that lined the tiny room, but I was fascinated by this little kid. He stared at me with these hazel eyes that emitted a look of such intense wonder and curiosity. He pursed his lips and tilted his head to one side. I understood that this kid couldn't afford to go to school and this was his job—running this game hut for some money-making land-lord. He walked around like a little boss and checked in with all the kids playing games, selling them glass bottles of Fanta and Coca-Cola, but turning to look at me regularly.

I made my way over to Akash, who was now completely engrossed in a game of foosball, and asked if it was obvious that I wasn't from India. "Yes, Rajiv, it is quite obvious. You are clearly a foreigner. Your stance, your build, even your confident gaze is telling us that you are from far away." I was momentarily proud, then remembered my goal of becoming more Tamil. I looked around and took cues from the other boys' posture—I slouched a bit and softened my gaze.

Nosey roped me into a Nintendo game. He was frantically hitting the buttons on the controller, twitching and jerking with every move of his character on the tiny TV screen. "Boys in India are quite rowdy, no?" he shouted through fits of giggles, his bum rising off the chair and then thumping back down as his character hopped over a fence, ". . . not like in America, no?"

I forced out a short, uncomfortable laugh and just raised my eyebrows. *Dare I tell him about guys being sent home from school for transactions of weed in the bathroom? Should I mention the cherry bomb firecrackers that exploded in the trash can outside the principal's office one afternoon? Or maybe I should tell him about our scandalous drama class teaching assistant—a three-hundred-pound, thirty-year-old who was doing the forbidden hokey-pokey in the backside of a waiflike tenth grader. No, I better not.* I had visions of returning to Petit Séminaire the next morning, only to be greeted with a scene of sinful earthly delights from an old Dutch painting, one of pure jungle madness, a bunch of brown boys violently beating their teachers with yard sticks and crucifixes while others engaged in various unmentionable acts in the paradisiacal courtyard. A shiver ran down my spine, despite the humidity. My street-crossing incident showed me that tampering with the way things worked could be detrimental.

"No, boys here are very different. That's for sure!"

My new set of friends, who dubbed themselves "the Dudes of Petit," made me a part of their gang at school and went out of their way to ensure I didn't want for anything. Once, I mentioned to them that I didn't have a clock in my hotel room and had forgotten to bring my watch to India. I returned to my room that night and found a package outside my door—a big, tacky, pink, plastic clock in the shape of a huge watch (with batteries inserted into the back). The following day in class, Karthik turned around and slipped a note to me:

l' horloge comment est - il? Karthikeyan

He was practicing his written French, and before I had a chance to respond, he slipped me a translation, either doubting his grammar or my comprehension:

How is it?
It is working
or not?

I tried to stifle a laugh and it came out of my nose as a loud, ruffled snort, momentarily interrupting the physics lesson. Karthik whirled around and I gave him a thumbs-up.

Akash began to feel like the brother I never had. At lunch, which I now participated in with my own tiffin container filled with food from my hotel restaurant, Akash helped himself to bits of my meal and offered me morsels of deliciousness that his mother had packed for him. He discreetly fine-tuned my eating habits (we all ate using our fingers), whispering to me that I was never to use my left hand, considered "unclean" in India, where it was used in conjunction with a bowl of water to clean one's bum after pooping. This explained why locals would stare at me while I ate in the hotel restaurant—I had been ripping apart my dosa with my poo-hand!

At the video game hut, as the other guys flocked to their games, Akash began sitting with me on the stoop outside, and we'd share our dreams of the future—I with my sights set on a career in front of the camera, and he with a passion for either law or medicine; he couldn't quite decide. He wanted to dedicate his life to a practice that would benefit his "fellow countrymen" in the noblest way possible. Akash was a philosopher, an old soul, and I loved that about him. "I feel as though I had met you long ago," he once said to me. "Perhaps we were brothers in another life. The universe works in strange ways. I am certain you were brought to India for more than you know."

My morning walk to school was eventually replaced by a faster mode of transport, when Akash insisted on picking me up at my hotel every morning to take me to school on the back of his motorbike—all the boys had one, and his commute entailed passing by the hotel any-way, he said. The first time he showed up with his bike, I hesitated, hemmed, and hawed, and then sighed deeply and got on the seat behind him, holding on tightly as the motor whirred to life and we whizzed off into the street. No one wore helmets and they all rode their bikes haphazardly, according to the rules of the road here, which were—*there were no rules!* My view from the back of the bike gave me a different perspective of this town—moving at a faster pace gave me more to look at, kids crammed into the back of rickshaws on their way to school, tightly clutching their brightly colored lunch bags to their chests while other kids walked to school on the sidewalk, with-out shoes; buses backed up with no warning; cars cut us off within a hair of colliding; and flatbed trucks carted around huge loads of cargo, precariously piled high, with no sign of being securely anchored. *At least if I died, it would be in pursuit of my dream.* "Killed in a crash in India while doing research for the role he was born to play," the obituary would read. "A tragic loss of a life full of such potential. We mourn together."

After-school excursions with the gang became a daily routine when the boys found out about my checklist of places that I wanted to visit in Pondicherry. "We will take you," Deepak said, putting his arm around my shoulder as we were walking out of class one day. "You must see Pondicherry as a local, not as a tourist."

That afternoon, I overcame my initial fear of putting my life in the hands of these sixteen-year-olds. The warm wind was blowing through my hair and drying out my sweaty shirt as our four motorbikes snaked their way through town. I saw more of the city on the back of Akash's bike, narrow lanes and alleys that I had not traversed on foot. I caught fast flashes of new scenes all over town—on the side streets, men pushing their carts of fresh fish and vocally advertising the catch of the day; an old shopkeeper whacking the corrugated tin roof of his stall with his umbrella and shouting at the pack of roguish monkeys that had just stolen big bunches of ripe yellow bananas from him. Two women were adorning a roadside idol of Lakshmi, goddess of wealth, with fresh flower garlands. The nondescript location seemed completely random, surrounded by piles of garbage and flanked by mechanic shops, and with all the other temples in town, I wondered why these two women were worshipping here.

We rode through a crowded marketplace full of activity: a woman squatting on the ground, cutting banana leaves into quarters—the same banana leaves that lined the plates at my hotel restaurant (banana leaves are huge, about four feet long by two feet wide, and have lots of uses in South India because they're food-safe, waterproof, and very flexible). The market was thick with people and as our bikes slowed down, I saw locals haggling with vendors who sold all kinds of things, from mangoes and ginger, to plastic buckets, bars of soap, and twig brooms. Small boys, no older than seven, would be scurrying by in threadbare clothing, carrying huge baskets of pineapples balanced on their heads, while men emptied giant burlap bags of tiny purple onions onto the tarps on the ground.

We left the market and Akash revved the bike up to its full speed;

roadside details blended into a blurred ribbon of vibrant colors. It was thrilling, twisting and turning through town with the rustling motor reverberating under us—until he turned to me, taking his eyes off the road, and randomly told me that his palm-reading grandmother foresaw his tragic death at a young age.

I quickly changed the subject; our conversation turned to the movie version of *Life of Pi* and he suggested that I tell the producers to film in Pondicherry. I tried to relay to him the insignificance of my opinions even if I were to get the part, and that there was only a very small chance of me actually getting the part. He cut me off midsentence, "No, no, Rajiv, you musn't say that. There's a very BIG chance," he yelled over the bike's motor, "you *will* get it; I can see it in your bright eyes—your future is bright." I couldn't help but smile.

Soon, Akash stopped the bike as he waited to make a turn and I noticed three children, mostly naked, filthy, and with matted hair. They were laughing and giggling as they passed a tiny, helpless, newborn puppy back and forth. One of the girls stepped aside, squatted a bit, and just began peeing on the ground, a small cloud of dust rising up as her urine hit the packed dirt. Then she ran back and joined the group. The puppy whimpered and the kids put it down and danced around it. After Akash's engine started to purr and we rode away, I lingered on what I had witnessed, wondering what would become of that puppy—imagining its future searching the dirty streets for food, sleeping wherever it could, trying to avoid getting killed by the crazy traffic—and then I realized that those kids, now laughing and running around, seemed just as ill-fated as the dog. This was India, and I challenged myself to not look away, to see this country for what it truly was and to accept it as such.

I settled into my hotel room later that night and longed for a Western staple that I had previously taken for granted—a plain old shower, a thing of beauty; you turn on the faucet and water comes gushing out of the tub spout. One quick pull of the diverter and the water is redirected to come sprinkling out of the showerhead like rainfall. My hotel was one of the fanciest in Pondicherry—about nine hundred Indian rupees a night (about fourteen American dollars)! *However*, there was no shower in the bathroom, but instead, a little faucet jutting out of the tiled wall, about knee-high, and under it was an orange plastic bucket with a thin plastic bowl floating in the water it contained. Bathing consisted of stripping down and pouring bowlfuls of the ice-cold water on myself, which splashed all over the bathroom, soaking the entire floor.

The bucket with the bowl was also intended to be used in conjunction with the toilet, to wash one's bum. When I was little, I was potty trained with the rule that one's bum was only clean if it came in contact with water after pooping—and as a toddler, this meant sitting on the toilet seat and calling, "Maaaaa?" or "Daaaaad?" to come and pour a bowl of tap water carefully through the space left between my seated torso and the opening of the back of the toilet seat, a delicate procedure that, if successful, would entail a steady stream of water running between the valley of the butt cheeks, purging one's behind of all its sins. Ma was always better at it than my dad, who paid little attention to the temperature of the water, and would often end up pouring down a bowlful that was either scalding hot or freakishly cold, resulting in jerky contorting and shrieking in shock. The sacred water decanting, however, was always followed by me finishing it off, so to speak, with toilet paper. When I started elementary school it was extremely disturbing to learn that toilet paper was intended to be used dry—a conclusion I reached while staring at the faucet of the sink, so very far away, through the crack of the bathroom stall.

There was no toilet paper provided at the hotel in Pondicherry—it was a discovery that revealed yet another side to the bum-wiping saga:

that the water/toilet-paper combo was a kind of immigrant adaptation, holding on to an older practice while incorporating and welcoming a new one, in a new land. Here in Mother India, no one used toilet paper, as Akash had insinuated. Luckily, Ma had the foresight to know this and had stuffed about ten rolls of quilted, three-ply Cottonelle into my suitcase. I had initially assumed that she was filling the gaps in between my clothes so they wouldn't shift around—and I sure was glad that I didn't question what she was doing.

Nights in my hotel were the quiet alone time I used to process the new world I was being exposed to. As I envisioned the boys dutifully making their way through the prescribed homework for the day, I would open my own set of books and continue with my personal Pi homework—literature that I had brought along with me in the hopes it would be relevant to my activities in India. One of my books was *The Complete Idiot's Guide to Hinduism*. It was an attempt to finally understand what was behind the idol worship and symbolism that I had been so infatuated with as a child. When I finished the book, I was up to date with the ins and outs of the religion I had been born into. These practices were as old as the pyramids in Egypt—and thousands of years later, in both Toronto and Pondicherry, they were still alive and thriving. I was ready to be a groupie again.

The boys continued to help me make my way through the precious list of Pi sites I had assembled. One evening was spent visiting all the holy sites—the beautiful, whitewashed Jamia mosque (a central gathering place for the city's large Muslim population), the ashram of a famous saint, Sri Aurobindo, and finally, an ancient Hindu temple by the ocean dedicated to the elephant-headed god, Ganesha.

"This is a significant place of worship," Deepak explained as we got off our bikes and made our way toward the temple's entrance. "The statue inside is famous throughout all of India."

Nosey chimed in, bobbling his head. "The French colonists removed it from the temple and threw it into the deep ocean, but it reappeared in its original setting the following morning. Repeated attempts to remove and sink the idol proved in vain . . . it would continue to magically return to the temple."

My breath was taken away when we turned the corner and came face to face with a spectacularly huge, live elephant festooned with garlands and bells, stationed in front of the main gate. One by one the boys stopped in front of the creature, bowing as the elephant blessed each one of them by touching the top of their heads with its trunk. When it was my turn, I stepped up and felt incredibly small, holding my arms close to my side and waiting for its trunk to make contact with my head. My skin pulled tight around my skull, not knowing how far the elephant's trunk was or when it would touch me. It was incredible seeing the animal up close—its skin was a slate color and amazingly thick, like the rubber on a car tire, but marked with tiny wrinkles. Its trunk finally touched me with a light *tap, tap, tap*, almost as if it had been searching for something in my hair. I looked into its eye, like a human's, yet with an orangish iris, its eyelashes about an inch long, thick and bristly. Making eye contact with this magnificent being left me somewhat unsettled, realizing it was subjected to a life of servitude.

My uncle in Toronto once told me that when he was a student in India, the temple next to his school had a baby elephant that he would give a little candy to every day. He returned to that temple thirty years later, while on vacation. A temple worker confirmed that the fully grown elephant was the same one he had befriended—and when he gave it a candy again, all these years later, tears streamed down the elephant's face as it caressed my uncle's head with its trunk.

We removed our shoes at the entrance and the boys and I stepped over the holy threshold into the temple. The cold granite floor felt refreshing against my bare feet. This was true sacred ground. I felt a hush.

Everything was made of carved stone—the walls, the altars, the ceiling. I felt strangely out of place here—I had outgrown my enthusiasm for religion, and hadn't been in a temple for quite a while. As I grew out of my childhood habit of practicing two religions, I had settled on Christianity by the time I was twelve, fervently going to church with my aunt on Sundays. But the hard and fast rules, the insistence that a person could only be "saved" if he knew Christ, and the notion of "blind faith" without questioning the reasons and motives of these strict codes made me leery of the authenticity of organized faith, and eventually left me bitter about having to adhere to a prescribed form of worship.

It was dark and cool in the temple and the smoke from oil lamps and incense filled the air, which felt intensely charged as we neared the idol at the center of the building. I noticed signs that stated "Hindus only, beyond this point." The central chamber that housed the idol was dark, save for a few brass lamps hanging from the ceiling, which were fueled with ghee or coconut oil—it was Friday, the holy day, and the room was packed. Three Brahmin priests, shirtless (save for a single holy thread that ran from the shoulder to the waist) and wearing orange loincloths, chanted in Sanskrit as one rang a brass bell he held in his left hand while circling the idol with a small camphor flame on a brass tray in his right hand. The nasal chanting, coupled with the echoing bell, tugged at something inside me, and my eyes filled with tears. I was embarrassed and turned away from the boys, pretending to inspect some carving in a corner.

As a child, I'd stand with my parents as the Brahmin priests would bathe a seven-foot-tall granite statue of Vishnu with milk, honey, and turmeric water, then shut the doors of the little room that housed the idol, and we'd all wait in silence. A few minutes later, the doors would reopen, and Vishnu would be dressed in fine silks and glittering jewels. I'd look around me as the ladies and men reverently gasped and fluttered their eyelids. The men would fall to the ground and do a few push-up-like moves. I was told that we were looking at God. And God was colorful, flashy, and had a pleasant smile on His stone face. We'd stroll around the temple and visit the other gods and goddesses—Meenakshi, tiny waist, big hips, pretty in a purple sari and wearing a ten-foot-long fresh-flower garland; Murugan, god of the Tamils, young and handsome, riding on a peacock; and beside him were his two wives, Valli and Deyvanai. This was all fodder for my wild imagination as a child, but as I grew older and continued to practice two faiths, the Christian pastors who learned of my ways made it clear that Hinduism was a no-no and, condemning these ancient rituals, insisted that I run far, far away from these stone idols, which were the devil's means of luring me off the path to the one true God.

I was about ten years old when I began asking Ma questions about what it all meant, in an effort to give her the opportunity to make a case for Vishnu and his posse, so I could make a final, informed decision. When Ma's repeated response, tinged with an edge of annoyance, continued to be, "That is the way. It is just the tradition; that's all . . ." my attitude toward the Hindu religion went from enthusiasm to disdain, dismissing it as superstitious paganism and nonsense doll worship, turning my faith fully to Christ . . . before his church, with its rigid exclusions of all other faiths, turned me off religion entirely.

Now, in Pondicherry, I had a refreshed perspective. As we continued to stand before the stone statue of Ganesha, I finally understood that he was just a point of focus, an ancient means of concentrating on an *idea* or notion of an energy that ran through the entire universe. This made sense to me. Hinduism was all about consciousness. I looked around me and noticed the locals, dark-skinned Tamils from all walks of life, gathered here to worship. India, filled with such poverty and suffering, was a place where religion was alive and thriving. However unreal, however far-fetched these ideas and concepts might be, it helped these people get through each day, in some way. Their suffering, in the context of their faith, fit into some kind of order, with a reason for its existence, and this simple notion made it that much easier to deal with. I stared up at the elephant-headed god, cozily surrounded by masses of flower garlands. Ganesha, *Lord Overcomer of Obstacles*. I subtly looked to my right and left—Akash, Nosey, Deepak, and Karthik all had their palms together in prayer, facing the god, but their eyes were closed. I closed my own eyes and sought out the obstacles that I was currently struggling with.

"Scientists in the West peer through powerful telescopes, looking deep into space in the hopes of learning about the universe, while the Hindu approach couples inspection of the world around us with a self-disciplined *inner* journey . . ." I recalled, from my handbook on Hinduism. Now I was ready to put it into practice—focusing and looking into the depths of consciousness in my own mind. *Know thyself. Inquire. Be free.* Hippie talk? Maybe, but all this was being revealed to me at just the right time.

In that crowded inner chamber, Akash took my hand once again, and walked me even closer to the stone idol of Ganesha. The priest continued to circle the idol with the camphor flame, and then he stepped down from the altar and brought the tray of fire to the worshippers. We were pushed together as people crowded in and reached toward the flame with both palms, quickly making contact with it before touching their fingers to their foreheads. "The fire shows us to God," Akash whispered as we both reached in, "and we come in contact with it to accept his blessing." Another priest followed closely behind and marked our foreheads with red Kunkumam powder, a sign that we had received the deity's blessing, but also a reminder of the "third eye"—the most important means of viewing our external world, through our *mind's* eye. Karthik, Nosey, and Deepak were behind us and as they knelt to the ground, I joined them and followed along.

"Ask for what your heart desires," Akash said in his lilt, "and all will be granted." I closed my eyes, and when our heads touched the stone floor, my tears began to flow. As three priests chanted in unison and the ringing bell continued in tempo, I wished for my efforts to prove fruitful, and not be in vain. In that temple, in that small Indian city so far from my home, I was now incredibly comfortable, finally connecting to a part of my identity that had never been fully realized. Here, a world apart from my parents, I felt closer to them than ever before. This was the world they came from, and I had finally become a part of it.

"You cannot leave India without having Pondicherry ice cream," Deepak insisted later that evening as the boys and I walked along the seashore, stopping to purchase chocolate and nut-covered bars of deliciousness from a vendor on the boardwalk.

"You are truly a good person, Rajiv," Akash exclaimed randomly, in between bites of his pink ice cream bar coated in crushed cashews. Karthik and Deepak made sounds of agreement and nodded with their mouths full. "Not like another boy who once visited us from America," Akash continued. "He showed us pornographic magazines he had brought with him. Very corrupt fellow, he was."

We stopped and posed for pictures together under the huge statue of Mahatma Gandhi. They took me through the old French quarter of town, streets lined with well-kept colonial-looking houses painted in a variety of pastel shades. Ladies had laid out elaborate *kolam* patterns on the ground in front of their houses, using white rice flour. When I asked questions about culture and customs, my four friends eagerly shared their insights and opinions. I marveled at how mature they were for sixteen-year-olds, but also how naive they were about things that seemed inherent to teenage culture back home—clothing, music trends, and sex. When the conversation turned to the rampant corruption that plagued politics in India, Deepak piped up, "*Raaa*jeeve, we have a saying in India: even a dead man would open his mouth for a rupee!"

The Dudes of Petit gave me a glimpse into what my life might have been like had my parents not immigrated to Canada. My lonely dinners at the hotel restaurant were soon replaced by home-cooked ones at the boys' houses. It started with dinner at Deepak's, but once the word got out that I had visited one boy's house, the invitations aggressively poured in from all the other boys' parents and I was made to promise that I'd make time to join them for a meal. These boys meant so much to me, and I wanted to do whatever I could to show my gratitude and contribute to our budding friendships. But I also saw this as a valuable research opportunity—a true grime and grit exposure into the kitchen cupboards of Pondicherry.

In every home, I was treated with an overwhelming amount of hospitality—the food overflowed from my plate and I was constantly asked if I wanted anything else to eat or drink. At Karthik's house, I relished the new experience of sitting on the floor and eating our rice and curries directly off of banana leaves laid on the ground (in the place of plates)—as Ma and my dad had often described as being uber-traditional. I made sure my left hand was securely tucked into my lap, far away from my food.

I had one shirt that was my go-to article of clothing for these visiting dinners and special occasions in India. It was a white linen button-up dress shirt with short sleeves that I had bought just before leaving Toronto—I was in H&M and was impressed with how thin the shirt was, but also that it had a subtle white-on-white plaid pattern woven into the cloth. The shirt was too scandalous to wear on its own (nipples visible) so I bought a thick, white tank top that would go underneath. I'd hand-wash the shirt back at the hotel after each outing.

I spoke Tamil, to the best of my ability, to Deepak and Karthik's parents. Akash's father (a lawyer) was eager to practice his English.

I became versed in local social etiquette, buying garlands from the flower ladies on the side of the road and offering them to the boys' mothers. The "aunties" (as I addressed them) would accept my gift with both hands, close their eyes, and reverently touch the garland to their forehead before hanging it on a statue of a Hindu god in their home altars.

Once, at Deepak's house (where I learned he was a mama's boy—she'd lovingly call him "Deepuuuuu," which the dudes and I used to heckle him with), his mother was attempting to apply henna onto his younger sister's hand. The two were seated on the front stoop of their house, where the early evening light was its brightest, and I noticed the mother doing a terrible job, making noises of frustration between her teeth as she continued to struggle with a plastic cone of henna paste. I offered to take over. The two of them looked up at me, bewildered. She handed the henna cone to me somewhat hesitantly, perhaps feeling obliged to accommodate the request of her guest.

What she didn't know was that I had a knack for applying henna designs. It began as a fluke when I was about twelve and a Muslim friend of mine in elementary school, Syed, noticed me carefully piping out paint onto a canvas in art class. He asked me whether I might go to his house that evening and do henna on his sister's hands for the festival of *Eid*, and after warning him that I had never done it before, I consented to taking a shot.

His twenty-year-old sister rolled a sheet of plastic into a tight cone, filled it with henna paste, and then carefully cut a tiny hole at the tip.

She handed me a pattern book full of traditional designs to refer to, and told me to relax and have fun. Three hours later, I had her hands and feet covered in leaves, flowers, and paisleys. When the henna design started drying, she gently moistened it with a cotton ball soaked in a viscous mixture of lemon juice and sugar, and then held her palms over the warm smoke created from cloves heated in a cast-iron skillet on the stove—all part of the process that would help darken the henna stain, she said, which would be revealed the following morning, when she flaked off the henna paste after a night of allowing it to soak in.

Syed's short and stout mother pulled her headscarf tight to her head and casually handed me a crisp hundred-dollar bill on my way out, and my jaw hit the floor. I saw a business opportunity here, and after honing my skills on my sisters' hands for weddings and religious functions, word of my skills spread around the local Muslim and Hindu communities. I eventually began making quite a bit of money from my little henna business.

Deepak's mom covered her mouth in awe when she returned to the room a while later and her daughter's hands were covered with traditional intricate filigree designs. The dudes were flabbergasted as well and I was proud that I possessed an obscure skill that was rooted in their native traditions.

The most vital elements of what I needed to learn from the boys were relayed to me without them even knowing it. It was how they addressed their parents and how they truly listened to each other, quietly, intently. Their very way of being. They had so little, but seemed so grateful for what they *did* have. I guess the same could be said for most of the people I met in India. I would leave a ten-rupee note (thirty American cents) as a tip for the waiter at my hotel restaurant (an older man, sixty or seventy). Ten rupees was probably an entire day's wages for him, and he would always open the billfold, pick up the note, and touch it to his closed eyes—the common gesture that signified he was thanking God, even though *I* was the one actually tipping him. But I was coming to understand that God, to him, was really the force of the universe, an infinite series of intricately connected events that somehow brought this ten-rupee note to him, and he was acknowledging and appreciating this. That appreciation was probably a reason why the locals smiled frequently—and their smiles seemed warm and genuine. It gave me pause to wonder why it was rare to see such smiles on the faces of North Americans on a regular basis. In India, one's spiritual life and social interactions were held in great esteem; relationships were valued here.

One of the things I was repeatedly asked, by people like Father Antonisamy's servant, Akash and Deepak's parents and siblings—even the flower ladies—was that I "remember them" after we parted ways. It wasn't just a salutation, the casual and empty "take care" that we use in the West. They looked me in the eyes and made this request with such earnestness that I wondered why it was so important to them. Maybe because to many of these people, their memories were all they had, so they cultivated them, collected them, knowing that they could look back and relive the small moments in their lives that brought them joy. Maybe the material obsessions we were after in the West were what plagued our minds with stress, fear, and feelings of emptiness that left us constantly dissatisfied with our lives and always wanting more than we had—bigger, better, faster, and flashier. More gigabytes for our handheld nooses.

The boys were some of the most honest, genuine friends I ever had. They made me see a new side to my own motivations, and I began to ask myself why exactly it was so important to me to land this part, fame and fortune aside; why was there this desperate need, a quenching thirst inside of me, to be a part of this film? The boys had no grandiose dreams of becoming movie stars or super heroes; they would roman-tically talk of changing the face of India. I guess landing the role of Pi was a challenge that I felt would push me to become the best possible version of myself. I remember sitting with Akash one afternoon, re-cording his voice as he read aloud from my battered copy of *Life of Pi*, capturing his accent while he spoke the very words that I might even-tually be auditioning with. It was astonishingly clear that *this* was the realest version of Pi. These boys inherently possessed the qualities of dedication, discipline, innocence, and good nature that the role would demand. I looked to them and saw a potential reflection of myself that was hauntingly beautiful. No six-pack or bulging triceps. No sex lines. It was all on the inside.

From: yann_martel1963@yahoo.com

To: rajivsca@yahoo.ca

Subject: RE: Updates

Date: Sat, 09 Apr 2005 02:17:34

That's right, Rajiv; Night has dropped out. He was stuck artistically, I think; he just didn't know how to do it. And he wanted Pi in his filing cabinet, to be pulled out when he wanted. But Fox didn't want to wait.

It seems now that indeed it will be Alfonso Cuarón (*Y Tu Mamá También* and the latest *Harry Potter*) who will be coming up to bat. It will be his next movie, after the one he's working on now, based on a PD James book.

Don't know when production would start. Perhaps sometime in 2006, but I don't know. But everything is still tentative, as is everything in Hollywood.

Greetings from Panama.

Yann

6.

M A HAS AN OLD LEATHER-BOUND photo album from her child-hood filled with flaking sepia photographs of life in Ceylon during the forties, fifties, and sixties. The pictures feature a repeating detail—strands of white jasmine garlands hang from the thick, black braids or tight, round buns of hair on Ma, my grandmother, and other female relatives.

One tiny jasmine flower bud, freshly opened, measuring only a half inch wide, has the ability to perfume an entire room by subtly pulsating the air with a fragrance that is soft but also piercingly sweet. The closed buds are even more fragrant than the open flowers, and a short strand of jasmine garland is made up of hundreds of tiny buds. Their unique scent, unlike any other flower, marked my time in Pondicherry.

"Four feet, ten rupees!" the flower ladies in Pondicherry would call out in Tamil, soliciting their wares from the edge of the sidewalk where they were seated. Every morning, as I walked to Petit Séminaire, I watched with wonder as women and young girls made their daily flower purchase and then, right there on the sidewalk, lifted the garlands to the backs of their heads and methodically clipped them into place. I was drawn into what seemed like a private moment, displayed in public. These women walked around all day with their hair garlands and there was something wonderful about seeing them withered and wilted at the end of the day.

I started my own little tradition of buying a length of jasmine garland on the weekends, when Father Antonisamy would drive one of the school's cars and take me on day trips to see the rural areas that surrounded Pondicherry. My Tamil was getting better by the day and I could hold my own while conversing with the flower ladies. Father Antonisamy continued to speak to me in English, since it was one of the few opportunities he had to use the language. He'd pull up in front of the hotel in a white Maruti Suzuki; I'd hop in and hang the garland from the rearview mirror, and we'd be off. The garland would sway from side to side as the car bumbled along the narrow red-dirt roads that took us outside the city.

Father Antonisamy explained the flower's significance in Indian culture, "Jasmine garlands are a symbol of auspiciousness and prosperity here, but superstitions aside, the scent is known to release chemicals in the brain, feel-good chemicals." I knew exactly what he meant; the smell from these garlands was almost hypnotic.

Botany, plants, and nature were a passion of Father Antonisamy's. During our drives, he would pull the car off the road when he spotted breathtaking banyans or gigantic tamarind trees bearing fruit. He'd deftly pick a few of the ripe, cocoa-colored, beanlike pods and offer me a taste of the sweet and sour fruit, pulpy and unappealing in its appearance but distinctly unique in its flavor, refreshing as a snack on these hot afternoon adventures. Ma used tamarind in coconut chutney, eggplant curry, and various other Tamil dishes, but I grew up seeing it only in packaged form—an unappealing block of brown, taffylike paste compressed together and wrapped in clear plastic.

Once, Father Antonisamy pulled me out of class on a particularly boring afternoon of physics and calculus to take me to the botanical gardens at the center of town.

"I have been waiting for the most opportune time to bring you here," Father Antoisamy said as he walked me through the gates of the gardens, a large neoclassical archway with the French words "Jardin Botanique" spelled out on a sign. In *Life of Pi*, the botanical gardens were where the family had set up the Pondicherry Zoo—it was where Pi lived. I had told Father Antonisamy that it was one of the places in Pondicherry that I wanted to become more familiar with.

"Take your time, and do not feel rushed," he offered, "I have cleared the entire afternoon for us to look around at our leisure."

The gardens weren't full of the spectacle and mystique of the Hindu temple, nor were they home to exotic animals like the Toronto Zoo, but walking through this unassuming grouping of trees, shrubs, flowers, and open lawns covered in patchy, yellowy grass warmed my heart. Yann Martel's imagination had taken this place and transformed it vividly into Pi's world. As we strolled along the wide pathways, paved with dry, red Indian clay, under gigantic boughs of pink, purple, and orange bougainvilleas in full bloom, I sunk into my own imagination a bit, envisioning myself as Pi, living on those grounds. *If this were my home, my own garden . . .* I wondered.

Immensely tall palm trees lined the avenues and offered us shade as Father Antoisamy pointed out plants, monuments, and statues that were of notable interest. He had rummaged through his files and found a thirty-year-old, yellowed brochure that was handed out in the garden's heyday, and somehow knew that I'd appreciate the nerdy details.

My childhood hobbies had included growing all kinds of weird plants in glass jars and old fishing tanks, so I was fascinated by his botanical knowledge. When we started talking about the carnivorous Nepenthes (pitcher plants), we fell into a frenzied state of plant-obsessed madness!

On my last Sunday in Pondicherry, Father Antonisamy invited me to accompany him to a small inland village. He traveled there every week, giving a sermon to about fifty villagers.

"Surendra," he said, "you will benefit greatly from witnessing how these people live. I myself am humbled when I am reminded of a simpler life."

I was wearing my favorite white linen shirt that morning. My obsession with linen was partially due to the fact that it has the incredible ability to absorb ten times its own weight in moisture, wicking away perspiration from the body and cooling it down. Images of the British in colonial India came to mind, clad in linen suits and dresses as they trekked through wild jungles.

Father Antonisamy and I matched that Sunday—he in his crisp priest's cassock and I in my spotless white shirt. The air conditioner was turned on and the jasmine flowers had filled the car with their scent. We drove mostly in silence, comfortably enjoying each other's company without having to say anything.

We arrived at the tiny village and he parked the car on the curb of the main road. The village itself was made up of about thirty little mud huts with woven roofing made of dried palm leaves. Father Antonisamy pointed out the building that would serve as the chapel for the day and suggested that I wander around and explore while he gave his sermon.

I could hear the voices of the villagers singing Christian hymns in Tamil while I slowly made my way through the rows of huts. In one home, a small television sat on the packed dirt floor, with a man lying on a straw mat watching intently. Two dark-skinned women in thin, brightly colored cotton saris were outside their huts, at the only source of water in the village—a pipe that jutted out of the ground, with a little faucet attached to it. The women smiled and looked at me inquiringly. They both had gold nose studs pierced into both of their nostrils. I gave them a friendly wave.

Things were quiet; my tour was over in five minutes and I sat outside the chapel while Father Antonisamy finished his sermon. "Remember to treat one another with kindness and respect," I heard him preach in Tamil, "show love and consideration to those who are less fortunate and those who are in desperate need of help."

We had driven halfway back to Pondicherry late that afternoon, when we noticed people gathered on the road. Father Antonisamy slowed down the car as we neared the crowd, mostly men in loincloths and sarongs who were standing by a big, white transport truck that was in the middle of the road, flipped on its side. Two police officers, dressed in khaki uniforms and carrying batons, turned to face us, and one held his hand up to indicate that we should stop. I started getting nervous— the boys had told me stories of corrupt police officers, rampant throughout India. They both sauntered over to the car with menacing looks and motioned for the window to be lowered. Father Antonisamy and the officers quickly exchanged words in Tamil that I couldn't quite follow. Then he referenced me to the police officers by nodding his head in my direction, and pleadingly said in Tamil, "But I have a guest with me, it would be very inconvenient. Please, this is not suitable . . ."

The officers began to sound somewhat aggressive while Father Antonisamy continued to plead with them about something, his hands still on the steering wheel. When they turned away and headed back toward the crowd, I assumed we were free to go, but Father Antonisamy didn't move the car.

"There has been an accident, Surendra," he explained, and I could hear the frustration in his voice. "A man on his bicycle was hit by the truck and is injured. The officers are insisting that I take him to the hospital in town."

"Why don't *they* take him?" I asked, confused.

"This is exactly what I was asking them myself, Surendra," he said, shaking his head. "They say they must remain here to survey the situation, but here is a perfect example of the political corruption we are plagued with—they simply do not want to soil their vehicle."

I didn't quite understand what Father Antonisamy meant by "soil," but just as I began to guess, the officers headed back to our car, followed by a group of villagers who were carrying the injured man. His dark brown skin was glistening with sweat and his blue-and-green–plaid sarong, tied up to his knees, was covered in dirt from the road. The white, sleeveless undershirt he was wearing was torn in places, and he was writhing around in pain. The major injury appeared to be his right hand, covered with a yellow cloth bag that was wet with dark blood. The villagers opened the back door of the car while Father Antonisamy attempted again to convince the officers to take the man to town themselves, but they ignored him, not making eye contact, and simply watched as the villagers lay down burlap sacks on the black leather upholstery in the backseat. And then they gently dumped the man into the car and shut the door. Now this guy was our problem.

"*Aiyo! Aiyo! Amma! Kadavulay!*" (Oh my God! Oh my God! Mother! God almighty!) the man was shouting in Tamil, continuously, as we picked up speed and began down the road again.

"Don't worry," Father Antonisamy yelled to the man in Tamil, quickly glancing into the rearview mirror, "we will be in town soon." Then he turned to me and whispered in English, "Surendra, I am extremely sorry for this inconvenience. Please . . . don't look back there."

Well, of course I looked back there. The man was rolling back and forth, his head jerking violently, grasping his right wrist tightly with his left hand. The yellow cloth bag slipped off and I could now see that all the fingers of his right hand had been partially severed, dangling from tendons and bits of bone. Everything was red and bloody. I must have gasped or cried out in shock, because Father Antonisamy was turning to me and begging me not to look back at the man. "I will faint if I see blood!" he yelled. " You will also faint! Please, don't look!"

His hand was dripping with blood and I was looking around for something to tie it up with. I looked down at my clean, white linen shirt. I paused just long enough to think, *I know—I'll use my tank top instead!* As I quickly unbuttoned the linen shirt and started to pull off the tank top, Father Antonisamy became even more frantic. "*No*, Surendra! Please! Do not inconvenience yourself! You will faint!"

As much as I respected and admired Father Antonisamy, I just wanted to shout, "*Shaaaaadddaaaaap, already!*" but I blocked out his yelling and climbed into the backseat. The man was still crying out in pain as I gingerly wrapped his hand in my tank top. Within a few minutes, I could see blood starting to seep through the thick, white cotton. My own hands were now bloody.

After wrapping up the man's hand, I rummaged through my leather satchel for a small bottle of hand sanitizer, taking in the severity of the situation and wondering with fear whether I had any open wounds or cuts on my hands. I rubbed the gel all over my palms, smearing around the blood that had dried onto my skin and wishing I had something to wipe my hands with.

When we reached town, Father Antonisamy honked his car along all the main streets, weaving through traffic to the hospital. ER workers eased the man out of the backseat and into the hospital, where he was rushed into surgery. The man's blood had dried on my hands. Father Antonisamy and I said little to each other on the ride back to my hotel.

⌒◍

"A train still runs on Sundays . . ." is a detail from *Life of Pi* that appeared early on in the book.

It was about four in the afternoon, and the botanical garden was full of people—Indian families sitting under trees, picnicking or lounging on benches and enjoying the shade of the huge jackfruit trees. I had found the train. And it was actually running . . . this much was true—it still ran on Sundays. The ticket was three rupees, and after safely stowing away the thin, yellow ticket stub (a valuable memento) in my copy of *Life of Pi*, I got into a little compartment surrounded by kids and toddlers. The train slowly made its way through the botanical garden, and the kids laughed and smiled to their parents, who were following nearby on foot.

I perused the worn and battered paperback *Life of Pi* that had brought me here. Then I opened it up to one of the early pages of the story and found exactly what I was looking for: "A train still runs on Sundays for the amusement of the children. But it used to run twice an hour every day. The toy train had two stops: Roseville and Zootown. Once upon a time, there was a zoo in the Pondicherry Botanical Garden . . ."

I hadn't noticed the train when I first visited the gardens with Father Antonisamy, in the middle of the week. But now it was Sunday afternoon. Yann had taken the factual children's train and woven it into his fictional Pondicherry Zoo.

I sat on the train for three trips around the gardens and although I was trying my best to enjoy the ride, I was haunted by the gruesomely vivid image that had seared itself onto my mind—that bloody hand with its severed fingers, tendons exposed. Could that man's hand be saved? Was that man even *important* enough, from an Indian social perspective, to warrant proper medical attention? If so, who would pay his medical bills? Father Antonisamy? I wished with all my might that I had turned down Father Antonisamy's invitation to accompany him. I wished that we could have left town a little later, or a little earlier, fatefully avoiding the scene on the road. I wished, for a moment, that I had never come to Pondicherry in the first place.

The next morning was Monday, my last day in Pondicherry. I was a bit late getting to school and as I walked through the front gates, everything was quiet—the boys had already gathered for their morning assembly in the courtyard and I could faintly hear Father Antonisamy's voice through the loudspeaker. As I got closer, I began to make out what he was saying in Tamil. I stopped behind a pillar, out of view, and listened. "We fear the ways of the West, deeming them cold, too forward and devoid of tradition," he said. "But yesterday I witnessed the compassion and care for a fellow human being that was unaffected by caste or creed. I myself refused to help a man in desperate need. It took someone from so far away to show me the error of my ways and the ways of this country."

The assembly came to an end and hundreds of boys made their way out of the courtyard. First, it was one small boy, about ten years old, who noticed me. I remembered him; once, during lunch, I had a pack of Skittles that I had brought from Canada and was sharing it with the Dudes, when he boldly came up to us and asked whether he could have one. Deepak pushed him away, but I told him to come back, and poured a few of the candies into his open palm. He was a cute little kid and his heart-shaped face lit up when he popped them into his mouth, so I gave him the whole pack. He ran away excitedly, and shared it with his group of friends. He now stood before me and took my hand, shaking it.

Then there was another boy shaking my hand while saying, "Thank you for helping a fellow Indian." And another, "Thank you for your kindness." And yet another. There was a crowd of boys all around me, each waiting to shake my hand. Tears welled up in my eyes.

The Dudes of Petit—Akash, Deepak, Nosey, and Karthik—squeezed their way through. "Thank you, *Raaa*-jeeve," Akash said quietly, smiling with his eyes twinkling. He extended his hand. I opened my arms, pulled him close, and hugged him. "Please don't forget us," he whispered.

⁓

The wheel on the bottom of my suitcase had annoyingly broken off in transit to India, with a sharp bit of plastic now dragging on the floor as I pulled my luggage to the entrance of the hotel. I was wearing my freshly washed linen shirt, which billowed in the afternoon breeze as I waited for the car that I hired to take me back to the airport in Madras. The driver pulled up and opened the trunk, and although he moved close to pick up my suitcase, I had begun lifting it on my own. I felt a pull on my shirt and then heard a *rrrrriiiiiiiip*. The sharp shard of plastic had latched onto the fine linen, which now had a gaping hole in it, about five inches long.

Pondicherry was saying goodbye. I had come here as a complete outsider but was now a part of the chaos, the unexpected, the loss and gain. I had hesitated to use this shirt when it was needed most and now it was worthless. I couldn't help but smile to myself, shaking my head and sighing. Wherever the message was coming from, whatever the lesson I was supposed to learn, I got it—I understood. I didn't need this shirt to remember it all. I would never, ever, forget.

From: yann_martel1963@yahoo.com

To: rajivsca@yahoo.ca

Subject: RE: Hi there!

Date: Sun, 5 Jun 2005 08:39:14

Dear Rajiv,

Things are in flux. Night is out and Fox hasn't yet
filled his big shoes. No, still haven't seen *Mean
Girls*. My girlfriend did, and she enjoyed it. Panama
hats are actually made in Ecuador; they got the name
Panama hats because at the time, they transited
via Panama (and its famous canal) on their way to
Europe. They have hats here they call Panama hats,
but I think they're just hats made in Panama and not
actual Panama hats. Or they're imitations. There,
all you ever wanted to know on Panama hats.

Yann

7.

IT WAS A SWELTERING-HOT JULY afternoon in Toronto, and I sat in the corner of Daniel Stong's log cabin, gently maneuvering a tuft of sheep's fleece. As it twisted into a fine thread and wound itself onto the wooden bobbin of the antique spinning wheel, the year 1838 carved into the deeply patinated wood, I sat in silence and contemplated my situation. A huge fire was burning in the fieldstone fireplace beside me, with large copper and brass pots hanging from the crane, bubbling with plant dyes for the wool. I was dressed up like a pioneer, wearing a long-sleeved plaid shirt and striped cotton trousers held up with suspenders that were concealed by my taupe-colored linen vest. Sweat beaded up on my forehead.

No *Life of Pi* movie. No audition. No school. Back to my summer job.

My older sister spent her summers working at the bank, with Ma. My younger sister was taking extra courses in summer school. I felt incredibly lucky to be spending my summer, just like the previous four summers, in my safe place, working as a historical interpreter at Black Creek Pioneer Village—the greatest summer job a boy like me (a chicken-keeping, wool-spinning freak) could have.

Sitting on the pine floor of Daniel Stong's log cabin as a second grader, I had felt an instant connection with the pioneers who had inhabited this tiny dwelling. When I began volunteering at Pioneer Village as a teenager, Stong's log cabin (First House) quickly became my favorite building to work in. Over the years it had become a home to me, a hallowed place, not only because of its breathtakingly authentic feeling of stepping back in time, but because of the interpreter who had worked here for over twenty years, Kate Rosen. She was in her late forties, soft spoken, and had the innate ability to bring this log cabin and its inanimate objects to life. I was inspired by how dedicated she was to everything she turned her focus to—whether it was wiping off the pair of iron scissors after each use to ensure they wouldn't rust, or listening to me vent about the shit my dad was putting my family through. When I spoke to her, she'd look me dead in the eyes and genuinely made me feel like I was the only other person in the world. There were moments in that house where deep conversation, not just about my home life but about our mutual obsession of all things past, left us both in tears.

Having her as a mentor at work gave me the tools to do what she did best—historical interpreting; Kate was a genius at engaging visitors. I would sit beside her and sort wool as she captured the attention of both four-year-olds and obnoxious teenagers, knowing exactly what to say or do to draw them in and leave them with a sense of wonder for the arduous lives of the pioneers.

"I don't know, Rajivski," she once said to me nonchalantly as I marveled at the attention she was giving to dusting the bottom rung of one of the old rush-seated chairs in the cabin, "I sometimes feel like these things have a way of responding to you, if you take care of them."

Kate retired the summer I graduated from high school, and when her position opened up for First House, I went from part-time volunteer to full-time, seasonal employee. I knew I had big shoes to fill, but I continued in Kate's tradition, treating that house like it was my own.

That summer was my second year in Kate's old position, keeping the flame of Daniel Stong's legacy alive. My return from India in the spring had entailed a brief period of culture shock. Whizzing home on the highway, stocking up on supplies at Wal-Mart, and stepping back under the warm and evenly pressured flow of my beloved shower took a bit of time to readjust to. I missed the Dudes of Petit, the flower ladies, and eating off of banana leaves. Now I was lingering in a place of purgatory, wondering what was to happen with my Pi goals.

When I left for India, I had envisioned coming home with some kind of indication that *Life of Pi* would begin production and I'd have an audition to pour my soul into—but now the project had been abandoned, and with no director attached, it was unclear how long it would take to get things back up and running. I was surprised at myself for not feeling defeated or discouraged. Something inside told me that I didn't need to worry, that I was the only guy who could play this part, and that when it did come up for grabs, I'd be ready.

So, there I was that summer morning, spinning, contemplating, and reminiscing, when the light that streamed in through the open front door was blocked momentarily. I looked up to a group of a dozen eight-year-old kids in neon yellow summer-camp T-shirts stepping into the cabin with their teenage camp counselor, a heavy-set black girl wearing a bandanna. The tiny room was now crammed full of people.

"Hello," I began, taking my eyes off the strand of wool that I was spinning and looking up at them briefly. "This building's called First House because it's the oldest one in the village."

The kids peeked into the two small bedrooms and quietly gazed in awe at the details—how small the beds were, the bumpy look of the straw-filled mattress, and the little doll made out of corn husks that lay in the wooden baby's cradle. Two boys were standing in front of the fire, staring at the flames in a trancelike state.

"This building is original to the site. Everything else was moved here, but this little log cabin was built right here in 1816, when all the surrounding land was a huge old-growth forest. The farmer and his wife chopped down the gigantic pine trees that were growing here, shaped them into square logs, and put this house together before their first winter here. See those marks on the walls?" I asked, guiding them with my gaze. "Those are from the farmer's adze—the tool he used to square the round log."

The kids were now looking at the walls and ceiling, and one girl ran her hand along the log beside her, touching the adze marks.

"How many people lived in here?" the camp counselor asked.

"Nine," I said casually. And then, on cue . . .

Gasps and shock. "Where would they all sleep?" another girl asked, incredulous.

I continued to spin in the corner while talking them through the three rooms of the cabin.

"After clearing the land for their farm and building the outbuildings for their animals, the family built a bigger home, the one we call Second House—that one over there," I said, pointing through the open doorway to the huge, red, two-storied clapboard house across the yard.

The group gathered around me at the spinning wheel. I shifted the conversation to my task at hand.

"These are called carders," I explained, opening up the pair of large, flat, rectangular brushes that resembled the comb we used to brush Meesha's fur. "They take the mats and tangles out of the fleece." I picked up a bunch of sheep's fleece that I had washed and dried out in the sun the day before, and spread it out evenly onto the tines of one of the carders. Then I clapped the two carders together, sandwiching the fleece between the two sets of tines, and pulled the brushes in opposite directions. Five or six strokes and the fleece was straighter and fluffier, and all the fibers were running in the same direction. The kids were spellbound, completely silent as I took my time and continued with the process.

I opened up the carders and laid the empty one on my left thigh while I gently rolled the carded fleece off the other carder, into a sausage-shaped roll of cloudlike wool, wispy and light.

"At this point, the wool's called a rolag," I explained, "and now I'm ready to spin." I cradled the delicate rolag in my palm and started the spinning wheel, giving it a firm clockwise turn and then placing my right foot on the pedal to keep it going. The silence remained as I picked up the strand of thread that came out of the bobbin in my right hand and attached the rolag to it as it spun.

The kids had their eyes glued to the bobbin. The light and airy fleece quickly twisted into a fine and strong woolen thread.

Just as I settled in to enjoying the moment, an icy breeze sent a shiver down my spine and the pleasant mood was sucked into an invisible vortex as Wendy, my thirty-something supervisor, darkened my door. She slipped into the back corner of the house, shrouded in shadow and wearing her favorite article of clothing, a long, taupe-colored, sleeveless linen shift that looked like a potato sack. I knew what she was here for—to see whether I was implementing her recent edict of incorporating gender issues and class structure into my interpreting. Fucking boring as shit.

One of the camp kids looked over to the big basket that sat beside me on a low wooden bench, containing about a dozen different skeins of yarn we had produced, dyed a rainbow of colors.

"Those pots hanging over the fire have dyes in them right now," I explained. Through the corner of my eye I could see Wendy, her head cocked to one side, with a clipboard under her arm while she impatiently tapped her foot on the floor. "The big copper pot has rhubarb leaves in it," I continued, as the kids made their way over to the hearth, "which will make green dye. And the small brass pot has bloodroot in it—it's a native plant with red roots—and it makes a bright orange dye."

One of the girls pointed to the drying herbs that hung from the pine ceiling over the fireplace. "Are those for dye?"

"No, those herbs are for cooking and medicine. The pioneers would have used all kinds of plants for a lot of different purposes."

The group returned to me and the spinning wheel. The foot-tapping started to get faster.

"You know, the color of someone's clothes two hundred years ago usually said something about their rank in life." I had decided to give ol' Dementor Face what she was here for, and instantly she stopped her foot tapping and began nodding. "Most people could make every color from plants that grow around here, except for two colors—can you guess what they were?" Various attempts by the kids led to the right choices—red and blue. "Nothing that grew in North America produced blue dye—so they'd have to purchase that dye if they wanted blue. It was an expensive dye called indigo and it got its name from the fact that it came from India. In the year that Daniel and Elizabeth Stong built this cabin, blue clothing meant power or status—like royal blue or navy blue . . ."

One of the kids piped up, "What does indigo look like?" "Well, it's a plant with little, green leaves—but if you went to the store to buy it . . ." I got up from the spinning wheel, walked to the corner cupboard, and pulled out a small round stainless-steel tin, " . . . you'd buy a block, like this." I popped the lid off the tin and showed them the small cube of blackish-blue indigo that I had brought back from my trip to Pondicherry. It was one of the essentials on my "things to buy" list. "And then you'd crush this into a powder before you used it."

The kids took turns handling the small rocklike cube of blue dye. One of them asked, "So, you mix the powder with water?"

"Well . . . it actually doesn't dissolve in water. Can you guess what they used?"

None of them spoke up.

"Urine," I said. Blank stares. "Pee." Their eyes widened. "Yup, they'd collect a bunch of pee and put it in a crock. Then they'd put it in a warm place and let it ferment."

"*Ewwwww, gross!*" The kids shouted out in unison, sending Wendy out of the building.

When the kids had no more questions, they said goodbye and walked out. I was alone for only a few minutes before my door was darkened again—this time it was my neighbor working in Second House.

"What did *she* want?" Laura asked, placing another log into the fire, pops and cracks abounding, while I continued to spin. Laura was just a few years older than I, and was dressed in a floor-length gingham pioneer dress, complete with a starched white cotton house cap that covered the long, blonde braids she had coiled and clipped to her head.

"Oh, you know, the usual—shoving Victorian class structure and the plight of women down people's throats. She walked out of here rolling her eyes."

"I hate that *cunt!*" Laura growled.

My spinning slowed down momentarily.

"What's a *cunt?*"

The brass ladle in Laura's hand froze midstir and she turned her head to face me.

"Rajee, come on. Are you fucking serious? You don't know what a cunt is?"

"No, I've never heard that before. What does it mean?"

Laura was shaking her head. "Vagina! Cooch. Pussy. Penis flytrap. Labia majora. Labia minora. Actually, labia *men*orah, if you're Jewish—"

"*Okay!*" I shouted back, focusing on the strand of yarn I was spinning, "I get it!"

"Good. Don't forget it; it's basically my favorite word. You should use it sometime."

Laura was one of my favorite interpreters who worked at the village, but there were over a dozen of us—an old tinsmith who spoke in a shrill Cockney accent and rolled his own cigarettes, an eighty-year-old Gepetto-like Dutchman who was an incredible woodworker, and a seamstress who looked like the old woman who lived in a shoe with two long, snow-white braids that served as the prototype for Laura's preferred historic hairstyle. Her face was weatherworn and reminded me of a shriveled apple-faced doll—she seemed like she was a hundred years old and fascinated me to no end. These were the old-timers, the ones who were there when I had visited in second grade and were still working in their buildings as masters of their trade.

I loved my job. Nights with my dad left me feeling trapped and unsafe, but my bus rides to work in the mornings settled my nerves. The work itself was hard—sweaty in the summer, dressed in four layers of clothing and slaving away beside open fires—but the setting was idyllic. We had our busy periods, with lines of students or tourists snaking outside. But on rainy weekends, or on weekdays after about three o'clock, when the school groups would all leave the village, things were often still and quiet, and there were long stretches when I'd be completely alone in my building. This was my favorite part of the job—quietly working on my manual tasks. Sometimes, I'd leave the log cabin with a huge wicker basket and a pair of hand-forged scissors and walk down to the creek, foraging for plants to be used for dye.

My days in Daniel Stong's First House always began a few minutes before visitors arrived, as I'd open the corner cupboard and pull out a few sheets of newspaper to roll up and start the fire. It never ceased to bring a smile to my face when I'd happen upon one of my *Mean Girls* costars on the pages of the *Toronto Star*. While the articles and pictures chronicled Lindsay Lohan's fall from glory, Rachel McAdams was now the *it* girl, and Tina Fey was steadily becoming the queen bee of comedy. Somehow, it seemed wrong to roll up her picture and watch her face burn in the morning flames of the fire, so I'd just fold her up and take her back to the staffroom at lunch, to be deposited into the clean and peaceful recycling bin. Tina had once expressed an interest in the wool I was spinning (she was learning to knit while pregnant with her first child), so I saved up a few skeins, dyed them light pink with red onion skins, and sent them to the set of *30 Rock*. It made me happy to imagine Ms. Norbury, now Liz Lemon, knitting away with the yarn I had spun.

The blazing summer heat of July became unbearable one afternoon, and as there were no visitors around, I moved to the front stoop of the cabin, sorting a freshly shorn fleece, pulling apart tufts of raw wool to prepare it for washing. The long, lazy, buzzing drone of the dog-day cicadas rang out from the black walnut trees overhead. My hands were working away steadily, covered in lanolin. *What next?* I wondered. It wasn't a little "next" but a big "*next*." It was the next step connected with *Life of Pi*. What's my next move? I looked out at the flock of Border Leicester sheep grazing in the apple orchard nearby and spotted the naked-looking ewe whose fleece I was sorting. *I've gotta learn how to swim.*

"No!" a voice in my head shouted, "scary!"

"Shhh . . ." another voice said, "this is important."

Pi is an excellent swimmer, but I didn't even know how to float. I was working on a clump of the fleece that was matted with bits of straw in it. As I gently pulled apart the curls, the crisp, golden straw cracked into even smaller pieces and flitted down onto my lap. In the novel, Pi flaunts his skill of swimming the butterfly stroke and his long voyage across the Pacific entailed numerous occasions where he jumped into the water, to get away from the tiger. What would the filmmakers think if they found out that I couldn't even float and had a huge fear of swimming? I reached a clump of wool that was matted together with a little bit of sheep poo. *I really should be wearing gloves*, I thought—but they wouldn't have worn gloves to do this a hundred years ago. Meh, shitty hands, *whatever*. All they eat is grass, anyway.

Ma and my dad didn't know how to swim and their fear of the water kept me and my sisters away from pools. When we'd go to the beach, we'd only go into the water knee-high, before Ma would shout, "No, no! Stop! Careful! Don't go further! You will drown! Stop, child!" Yann had mentioned in *Life of Pi* that people who grew up by the ocean often didn't know how to swim—he was right in my parents' case. It wasn't part of Tamil culture to strip off into ones skivvies to sea bathe.

I looked up from my shitty hands and spotted two ladies in their seventies heading in my direction. They were both wearing wide-brimmed straw sunhats and one of them was using a walking stick, hobbling down the path that led to my building. I hastily picked up the pile of wool and took it into the house, and then washed my hands in the wooden pail that sat in the corner before resuming my post at the spinning wheel.

The lady with the cane peeked in, noticed me in the corner, and then turned to her friend behind her, "Oh, *look*, Evelyn," she gushed excitedly in an uppity British accent, "this must be the *slave* cabin!"

My eyes almost popped out of my head. I was going to correct them, but decided against it. It was an honest mistake—everything in our village was "historically accurate," except me. I had to hand it to

Wendy; she hired me even though there was absolutely no way there were Tamil people spinning wool in log cabins in the backwoods of Ontario in 1816.

The two ladies were now standing in front of me, ogling with huge grins on their faces as I started spinning and talking about the process. One of them cleared her throat and leaned in, putting her weight on her walking stick. "I have a question for you," she prefaced in a hoarse whisper, "are you . . . an Ethiopian?"

"No," I said, caught off guard, "I'm Tamil. My parents are from Ceylon—Sri Lanka."

"Oh . . ." the other lady said quietly, smiling widely, revealing her set of yellowed false teeth, "with your curly black hair, your dark skin, and your very white teeth, we thought perhaps you were an Ethiopian."

It was rare for me to be left speechless by our visitors, but the two British ladies had managed it.

❧

The groundhog population at the village had reached an all-time high by the end of August. Our historical outbuildings housed horses, sheep, pigs, ducks, turkeys, and chickens, but there were an equal number of wild animals that made their homes on the outskirts of the property, where marshes, ponds, reeds, and woods created a sanctuary amidst the urban sprawl.

The groundhogs posed a problem because they fed on the prized plants that were grown on-site in our historically accurate gardens. The head gardener, Luke, a spindly Ichabod Crane type, was frequently chasing the fat, little balls of brown fur out of the herb garden, the berry patch, and the field of heirloom vegetables that grew behind Second House. He wasn't allowed to kill them—the village was technically run by the Toronto and Region Conservation Authority and their mandate was heavily connected to preserving the "natural" heritage of the city.

I was always thrilled when I caught a glimpse of a fat groundhog running across my path as I walked from the staff room to First House. The little furry creatures had such a dignified air to them—I imagined them as distinguished old men wearing top hats as they bumbled about with their huge, fatty behinds that jiggled with such a pleasantly gratifying motion.

One afternoon I did a bread-baking demonstration using the iron cookware that sat by the hearth. I mixed together my ingredients in a big stoneware bowl on the wooden table as kids gathered around me. A few hours later, another group of kids watched me put the loaf into the Dutch oven and place it onto a bed of coals. I shoveled more hot coals on top, surrounding the pot with radiant heat.

Sadly, there weren't any visitors left in the village in the late afternoon when I opened the Dutch oven and revealed a perfectly baked rye loaf, which I picked up with a piece of linen toweling and let cool on the table. The cabin filled with the smell of freshly baked bread as I left the house with a basket and scissors to collect some goldenrod.

I was busy cutting off the bright yellow blossoms, when, out of the corner of my eye, I noticed a groundhog had his two front paws on the front stoop and was looking into the house.

"Oh, shit!"

I threw aside the basket and ran over to the cabin, assuming the groundhog would scamper off. Instead, he glanced at me over his shoulder and then hopped up, into the house.

"Fuck!" I cried, following him into the dark cabin. A wild animal in a house full of two-hundred-year old precious artifacts was a disaster in the making.

As I walked into the cabin, he shook his fat bum and scampered off into the children's bedroom, his nails clicking on the wooden floor as he ran under the bed. I was shaking. I didn't want to scare him even further, but I needed to get him out of here. I quietly walked over to the bed and slowly crouched down to look underneath. No groundhog. My panic rose when I saw a small hole in the wooden floor that I hadn't noticed before. It looked like it was some kind of vent. I quickly pushed aside the painted wooden child's bed and looked down the hole. Darkness. Then I heard the scampering of little paws. In all my years of working in this building, I had never thought about what was under it. I had no idea if there was a basement or cellar down there, but I felt I needed to work fast—I couldn't bear the thought of this little top-hat-wearing groundhog being hurt, or worse. *He came for my bread!* I thought, as I ran to the staffroom. My coworkers were leaving in their twenty-first-century clothes. I realized the village was closed now, and everyone was going home. I ran into Wendy's office, but she wasn't at her desk, so I ran down to the staff phone and called the head of the maintenance department.

"There's a groundhog in my house, Donald—it fell into a hole in the kids' room!" I wheezed.

"I'll go over there right now," he said. "We've gotta scare him out of there; can't have one of those pests in the building."

I didn't trust him to handle the matter with the groundhog's well-being in mind, so I flipped through the phone book and found the number for the Toronto Wildlife Center.

"Don't scare it," the girl on the phone instructed calmly. "Go over there and make sure he doesn't scare it—it'll be frantic and won't want to come back up; it'll probably try to dig itself out and if the basement is concrete, it'll hurt its paws. Get some peanut butter . . . or some of that bread you baked and put it at the end of a long board or plank of some kind and put it down the hole; hopefully he'll climb back out. Call us back if he's not out in an hour and we'll send someone to help."

Back at the house, Donald was stomping on the wooden floor, shouting, "We've got to get him out! We've got to scare him out!" Donald had opened up a trap door in the floor, about two feet by three feet, something else that I had never noticed before.

"Stop, Donald!" I whispered frantically, "stop stomping; I called the Wildlife Center and they said not to scare it! And there's no way for him to get out; we need to put something down that hole!" I ran out of the house to look for something. The orchard where the sheep grazed was surrounded by fencing that was made up of split logs and I was able to pry one loose. I stuck it down the hole. It hit the floor of the cellar and then projected above the opening of the floor about a foot.

"Good thinking," Donald said, walking out of the house. "Well, then, there's nothing more we can do. Just lock the building up and he'll come back up."

"And what's he going to do once he's up, in a locked building overnight? Huh? We can't just leave him in here all night!" I followed him outside, trying to keep my voice down.

"There's nothing more we can do; he'll be fine until the morning," he said, turning his back to me and leaving. "I've got to get home."

I was trembling and drenched in sweat. I moved cautiously as I walked back into the house, ripped apart the loaf of bread, and jabbed a piece of it onto the pointed end of the wooden fence post. Every now and then I heard a faint scampering sound below me and wondered whether the groundhog was attempting to dig itself out.

Now Wendy was at the door; I guided her out of the house, telling her it needed to be quiet, and then I filled her in on what was going on.

"Well, Donald says that we need to close the building," she said, sighing. She was wearing her potato sack dress again.

"Donald's an idiot. We need to wait here for it to come out or we need to call the Wildlife Center to come and help."

"We're closed, and Donald's going home, Rajiv," Wendy said, impatiently. "He's my boss, and those are his instructions."

She pressed her lips together and was looking at me challengingly.

"Well, I'm not leaving."

"He's my boss," she repeated slowly, through gritted teeth, "and I'm *your* boss, and you have to listen to me!"

"I'm not leaving here until that animal is safely out of the house."

Wendy had her hands at her side, balled into tight fists. I had never seen her so mad. She fumbled around for something to say and finally blurted out, at the top of her lungs, "You can't always get what you want!"

What? Was *that* her best retort? That I couldn't just get what I wanted? Oh, *hell, no.*

"Watch me," I said flatly, turning away from her and sitting down on the ground outside the house.

She fumed for a few seconds before she abruptly turned on her heels, creating a cloud of dust from the dry sandy gravel, and headed toward the main building.

"*Cunt,*" I said aloud to myself. Laura was right, it was a good word.

I sat with my head in my hands for about ten minutes, sad that I might have put my little furry friend's life in danger. I was exhausted and weary.

Today is the day I get fired, I thought. *Look around, this is probably the last time you'll be seeing these buildings, the huge black walnut trees beside Second House, the sheep grazing in the apple orchard.*

My thoughts turned to *Life of Pi*. I couldn't help it; I thought about the movie every day, but with the project being in limbo, I tried my best to push it out of my mind and be patient.

"Yes, and while you're being patient, you can *do* something," one voice in my head started up.

"Like what?" the other voice retorted.

"Like swimming . . ." the first voice said, in a challenging tone.

"No! Scary!"

"They've got three pools on campus at U of T . . . and you'd make Ma happy, working on getting that stupid degree. Go back to school."

Fine, I decided, I would man up and conquer my fear. While chipping away at a degree in art history and classics, I'd fill all my spare time with lessons at the university's three swimming pools to continue my Pi research. Just thinking about swimming made me short of breath. "Scary," the voice in my head repeated. "This is a good thing," the other voice said, "Push yourself. Grow."

And then, there at the door of the cabin, was a little furry face. I couldn't have been happier if it had been the Blessed Virgin herself. The groundhog twitched his big black nose and turned his head, his tiny, beady eyes looking from side to side. He had two buckteeth that stuck out over his bottom lip. I was far enough away from the door to not be a threat, I felt. Then the little ball of fatty fur plopped down out of the house. I noticed his paws were bloody and my stomach turned. He stood there tentatively for a brief moment and then bolted off around the cabin into a wooded area, just as I caught sight of Wendy returning with the head of all of Black Creek, a short woman with a boy's haircut named Marty who was wearing an outdated, oversized '80s-style blazer.

The two of them made their way down to me by the front door of the cabin.

"Well," Marty said in a fake, sweet tone, smiling, "was that the problem, the one that we just noticed running off?"

"Yeah," I replied, in an equally fake, sweet way, "that was him."

"Great!" Marty exclaimed, lifting her palms up to the sky and casually shrugging her shoulders in Vana White fashion, "problem solved."

"Yeah," I repeated, looking at Wendy, who now had a fake smile on her face, as well, "problem solved."

I was surprised I hadn't gotten fired.

Back in the house, I wrapped the rest of the bread in a piece of linen.

"This is all your fault!" I reprimanded the loaf and put it in the dark cupboard. I closed the four sets of double-hung windows, gathered my things, and pulled the big red door of the cabin closed behind me. My response to Wendy sprouted in my mind as I put the giant metal key into the old iron box lock and turned it counterclockwise, hearing a loud, satisfying *click*.

I *can* get what I want. And I will.

Dear Rajiv,

Yes, it's true. A long, torturous process has finally
delivered the best possible scenario: Jean-Pierre
Jeunet. I'm delighted. I love his style and his
lightness of touch. And he's clearly matured as a
director and screenwriter. I'm very curious to see
what he will do.

Hope you're well.

Yann

8.

THE TALL, BLOND, SHIRTLESS GUYS strutting their stuff as they sauntered by, chugging protein shakes or emerging from the showers after an intense session of water polo, seemed sort of unreal, like Norse gods looking down their noses at this waiflike, troglodytic creature (me) lurking in the shadows. Almost everyone in Scarborough, the neighborhood where I grew up, was an Indian, Chinese, or Caribbean immigrant, and it was extremely rare to see a real, bona fide white person in the flesh. One was more likely to see a pack of thirteen Arctic wolves that escaped from the zoo convening at the main intersection near my house (yes, this *did* really happen once) than the bodies that passed me in the men's locker room of the University of Toronto Athletic Center.

This was the very first swimming lesson of my life, Swimming Basics, and as if learning how to swim wasn't going to be hard enough, I started hyperventilating as I pulled off my shirt and lifted my feet out of my jeans, catching glimpses of the glowing, alabasterlike bodies in tiny Speedos that were the living and breathing versions of the classical Greek and Roman statuary that filled the art history textbooks in my backpack.

A giant maze of bright yellow lockers, the color of a school bus, all edged with rows of wooden benches, knee high, served as the garish backdrop for my new venture. As I stripped down, my anxiety was exacerbated by the boisterous, jockish sounds of guys roughhousing—the words "dude" or "bro" plaguing every sentence that was drawled out in these deep, bass voices.

These guys were *cool*. I was not cool. I tried not to stare at their perfect, blemish-free, hairless skin, pulled taut over their muscular frames. Any single one of them could have been used in an anatomy lesson to illustrate every body part in its ideal form. These male, teenage sex icons exuded the very essence of lustful youth, extracted, boiled, and concentrated into this one room in its most meaty, fleshy, physical form, no mindful sentiment attached to it—pure wantonness based on that which could be seen, touched, caressed, and groped. I was now treading on new ground, in a world where I felt unwelcome.

I anchored the nubby, white gym towel to my chest using my chin, covering pecs to knees, as I pulled on my swimming trunks. I wanted to hide every part of me, the bumpy and inflamed skin on the back of my thin arms, my bony shoulders, and my chicken legs covered in a carpet of hair—*sick*. God forbid my towel slip off and anyone catch a glimpse of Willy the Anteater—he was uncircumcised, with just a little too much foreskin, you see. The one consolation to poor little Willy was that he looked exactly like the one on Michelangelo's *David* and I had recently read, in my textbook on Greek sculpture, that the ancient Greek aesthetic actually preferred *discreet genitals*, small in size—this was considered true elegance. Hmm. The ancient Greeks would have loved my penis. Sadly, I wasn't learning to swim two thousand years ago in the palaestra behind the temple of Artemis; this was Toronto in the twenty-first century, and I was being stopped on a daily basis by kids at school asking me whether I was "really Kevin G.," the last thing I wanted was to shatter their image of the rapping mathlete/badass MC by searing an image of Anteater Willy into their minds.

As I emerged from my towel cocoon, wearing my long, billowy swim trunks, and made my way, shirtless, from the locker room to the pool, that first day I felt as though I was walking the gauntlet— scrawny-ass ribs visible, pancake chested. I mustered up all the courage in me to slowly tiptoe over to the shallow end of the pool and, holding on to the metal hand rails, descend into the liquid world. As the water crept up over me, I felt as though it were physically pushing all the air out of my lungs, until all I had left were a few tiny mouthfuls.

In that very first swimming class, Meghan, the instructor, told us all to hold a flutter board and kick while she assessed our level of comfort. The water, at its shallowest, was up to my collarbone, and I kept one hand on the edge of the pool the whole time, knuckles white from my firm grip, fearing that I'd lose my balance and drown. Meghan had to gently coax me into letting go of the wall and taking hold of the flutter board with both hands, and eventually, as I gasped and wheezed and flailed my legs about frantically, my long and billowy trunks completely slipped off, exposing my brown bum to the other seven non-swimmer losers in the class, with Anteater Willy having a clear view of the bottom of the pool! The horror washed over me and everything went blurry as I stood up, crouched deeper into the water, and pulled my shorts back on, before jumping out of the pool and running back to the changing room. My first lesson was over in fifteen minutes.

I returned to class the following day wearing a new pair of Speedos jammers, knee-length shorts that were sinfully tight, with no chance in hell of slipping off. And, thus prepared, I tried to pull myself together and get back in the water. This wasn't going to be as easy as Yann Martel laid it out in the novel when describing Pi's melding with the water, calling it "liquid light." Don't fight it, become one with it.

"Now, I want you all to take a deep breath, bend your knees, and put your head under the water, then come back up, like this," Meghan demonstrated. I did as she asked. "Great! So, no one here is afraid of putting their head in the water, great! Now I want you all to take a deep breath and just float on your stomach, like this." She effortlessly lifted her legs up, stretched her arms out in front of her, and lay motionless at the surface of the water. The six other people in class followed suit, but I just stood there. And I could feel my chest tightening. The long beams of late-morning sunshine that streamed in through a row of windows disappeared as a cloud passed over the sun.

"What's the matter, Rajiv?" Meghan asked, turning to me. She was my age, a second-year student, which made things feel relaxed, but I didn't quite know what the problem was—I just couldn't do it. "I don't understand how to take my feet off the floor of the pool—it just won't happen. When I lift up my feet, where do they go? They'll just land on the floor of the pool and I'll be standing again."

Meghan laughed lightly. "No, they won't; trust me," she assured. "You just . . . just spread yourself out and float, like this." And she demonstrated again.

In my attempt to really try to do it, I lifted my feet off the ground and spread my arms out, face in the water, and my feet instinctively searched for firm ground, quickly finding their safe place on the small white tiles of the pool's floor. "Nope, I can't do it."

Meghan turned to the other students, who were standing in the pool silently, waiting. "Okay, I want you all to just keep floating and try staying in for as long as is comfortable." Meghan took me over to a corner of the pool. She hopped out, grabbed a flutter board, and said, "Hold this. Spread your arms out, take a deep breath, put your face in the water, and you'll float." And I did it. And then she took the flutter board away from me. "Good, now do exactly the same thing, but without the board."

But I couldn't do it. "I need the board. The board was what made me float, I just can't do it on my own!"

My swimming lessons found a way of slyly following me home and making their way into my dreams at night. I had repeated nightmares where I was facedown in the beautifully blue water, pulling one slow stroke after another, feet kicking slowly, calmly, everything going smoothly, with only the sound of the water plugging my ears, muffling all other noise. Then, all of a sudden the floor of the pool would vanish and the depth of the water became endless, and I'd gasp, but there was no air. I couldn't breathe. Frantic, I'd be trying to grab the edge of the pool, but it wasn't there—and then I'd be jolted awake.

I pushed myself, three times a week, to get back into that pool. I developed a ritual of mental motivation as I pulled up my trunks. "This is what you need to do to become Pi," I'd remind myself as I'd climb the concrete steps from the basement where the changing room was to the pool on the second floor. "You just need to let go," I recited as I pulled my swimming goggles down over my eyes and pulled the rubber elastic tight. But then I'd cautiously slip into the water, and as the other beginners swam entire lengths of the pool and I was the only one still in the corner, monopolizing the instructor's attention, I would feel defeated, embarrassed with the pace of my progress, which was painfully slow. Meghan was never impatient, but I could tell that not being able to get me to float was becoming a personal challenge for her—she seemed to be disappointed, not in me, but in herself for not being able to figure out a way to get me to just do it, and I was beginning to see that these lessons were a sort of collaboration. We were each dealing with a personal issue, an obstacle that we were frustratingly seeking to overcome; I needed to *learn* how to float and she needed to *teach* me how to do it.

"Okay, do you trust me?" she asked me one day, just as I was starting to think that there was no hope for me. She had sent the rest of the students off into the deep end to practice treading, so the two of us had the entire shallow end to ourselves. "I'm not going to ask you to do

117

anything that's dangerous or scary, okay? I just want you to trust me, okay?"

"*Yes!*" I shouted enthusiastically, determined to snap myself out of the mental rut I was in.

"Take a really deep breath and lie on the floor of the pool, like this," Meghan said as she inhaled, went under the water and lay on the bottom of the pool, spreading her limbs out completely. She stayed there for a few seconds before she resurfaced. "Do you think you could just do that? It's easy . . ." she said casually. I promised I would give it my best effort, then pulled my swimming goggles over my eyes, took a deep breath and bent my knees, submerging my head below the surface of the pool and spotting a stream of small bubbles rising up from the air pockets in my swim trunks—*glug, glug, glug*—the world of water all around me. The locks of my long, curly hair seemed to transform into a lifelike creature with a mind of its own, a swaying wave of black seaweedlike tentacles, occasionally blurring my vision. I could see Meghan's pale legs standing nearby. Everything moved slowly and without sound under the water. I began to push my arms and legs out, stretching completely, trying my hardest to get to the bottom of the pool, my face grimacing as I refused to be defeated. I struggled. I fought the water. I failed.

I bobbed up, out of the water, pushing aside the clump of hair that was plastered to the front of my face.

"What's wrong?" Meghan asked in her good-natured tone, smiling.

"I can't do it . . ." I panted, disappointed with myself.

"Why, what's happening?" she remained calm and patient.

"I just keep floating." And as I finished saying the word, a cheeky grin spread across Meghan's face.

"Ohhhhh . . ." she teased, " . . . you're *floating*, eh? I thought you said you *couldn't* float." Her wet palm patted my bare back. "Good work, Rajiv."

"No!" I countered back. "Good, work *Meghan*."

My swimming progress was slow. Like, snail's pace slow. The dread of stripping off all my clothes (especially during the frigid Toronto winters) and jumping into the cold swimming pool eventually became routine—something that I never fully came to enjoy, but rather a task that I came to terms with.

Every lesson felt like a purification ceremony, a human sacrifice almost. "Here we are again," I'd say to myself as I unzipped my down-filled parka, pulled off my tuque and mitts (hand-knitted using homespun yarn from Black Creek, dyed with apple bark from the orchard). "You will remain dignified as you descend into the sacred waters . . ." I'd continue. Sweater off. Shirt unbuttoned. "And the gods will praise your efforts . . ." T-shirt off, then jeans. "You can do it, putcha' back into it . . ." Ice Cube's wise words of wisdom (sarcasm) echoed in my head. Long johns off, " . . . you can do it, putcha' *ass* into it!" Tighty whities—off—oh, hey Willy! Wiggle-wiggle-shimmy-shimmy, and the Speedos shorts were on. Red flip-flops on, and then the gauntlet walk through the changing room before walking up the sixteen concrete stairs to the second floor where the pool was, turning the corner and—*shiver. Oh, God!* The cold winter breeze blowing through the corridor as an exterior door opened nearby. Then, at the edge of the pool. Towel down, slippers off, and into the blue depths.

Meghan insisted that I spend as much time in the pool as possible, even outside of our swimming classes, so I began attending one of the three scheduled lane swims that took place daily, whenever I had a significant chunk of time between my lectures. Lane swims were much more intimidating than my official lessons, not just because I no longer had the safety of Meghan to guide and protect me, but everyone there appeared to be completely competent swimmers, and I worried that I'd just get in their way. *No matter*, I thought with perseverance, *I must soldier through it.*

As I showered in the locker room before one of my early attempts at lane swim, I was faced with yet another reason to dread jumping into the pool carefree. I tried my best to not notice the obese old man to my left, probably a retired geology professor, his ginormous belly spilling over his Speedos, the black fabric stretched beyond its limits. As he lethargically turned from front to back under the shower spout, making no effort at all to lift his huge hippolike arms to clean under them, I wondered whether he ever actually washed between the folds of his fatty belly, the folds of his fatty thighs or, worst of all, the myriad folds that made up his massive buttocks, the suffocating sweat pockets which probably housed a multitude of old, caked-on pieces of festering fecal matter that he was never able to reach. *That's why he swims*, I concluded. He just plunges into the pool and all those fat folds effortlessly float apart . . . and those microscopic bits of poo slowly soak up the chlorinated water and then, when fully saturated, gradually release themselves from his butt folds, floating off into the pool. He probably stands in the corner, I imagined, and discreetly pulls down his Speedos—releasing any constrained fat folds and allowing the water to come in contact with every last bit of butt cheek.

I turned away, only to notice the man to my right, another distinguished U of T alumnus, no doubt—an eighty-year-old that looked like he had just returned from Auschwitz, pure skin and bones in a light and airy pair of loose, neon orange swimming shorts. At least this one was lifting his arms and rubbing his torso with a green bar of soap, but then, as he turned his face away from me and revealed his back, I was horrified to see that it was completely covered in peeling skin—eczema wounds that were blistering and filled with puss, oozing out as the warm water rippled and cascaded down his bumpy lesions. Great. The bits of microscopic poo in the water could be joined by thin flakes of sloughing skin and puss.

I closed my eyes and pictured two veteran tailors at Henry Poole and Co. on Savile Row in London, one kneeling and one standing at my shoulder, making the final adjustments on the tuxedo that I'd be wearing to the Oscars. Hanging from the green-velvet-covered walls were the framed royal warrants they had been issued from their patrons over the previous two hundred years, the crown heads of Europe and various maharajahs and emperors from the colonies. Refueled with a sense of purpose, a reminder of why I had to plunge into a pool of heavily chlorinated microscopic unmentionables, I opened my eyes and returned to reality, accepting my plight.

My swimming lessons with Meghan took place in the smaller, more intimate twenty-five-yard pool on the other side of the Athletic Center, but lane swims were held in this giant ocean of a pool, Olympic-sized for swimmers who were actually training with the Olympics in mind. This fact was not lost on me, and no, it did not serve as inspiration, but had the complete opposite effect—embarrassment that these future Olympians, jumping off the numbered platforms and effortlessly flying through the water, had to share their second home with the likes of me. I hurried out of the changing room, pushing through a heavy set of double doors, the threshold into the sanctum sanctorum, the natatorium. I was hit in the face with the strong smell of chlorine and the rhythmic echo of arms piercing the surface of the water from dozens of swimmers pulling stroke after stroke in the cavernous space, *ca-chick*, *ca-chick*, *ca-chick*. The floor of the pool was divided into eight lanes by lines made up of black floor tiles that sat in contrast to the white ones. In the shallower end, blue floor tiles spelled out "Toronto" in huge capital letters. Blue and white bunting hung across the width of the pool at four intervals.

I was doing my best to focus on *my* swimming and not the dozens of merpeople who looked perfectly at home in the pool. I pulled my goggles down, slipped my flip-flops off, and went to the edge of the shallow end, conjuring up positive thoughts as I readied myself to jump in, when there, beside me, was an Asian man in his forties. No potential forms of pool contamination from this man, I surmised, looking him over briefly. As I tipped my chin into my chest, preparing to jump in, I noticed his feet. His toenails were hideously long, thick, yellowing, and curving over the edge of his toes, and in the corners of his nails were darkened gray areas—toenail fungus, no doubt. Festering in his warm, dark, humid socks, living in the crevices of his toenails, this cheese bacteria was happy to hide out and multiply, growing a nice thick rind until—*wham!*—his feet hit the water of the pool and then, as his legs languidly undulated in the flutter kick and his pointed toes helped to propel him forward, the water pressure would push its way into every nook and crevice of his body, where no toe fungus was safe. A string quartet could be heard harmoniously playing out a classical waltz as the cheese bacteria slivered out of the corners of his toes and joined the rest of the tiny demons in the water—the poo and the dry, dead skin.

Welcome to lane swim at the University of Toronto.

❧

"You just have to relax! Chill the fuck out. You need to be relaxed when you're swimming," Laura insisted as she took a modern carton of whipping cream out of her wicker basket. I was back at school full-time, but working at the village on weekends, for extra cash.

"I'm *trying* to relax! But the more everyone keeps telling me to relax, the more nervous I get!" I was working "relief" that day—delivering firewood, kindling, and buckets of water to all the buildings. We were alone in Second House.

My arms were piled high with heavy split maple logs. I was

restocking Laura's supply of firewood for the day, going back and forth between my wheelbarrow outside the front door and the little brick alcove in the kitchen's fireplace. The leaves had fallen off all of the trees and I welcomed the warmth of my winter costume—thick trousers made from brown woolen tweed with a matching vest and jacket, with real horn buttons. On my head was a moss green bowler hat with a feather in it. "It's nerve-racking," I sighed. "I didn't think learning how to swim was going to be so hard."

Laura emptied the cream into a ceramic crock that served as a butter churn. "It's because you're an adult—you're overthinking it. You should be having fun. Kids don't think about it at all, they just jump in and play, and that's usually how they learn. It's how I learned. My sisters and I grew up by a big lake and I can't even remember not knowing how to swim. Swimming is supposed to be fun, Rajee; don't make it such a big deal. Just learn to laugh at yourself and have fun," she said as she put the empty carton back in her basket, covering it with a piece of striped cotton cloth. It was a strict rule that visitors were not to see any traces of the modern world in our buildings.

The brisk morning air was infiltrated by the sound of an approaching school group—kids laughing and talking excitedly, and it got louder by the second.

I pulled my antique pocket watch out of my vest. Nine fifty-five.

The school groups had prescheduled "productions" in various buildings, where they got the chance to see and take part in a task that was specific to the building. In Second House, the production was butter churning. I spotted the approaching group, headed by a guide named Ian. He was always friendly and polite but had that *weird uncle* vibe. Maybe it was his penetrating gaze, or the matter-of-fact monotone in which he dictated everything—he sounded like an auctioneer from the backwoods. Today he had his pristine white hair slicked right back, and was wearing a navy blue parka with a pair of pressed chinos as he escorted about twenty third-graders into the kitchen of Second House. Laura had cleared the giant pine table in the middle of the room for the demonstration.

"Now, boys and girls," Ian began, "Mrs. Stong here has set up the butter churn and is ready to make some butter. Can anyone tell me what animal on the farm gives us what we need to make butter?"

A freckled third-grade hand shot up into the air. "A cow!"

"That's right," Ian continued. "And what comes out of the cow that we use to make butter?"

Another polite arm in the air before "milk!" was heard.

"Correct," Ian said, rubbing his palms together. "You milk the cow, and the cream separates from the milk and floats to the top of the pail. Then the little boys and girls would help their mother out by skimming off the cream and putting it into this here butter churn; isn't that right, Mrs. Stong?" A huge phony grin spread across Ian's face and his bulging eyes were magnified by his thin-framed glasses as he turned to Laura, who obligingly nodded back.

"Yeah, sure," she confirmed,. I could tell she couldn't wait to get this over with. It wasn't the actual butter churning she hated, but the phony show the guides would rope her into, calling her "Mrs. Stong" or, the title she despised most of all, "the Mommy."

"Now, Mrs. Stong, will you please show us the motion that we use to churn the cream into butter?"

A wooden lid was placed on top of the churn. The lid had a round hole in its center, from which a long wooden dowel protruded. This was the handle of the dasher, at the bottom of which (now immersed in the cream) was a cross-shaped wooden piece. Laura grasped the long wooden dowel with both hands, lifted it up a few inches, and then pushed it back down quickly. She repeated this motion a few times.

"See, boys and girls?" Ian whispered, "This is how we churn butter! It goes from cream, to whipped cream, and then from whipped cream to butter! Now, which one of you would like to help Mrs. Stong churn her cream into butter?"

Dozens of scrawny arms frantically sprung into the air, jittering. Ian picked a little Korean boy, all smiles as he made his way over to Laura and grasped the handle of the churn, at the very top. Laura silently guided his hands lower on the dash, giving him a better grip. The others would not be left out, Ian assured; they would assist by chanting a rhyme that was traditionally recited as the children would churn butter, "to make the job a little more fun, and keep the rhythm going," Ian added. "You're going to start pumping the churn," Ian instructed the little Korean boy, "and I'm going to say the rhyme. Then, boys and girls, I want you all to join in quietly. We'll get faster and faster as the cream turns into butter! Ready?" he asked to the room full of eager and excited faces.

Laura subtly turned to me stacking wood by the fireplace and we exchanged a glance. Then the kid started pumping the churn, up and down, up and down.

And then Ian softly began the rhyme in a whisper, his knees gently bouncing in tempo, "*Come, butter, come! Come, butter, come! Johnny's at the garden gate, waiting for his Johnny cake. Come butter, come!*"

As the cream thickened in the churn, the pumping became more exhausting, and every so often Laura reached in to help the boy with the churning. And with each sequence of the rhyme, more and more kids joined in, excitedly whispering while following Ian's movements, bouncing up and down on their knees, "*Come, butter, come! Come, butter, come! Johnny's at the garden gate, waiting for his Johnny cake. Come, butter, come!*"

Oh, God, I thought to myself, *surely there must be another rhyme we could be using for this.* The chanting was no longer a whisper. *"Come butter, come! Come butter, come! Johnny's at the garden gate, waiting for his Johnny cake. Come, butter, come!"* the kids were yelling, prompted by Ian, as the little Korean boy grasped the dasher with both hands, biting his bottom lip as he focused on his pumping, which now required his determined effort as the whipped cream thickened. *"Come butter, come! Come butter, come! Johnny's at the garden gate, waiting for his—"*

At that very moment, that miraculous moment when the fat solids of the cream separate and congeal, creating rich golden butter lying in a pool of milky, chunky white buttermilk at the bottom of the churn, the boy gave one final spirited hard and heartfelt *pump* . . . and if we could see the wooden cross at the bottom of the churn, in slow motion, we would see that it rose up above the buttery mess and then, *smack!* It hit the butter solids with an exhaustive *squish*, which violently *shot* the lumpy white buttermilk up the sides of the churn, erupting through the tiny gap of space between the dash handle and the hole in the lid and up, *up*, up into the air . . . and then . . . well . . .

The boy stopped his pumping. The room was quiet. Save for the *clack, clack* as I continued to stack firewood in the corner. The little Korean boy turned to Laura, looking up at her, "Oh, nooooo . . ." he moaned, "I got it all over your *face* . . ."

I dropped the log I was holding with a thud and whipped my head around just in time to catch Laura throwing both arms into the air and shaking her head.

"I can't deal with this!" she cried, running out the front door of the house. I jumped up from my task and flew to the door, holding the doorframe with both hands as I called out after her, "But Mrs. Stong, it's supposed to be *fun!*"

From: yann_martel1963@yahoo.com
To: rajivsca@yahoo.ca
Subject: RE: Progress
Date: Thu, 05 Jan 2006 22:42:48

Dear Rajiv,

Good to hear from you. Happy New Year to you, your
family, and the elephants in your backyard!

As for the movie, I was told that the studio is
expecting a draft screenplay some time in March,
and if they like it and things proceed normally,
shooting should start this summer, at the Fox studio
in Baja California and in India.

I wish you the best of luck with your casting hopes,
but I'm afraid it will be immaterial. Jeunet and
I have communicated back and forth about three
times and in his politeness he's been unfailing,
in his opinion of the book glowing, and in keeping
the door closed firm. Trust me, he told me. Which I
do. But it does mean that aside from making a few
recommendations early on, which he said he would
consider, I'm playing no role at all in the making
of the movie. So it's in the hands of Vishnu and
Hollywood. I imagine your efforts will be rewarded,
if not with this movie, then in another. India's
place on the map is increasing in size every passing
year, politically, economically and culturally. Look
at how Bollywood movies are becoming mainstream.

Stay well,

Yann

9.

"**Y**OU BASTARD! WITHOUT me, you wouldn't even *be* in this world!" My dad was drunk and livid. I was fourteen and, in a moment of desperation, I had come between Ma and my dad. She was usually insistent on handling him by herself, sending my sisters and me up to our rooms when things started getting ugly, but that night I ignored her protests. The three of us were in the hallway, at the foot of the staircase by the front door.

"I never *asked* to be here! You think I wanted this, huh? Do you think if I had the choice I'd want to be here, putting up with your crap? I hate you!"

"*Mahan*, stop!" Ma was trying to pull me back, "Enough! He'll hit you."

"Get *out!*" my dad boomed, both his arms raised over me, "get out of this house *now!*"

"You hit me, and I'm calling the police, you asshole, I *swear to God—*"

"*Mahan*, stop! Enough, go to your room!" Ma was now between me and my dad.

"*Get out!* This is *my* house, get out of here, you *bastard!*"

"Eyy!" Ma was screaming at the top of her lungs, "*You* shut up! *You* get out! *You* leave! Don't you dare tell him to go."

Ma and my dad looked like two wild animals willing to fight to the death. My dad dropped his arms, grabbed his car keys, and slammed the front door on his way out.

The air was still charged with crackling sparks. Ma turned to me, breathing heavily. "Are you hungry darling? Come, I'll make you something."

"No, Ma." I went up to my room, shut my door, and lay on my bed, staring up at the ceiling. I wanted my dad gone, for good. I wished, with every ounce of my being, that he would just *die*.

The phone rang a few hours later and Ma answered. It was a police officer. My dad had hit a car.

I got my wish, I thought. *He's dead. Finally.*

No one was hurt, Ma said, but the officer confirmed that the car was registered under Ma's name, and then told her she could be held accountable for the damages. My dad went to jail for the night and his brother bailed him out.

This was the end, Ma said after hanging up the phone. It was over, and this time, I really believed her.

The next two weeks were quiet at home—my dad had not returned since the blowup. He was staying at his brother's house. He had never stayed away from home for so long and, to Ma's relief, he had made no indication of coming back to try and patch things up. By the end of the second week, Ma had put the house up for sale and was looking for a smaller one, a house she could afford with her single income. My sisters and I collectively felt like we were finally free to start living our lives, the right way.

I came back from school one afternoon to find my dad in the living room, on his hands and knees, begging Ma to take him back. I stood in the hallway, out of sight, listening.

"No, no more," Ma was sobbing, "you've put me and these children through too much. You haven't even worked for two years. You have no job, you drink, and you've tortured us year after year. I'm finished."

"*Please*," my dad interrupted, "I don't want to lose my family! I'm sorry! I see now how bad I've behaved. I went to *jail*, do you hear me? They put me in jail! I've changed, I promise, I'll find a job."

I couldn't take it any longer. I turned the corner and walked into the living room.

"No, Ma! Don't listen to him! He says this all the time."

"I know, darling; I know," Ma said, her voice trembling as she wiped away tears.

"No, *mahan*, no; I promise," my dad cooed. My stomach was turning. He put his hand on my shoulder and I violently pulled it away, crouching down to plead with my mom, who was seated on the couch with her head in her hands.

"Ma! Please! Don't let him come back here—he'll just start drinking again. How many *years* have we gone through this, Ma?" My voice was breaking as I fought back tears. "How may times has he done the exact same thing, huh, Ma?"

"No, please—I promise—" my dad said over me.

"Ma, don't; don't listen to him. This happens year after year—you fight, he goes away and you say you're getting a divorce—and then he comes back and starts drinking again." I was full-out sobbing now. "It's just a pattern, Ma."

"I know, darling; I know," Ma cried.

"No, I won't!" my dad interjected, leaning in for Ma to look up at him. Then he turned to me. "Go to your room; leave us alone," he said, softly.

"*Fuck* you!" I spat.

"*Mahan!*" Ma looked up. "Don't say words like that!"

I looked my dad straight in the eyes. Knowing he was sober, and that he'd remember my words, I spoke slowly. "You are dead to me. You don't exist anymore. And if you think she's going to forgive you and let you come back here . . . you're completely stupid."

My dad just stood there and stared back at me, his eyes empty and his bald head beading with sweat. If it were legal to kill him, and I had a gun in my hands, I would have pointed the barrel right at his big, flat nose and shot him right in the face, and I would have enjoyed it—seeing his brains explode all over the white living room walls.

I went up to my room and fumed for a while longer, then my door opened and it was Ma, and my dad was standing behind her. She had a solemn, stern look on her face—the look of reluctant acceptance, of resolution.

"He said he has really changed . . ." she started.

"*No*, Ma!" I shouted.

She raised her voice. "*Mahan*, listen. This is the *last* time, the last chance I'm giving him."

"*No, Ma!*" I burst out in tears. "No! How could you *do* this? We were going to move on, you were going to sell the house."

My dad piped up quietly from behind Ma. "It's just going to take time for him to be okay with it."

"Ma, please, no." I had grabbed Ma by the shoulders and was shaking her, desperate to convince her to see the reality of this situation.

"*Mahan*, it's okay." she said, frustrated, sternly, almost as if she were convincing herself, too.

"No, Ma, it's not! You're crazy if you think he's changed!"

I was crying so hard I couldn't see. I grabbed my wallet from my desk and pushed past my parents. I ran out of the house and down the street. It was early October and although it was probably only five o'clock, it was already dark. I kept running. I ran all the way to the bus stop and waited. It was a cold night and all I was wearing was a ratty

Superman T-shirt. I was alone; this was the stop where the bus route ended and started again. The bus arrived and I got on. I had no idea of where I was going; I just rode that bus to the other end of the line.

I was numb. I was a zombie, aimlessly moving forward.

Two hours later, I was standing on the front porch of my pioneer village mentor, Kate Rosen.

She had invited me over for dinner the week before, when she introduced me to her husband, Eric, and their two kids. Now this was the only place I could think of going. I was trembling in my T-shirt on their front porch. I could see them through the white lace curtains, just finishing dinner.

A light flicked on above me.

"*Rajiv*?" Kate whispered, incredulous, "what's the matter?"

She pulled me into the house and took me to the dining table. Through sobs I told them what had happened at home, and then apologized for coming, but she and Eric interrupted and assured me that they were honored to help.

They put me in their guest room—in an old wooden spindle bed with a linen and wool coverlet on it that was woven in 1870.

"Rajiv, listen to me," Kate said softly, sitting on the foot of the bed as I nestled under the covers, "you come here whenever you want. And you can stay here, forever, if that's what you need."

I started crying again.

"You hear me? Whenever you want, okay?"

I nodded my head and wiped away my tears. "I hate that man, Kate."

"He sounds just *awful* . . . . crikey."

"He *is* awful."

"Well, you're safe now. Try not to think about it." Kate pulled out a tissue from the box on the painted pine table by the bed and handed it to me. "Nighty night."

I slept like a log. There was no noise in the house. No maniac to fear.

The next morning, Kate was setting the breakfast table while Eric toasted challah and the phone rang.

"Hello?" Kate answered. "Oh, hello, Mrs. Surendra." She pressed the speaker phone button and put down the receiver. The night before, Kate asked whether she should call my mom to let her know I was there—I shrugged; it didn't matter to me.

"The child belongs at home, Kate." There was an edge to Ma's voice.

"Well, he's very upset, and Eric and I are happy to have—"

"The child belongs at home. *This* is his home." No one said anything.

"Can I speak to him, please?"

I silently waved my hands across my chest and shook my head.

"He's in the bathroom; I'll tell him to call you."

"Yes, please. That child needs to come home, today. I will come and get him."

Ma drove her white Buick out to Thornhill and picked me up later that day. I got in the car and we said nothing to each other on the drive home.

It didn't take long for my dad to fall back into his drinking routine. I didn't say one word to him for the remaining years we lived under the same roof. Ma and my sisters continued in the drunken shouting matches with him, but I would stay in my room—or I'd leave the house.

I rebelled and spent many weekends and holidays with Kate and Eric. Their daily lives were relaxed, but also immaculately ordered, and I craved the sanctuary of their peaceful home. I'd go over to their place and we would embark on road trips that took us into the country. We'd spend hours at antique warehouses, looking for treasure. They liked collecting primitive painted furniture, Persian rugs, and ironstone soap dishes. I would look for old boxes of pen nibs for my calligraphy, and

Georgian silver—forks, spoons, and knives from the early 1800s that I'd add to my little section of the cutlery drawer at home (my sisters were revolted by the idea of using a fork that someone used two hundred years ago—I quivered with excitement at the same realization).

My dad couldn't help himself. He wasn't the only alcoholic in his family. He was broken and didn't know how to make the fix. This is how they coped, or how they *tried* to cope. Psychiatrists weren't really a *thing* in Ceylon. Neither was divorce. It took Ma twenty-two years of torture to break free of the cultural taboo that had bound her to my dad.

I guess my complete disinterest in a love life of my own had something to do with my parents' twisted relationship. For me, dating was a non-issue—it was never an option. Although Ma never came right out and said we weren't allowed to date, there was an unspoken cultural understanding (applicable to every Tamil household in Scarborough) that while we lived at home, our efforts were solely to be focused on productivity and success. The few times I did bring classmates home, to work on school projects, Ma's back would go up at the girls.

"Hi, Mrs. Surendra, nice to meet you," they'd say sweetly.

"Hello," Ma would snap, not looking up from whatever she was doing. She wasn't like this to my guy friends—and I knew exactly why; she didn't want me running around with girls, mixing with a "bad crowd," and doing "those things these Canadian kids get into." Based on the template of my older cousins, we were just expected to announce to our parents, in our late twenties, that we were ready to be married and had someone in mind—and this was a celebration—the union being a "love match," a rare contrast to the traditional arranged marriages that took place in Ceylon.

I was never bitten with the love bug, in any case. So, I found intimacy in my own way—in a love I expressed by pouring my heart and soul into my hobbies and the worlds that I had been escaping to since I was a child.

In fourth grade, pharaohs, pyramids, and mummies completely took over every aspect of my life during a unit on ancient Egypt. I painted the entire surface of my bedroom walls with hieroglyphics one weekend. Ma walked in, yelled, "What's the MATTER with you, child?!" and threatened to confiscate my art supplies. Little did she know that the hieroglyphics weren't just decorative, but I had painstakingly copied a protection spell from a book on ancient Egyptian ceremonies, so the walls, in a way, now held a sort of purposeful power. Lying in bed at night, surrounded by my tomblike walls, I imagined myself as a young Tutankhamen, secure under the Eye of Horus. This gave birth to the formation of an Egypt club with my cousins in which we'd have secret ceremonies with papier-mâché idols I had made of Isis and Osiris—we lit incense, chanted magic words while dancing and reciting ancient Egyptian poetry.

In sixth grade it was *Hercules: The Legendary Journeys* and *Xena:Warrior Princess*. When it was warm enough outdoors, my best friend, a Trinidadian kid named Reshad, would meet me every day after school and we'd set off on our horses (bikes) with swords (plastic) strapped to our backs, traveling the countryside (suburban Scarborough, made up of cookie-cutter-type subdivisions) looking for battles that needed our help (these were completely made-up and usually took place in an obliging park or field). On one of our epic journeys, Reshad and I rode our "horses" to the local Canadian Tire hardware store where I bought a metal stove-burner ring and a small bottle of bronze automotive touch-up paint, which was used to paint the characteristic designs onto my new *chakram*, making it look as close as I could to Xena's iconic round throwing blade. We luckily also happened to have a rare lapidary store in our neighborhood, the only one of its kind in Toronto, that sold rocks, minerals, and precious gemstones. Our horses carried us out there one evening and I found tiny round abalone paua shells from New Zealand, which I glued onto the stove ring to finish it off (this was a detail I had read about in an article published on the props used in the show). My *chakram* was complete. We threw that thing around all over the damn place. It hit trees and houses and sometimes cars, but a very worthy cause in our attempt to bring order to a war-torn world of despair.

And all this eventually led to my career as an actor. I had never given much thought to *why* I felt so compelled to make it as an actor. It took someone else to point it out to me; on my way back from India, I had made a brief stop in London to take a week-long acting class in Covent Garden. The instructor, a graying theater director, began the class by asking us why we were actors. "Just think about it for your-selves," he offered. "I don't want you to answer out loud." After a few seconds of silence he said, "My opinion is we're all in this for love. I think that somewhere in each one of our lives we were denied some aspect of love that we craved and needed. And that's what we seek from this profession. To be loved . . . to be wanted . . . to belong."

The realization of this was, to me, kind of twisted, but I admitted to myself that in my own case he was right. The prospect of playing the lead role in a story that had such a deep resonance with my real life would be the legitimization that my existence was worth something.

Just before I left for India, Ma left my dad and, this time, it was for good. They sold the house and parted ways. I vowed to never have any-thing to do with him again—to me, he was now a ghost. Ma found us a new, smaller home even closer to the zoo.

With my dad out of the picture, I no longer felt like I was running away from something, in pursuit of my dreams.

Life of Pi, the movie, was now the big-picture challenge, but swim-ming was currently the only thing in clear focus. I could now swim a half pool's length in front crawl while holding my breath. The whole breathing-while-swimming thing was light-years away. The pool was divided into three sections—slow, medium, and fast. I always made sure that I swam in the slow lane along the edge of the pool wall so I'd have something to grab on to while I came up for air (a frequent occurrence).

There were regulars who frequented the pool during lane swim, and I gradually became one of them. I slipped into the meditatively calm slow lane one afternoon and eventually passed the geriatric row of turtlelike swimmers, holding my breath and pushing myself to go as fast as possible so I could swim the entire length in one breath. Victory! Then, as I bobbed up for air, I noticed the lifeguard slowly descending the ladder of her elevated plastic white throne with feline grace. *Oh, shit*, I thought as I caught my breath, *she's coming over to me.*

"You should be swimming in the medium lane," she advised, leaning down to me.

I held my breath and slipped under the white-and-red buoyant pool dividers. I no longer had the wall to depend on, which made me nervous, but I somehow held it together, pretending like the wall was beside me while I swam two lengths of the pool, medium speed. It was a small triumph.

There was a lean, tanned, older lady who swam ahead of me in the conveyor belt of people that sequenced their way through lap after lap. Whenever I needed a break, I'd pause at the end of the pool and wait for her to reappear, using her as my benchmark for where I'd slip in again. She was in her sixties, and every now and then she'd join me at the end of the pool, making small talk.

I'd push myself to keep up with her and would manage to remain behind her for a few lengths, but as my arms and legs grew tired and my lungs were pushed to exhaustion, I'd start lagging as the other swimmers overtook me.

I was resting in the corner of my lane one afternoon, when the tanned lady displayed a water skill that I instantly coveted—an impressive flip and turn, an underwater somersault in which she pushed her feet off the wall to propel her through the water at the beginning of each length.

"You're getting better!" she noted a few months after we first met. "Are you ready to try a flip turn?"

"Oh, no!" I objected, "No way—there's *no way* I could ever do that!"

She somehow convinced me that it was easy and then demonstrated as slowly as she could manage. I couldn't exactly understand what was happening, but she talked me through the steps and then hypnotized me into trying it.

I swam to the other end of the pool as she followed behind. Catching sight of the wall nearby, I tucked my head into my stomach as she had instructed. I pushed. I turned. Having had no idea what direction I was facing or where my body was in space and time, I panicked, opened my mouth, and it filled with pool water as I pushed my head up, freaking out and blindly searching for the wall with my hands. I found the edge, came up, and then, still frantic, swallowed my whole mouthful of water.

"Oh my *God!*" I screamed, noticing the lifeguard jump down from her plastic throne and run over to me. She stood at the edge of the pool with the tanned lady to my left, as I continued to shriek out in shock, squeezing my eyes tightly shut, "Oh, no!" I cried. Most of the other swimmers continued to swim their lengths but a few of them had bobbed up to take in what was happening.

"What's the matter? Are you okay?" the lifeguard gasped.

"I—think—he . . . hit his head," the tanned lady stammered, her hand on my back.

"No!" I shrieked. "I didn't hit my head!"

"Then what's the matter?" the lifeguard repeated.

"I swallowed it!" I yelled. "I swallowed the pool water!"

The tanned lady and the lifeguard had matching puzzled looks on their faces.

"So? It's fine. Happens all the time. It won't kill you . . ." the lifeguard offered flatly before turning and walking back to the elevated platform.

"It's full of horrible things," I lamented to the tanned lady.

"We've all swallowed some of it. You'll be okay," she whispered. She nodded to me. I nodded back.

"I'm sorry I pushed you," she said, concerned. "I should mind my own business."

"No," I interjected, "I need to be pushed. I'm glad I tried."

Another nod of consolation from her, and then she was off, swimming breast stroke.

I remained at the side of the pool, shivering as I held on to the edge with my fingers. It was now a part of me. I had swallowed it. The poo, the flaking skin, the toe fungus. No one else seemed concerned as they continued to swim in soldierlike motion, back and forth. I took a deep breath, plunged my head back into the water, and propelled forward.

Dear Rajiv,

Alice and I just got back from an Anglican Easter
service. It was for families, so lots of screaming
kids and Jesus-baby-talk. Not quite my thing. I like
my religion a little more sober. But still a good
thing.

Hope you get that horror movie part you auditioned
for. Jeunet handed in a first draft; the studio liked
it and now he's doing some rewrites. I don't know
when they'll be shooting. I can't believe they'll
get it all together to do it this summer, but what
do I know. One of these years we'll be able to
uncross our fingers.

Alice and I went to a drive-in last night, Alice's
first time ever and mine in twenty years. Saw "She's
the Man" and "V for Vendetta." There were two other
movies on but we'd had enough. A fun thing, the
drive-in. Oh, yeah, our battery died. But it was
revived, in the spirit of Easter.

Stay well,

Yann

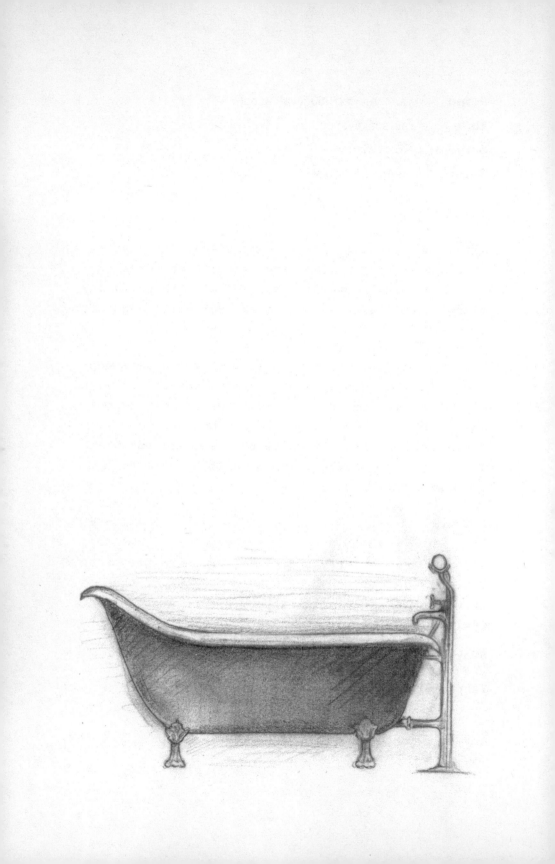

10.

THE CAR SWERVED SLIGHTLY onto the gravel shoulder and then jerked back onto the lonely country road headed north, flanked with snowbanks piled five feet high. Another car appeared in front of us and we slowed down, coasting well below the 60 km speed limit posted on the road. I was sitting in the passenger seat and Audrey, eighty years old, was driving. In the backseat was her family friend, Jenn, a schoolteacher—a pretty brunette in her late thirties, seated beside her huge golden retriever. We were all headed to Audrey's winter vacationing spot up north.

"Audrey—uh, you need to speed up a bit," Jenn called from the back. Audrey ignored her and continued to recount a story from her past. The car in front of us began to disappear, when all of a sudden my back jolted away from the seat as we revved up to 80 km and were instantly tailgating the only other vehicle in sight.

"It was at Lord Beaverbrook's annual spring dance," Audrey recounted, when she was again interrupted by Jenn, who was now hesitating as she leaned forward.

"Uh, Audrey, you need to slow down; you, uh—"

Audrey cut her off. "I was dancing with my beau at the time, Didd. Handsome. Tall. Gorgeous boy. Six foot three. I had a crick in my neck for a whole year from looking up at him."

As we swerved slightly off the road, Jenn piped up again, "Audrey, you, uh—"

"*Jenn,*" Audrey yelled, her ivory-colored kidskin gloves gripping the wheel tightly as she glared into the rearview mirror, "*shut up!*" I stared straight ahead, relieved that I had followed my instincts and kept my driving commentary to myself. "Just *shut up!*"Audrey continued. "*I* am driving. And *you* are in the backseat. And when *I* am driving and *you* are in the backseat, you sit there and you *shut up*! You *shut up* and you let me drive!"

Ladies and gentlemen, it is a pleasure, nay, an honor, to have the privilege of introducing you to my friend, Audrey.

I had met Audrey through Kate and Eric. And Kate had met her while working at the village—Audrey's husband, Bruce, a famed historical architect, was responsible for designing the Village way back in the fifties.

I became friends with Audrey unintentionally, beginning with tea at her house with Kate and Eric and then housesitting for her while she vacationed three hours north of the city on Georgian Bay, in her huge 1880s wooden houseboat that Bruce had saved, restored, and moored to a private island—her wedding present from him. Then one winter, she invited me to join her and her kids to go up north to their "winter cottage," Blagdon Hall, a stone cottage in the middle of nowhere, surrounded by acres of snow-covered hills where we would ski and snowshoe during the day and roast marshmallows while one of us played the guitar at night in front of the fireplace.

Being around Audrey always felt a little like hobnobbing with royalty. Audrey lunched with the elite in Toronto back when the grand mansions of the city had stables on their grounds. One of her old acquaintances was a Russian named Olga. "My mother-in-law would have me over for lunch in York Mills, and a few times Olga was there. We'd have watercress sandwiches and a boiled egg." Audrey spoke of Olga like she was the girl next door, but it was only after some questioning on my part that I discovered who this "Olga" really was—oh, you know, just the royal Grand Duchess Olga Alexandrovna Romanov of Russia, who never did find her niece, the famous Anastasia, she searched for after the assassination of her brother, the czar, and his family.

I'd stop in and visit Audrey every now and then, when I'd have Ma's car for the day. I picked her up one afternoon from the eye doctor, when her pupils had been dilated, and Loretta Lynn was playing on the radio. Audrey cranked up the volume to full blast and was blindly dancing along in the passenger seat as people who passed us gave us looks of pure confusion, perhaps assuming this was a real-life *Driving Miss Daisy* situation. She was distracting me as I drove, but I laughed and laughed all the way back to her house.

My lane swim sessions were improving as my third year at U of T wound down. I returned to the village again, but I had a thrilling new setup for the summer—I temporarily moved away from home and was housesitting for Audrey while she was away up north. I was to water the grass and feed the birds. For the first time in my life, I felt independent, like an adult, doing my own grocery shopping and coming and going as I pleased, answering to no one. I didn't have to bicker with my sisters about who left their dirty plate in the sink or whose pubic hairs were strewn across the toilet seat. Having a place of my own for the summer was more than enough compensation for the light work I'd be doing to take care of the house. I'd go to work in the morning and head back to Audrey's after a day of toiling away by the open hearth. Sometimes Laura or Kate would visit me and talk the evening away as the sun went down.

The phone rang one afternoon. It was Audrey. "It's gone. The houseboat burned down." I laughed awkwardly, certain I was missing the joke. "No, dear. I'm serious. There was a fire and the houseboat burned down. There's nothing left."

Audrey was on her way back to the city. It would be a few hours before she arrived, so I pulled her huge old single-speed bike out of the garage and rode to the corner store to pick up a basket of local Ontario peaches—in their prime for only a couple of weeks in July and August. Back in her kitchen, I cut up the fruit, mixed in some sugar and cinnamon, and left it on the counter. And as my fingers crumbled the lard into the flour in another bowl, I thought of what I might say to Audrey when she came home. Then I added an egg and some vinegar, as I had done countless times before. What was I going to say? My mind drew a blank. What do you say to someone whose house just burned to the ground? "At least you're alive?" *No . . . so generic.* "I'm sorry?" *Well, obviously. Damn. What do I say?* I rolled out the pastry and lined the tin. I drained off the liquid from the peaches, boiled it down to a syrup, and then added it back to the fruit—then I emptied the bowl of filling into the bottom crust. I figured I'd just say what I needed to say when I knew exactly what to say. I wet my index finger in a bowl of cold water and ran it around the edge of the bottom crust before adding the top crust, then I crimped the edges together with my fingers and the pie went into the oven. Audrey loved my peach pies . . . maybe I wouldn't need to say anything, perhaps the pie would say enough.

Two hours later, the entire place smelled like baking day as the pie rested on the counter, cooling down (the windowsill wasn't wide enough). Audrey walked in, with Lexi Looloobell's carrier. She let the tiny tabby cat out into the living room and then flopped on the sofa. I slowly sat down beside her.

"You know, I've been through a lot of shit in my life." Her voice was hoarse and she continued to stare ahead. "The third of July, 1957. I'm walking out of the drugstore, pregnant with Barbara, and holding the other two by the hands; Peter was four and Ian was two. Husband Jim was away overseeing a logging operation up north—"

"I thought his name was Bruce—" I interrupted.

"*First* husband, dear," Audrey clarified, her eyes blankly looking out of the window in front of us. "Jim. A forestry engineer. Beautiful man. I was walking out of the drugstore and a neighbor comes running down to find me in town. Jim's lifejacket and boat were found in the water. Jim was gone. Drowned in an accident. I don't know how I did it, but I picked up the pieces and moved on. Then I met Bruce . . . God, I loved that man. Nick was born—he was crazy about his father—they were best friends, Nick and his father. Bruce was often away on business, saving some old building from being torn down or giving talks about heritage architecture. He hated to fly. *Hated* it. His palms would get all sweaty, and I'd take his hand in mine and nudge him forward onto the plane. Life was good—busy, though. I never had the time to sit in a bath in the middle of the day, but there I was one afternoon— Bruce had left that morning, headed out east and the house was unusually quiet. And there I was at a quarter to twelve, in the bath listening to Gordon Sinclair on the radio. *Everyone* tuned in to Gordon Sinclair at a quarter to twelve. 'There's a Beechcraft down, off the coast of Newfoundland,' he said, 'they haven't found the plane, they think it's in the ocean.' Somehow, I just knew it. Bruce was dead."

Lexi jumped onto Audrey's lap and nestled in. I began, almost mumbling, hoping that the right thing would eventually just find its way out of my mouth as she finally turned to face me. She lowered her voice to almost a whisper. "I have a baseball bat in the closet, dear."

"Huh?"

"And in my will, it states clearly that I am to be buried with that bat," she continued in her whisper. "It's to get those two on the other side, for leaving me the way they did." She stuck her middle finger up above her head and made a funny face. I laughed quietly, but I didn't say anything. The mood was still somber. She turned back to stare blankly ahead. It was enough to just sit here and simply keep her company.

There was an old black-and-white photo in a pine frame hanging on the wall beside me. I had seen it so many times before, but we had never talked about it. Four cute little kids, about ten, eight, six, and two. The little girl had a black silk dress on with a big lace collar, and the fat toddler was grinning so widely his eyes were teeny, tiny slivers.

"I've learned a few things in my lifetime. My boobies may be down to my waist, but I've realized that no one wants to be around an old broad who complains all the time. Nobody," she sighed. "So, you put on a smile . . . even if it isn't real. Sometimes, you have to tell your mind to just shut the fuck up. And you put on a smile. And eventually," she turned to me, "it becomes real." She jumped up off of the couch with a bounce. "Now! I'm pouring us a drink!"

"Gin or vodka?" she asked as she headed to the kitchen.

"Oh, I don't drink, Audrey," I said. I was never pushed to explain why, but I had my personal reasons. My dad was one of them—I never, *ever* wanted to slide down his path, even in the slightest way. The other was that I was doing everything I could to maintain the naive and youthful mind-set of a sixteen-year-old . . . Pi definitely was a virgin in more ways than one. As Audrey continued to make her way over to the kitchen cupboard where she kept the booze, I called to her, "I'll just have some orange juice or something." She turned on her heels to face me, pointing her index finger at my chest. "Sit back down! There's no way I'm drinking alone. Gin and tonic, I think . . ." She bent down and was rummaging through the liquor cupboard.

I wanted to say no again, I was going to stand my ground and re-fuse the drink, but because it was Audrey, I pushed myself to not be such a hard-ass and at least *consider* the offer. Would there ever be a more suitable occasion than this to have my very first drink? I didn't think so.

Audrey was grinning widely, comically, as she pulled a large bottle out of the cupboard before noticing the pie cooling. "Well, look at this! Aren't you something, you've gone and made me a pie . . ." And as she rambled on, she poured, mixed, then handed me the drink, fizzing away with a wedge of lime floating at the top. She continued to go on about the pie as she raised her glass to mine, but I wasn't really listening. I was having my own conversation in my head. *Jesus, Mary-humping, motherfucking Christ*, I thought, *this is what it's all about*.

I brought the drink to my mouth and tipped the glass. I knew that I would never become my father. It burned a little as it went down and felt a little chemically. My very first taste of gin was not the illicit imbibing of some kind of poison associated with shouting, picking fights, and wallowing in self-pity, but an affirmation that I belonged to another kind of clan. I was lucky to be surrounded by exemplars of fortitude, courage, and perseverance, the epitome of which was now standing before me.

I named the voice in my head. That annoying little voice that would pipe up as I slipped into the swimming pool. While submerging my face under the water and splaying out my arms and legs, that voice began by saying, slowly, "*Uh-oh* . . ." I'd try my hardest to just ignore it, not responding as I started my kick and stretched one arm out, pulling the water underneath me while rotating my torso and lifting the other arm out and over. And as I'd start to see the floor of the pool descending deeper . . . oh, so much water going even deeper . . . the voice would gurgle, "No . . . you *can't* do it . . ." and my chest would begin to tighten, succumbing to the loudening voice, " . . . see? I *told* you. You *can't* do it, you can't relax . . . it's all water and you don't know what you're doing, *danger*, *danger*, you are going to drown . . ."

I named that voice in my head, and when I could ignore it no longer, when I was so fed up with hearing its constant, annoying, doubting whine from the peanut gallery, the frustration in me boiled to the brim of impatience and I yelled back, "JENN! SHUT UP!" As I turned my head and took a breath, putting my face back into the water and pulling another stroke, I continued, "*I* am driving, and *you* are in the backseat!" One stroke, two stroke, *breathe*, *dammit*. And although the voice was now quiet, I got louder, " . . . and when *I* am driving and *you* are in the backseat, you sit there and you *shut up*. Do you hear me, Jenn?! You SHUT THE FUCK UP and you let me drive."

I learned how to swim. It took five years, but I learned how to swim. Front crawl, back crawl, and eventually butterfly. I had put Jenn in her place, and I finally learned how to swim.

From: yann_martel1963@yahoo.com

To: rajivsca@yahoo.ca
Subject: Happy New Year

Date: Sun, 7 Jan 2007 23:11:47

Hello, Rajiv.

Happy new year to you too.

News about Pi. Let's see. It's still happening, though still no green light yet. That should be coming very soon. I've read the screenplay, which is very good, albeit still a little too long, I suspect. I should warn you that Jeunet cast Pi as a twelve-year-old, which strikes me as much too young, and I told him so. Not only because finding a good actor that young is unlikely, but also because of the story: twelve is just too young for a character as mature as Pi. I think he should go for a young actor who can make himself look even younger. But that's in his hands. He's the god of this project. What else? Will be shot in India for 21 to 28 days, then in Louisiana (!) for five months (seems they have a basin and swamps there), then the rest in LA in studio.

That's all I know so far. Jeunet was having a conference with the big cheeses at Fox between Xmas and New Year. Things may be proceeding as we speak.

Stay well. Good luck with pilot season in LA.

Yann

Hello, Rajiv.

Yes, very busy. Trying to finish my next book before mid-August.

Illustrated *Pi* is coming out this late fall. As for movie *Pi,* I believe the studio should be agreeing on the budget very, very soon. So, fingers crossed, a green light before the end of the month.

That's my news.

Hope you're well.

Yann

11.

MEAN GIRLS WAS NOW A bigger deal than it was when it was first released in theaters. Over the course of a few years, it had become a cult classic. I found myself in the strange situation of being interrupted while spinning wool at work only to be asked whether I was "the rapping mathlete, Kevin G."

I was still in the acting game, going out for auditions whenever they came up. My role in *Mean Girls* had given me just enough clout to be considered for any major "brown" dude, but I never did approach my career with the notion that one job would lead to another, and after playing Kevin G., I was adamant about not going back to auditioning for the monthly terrorist or IT guys in the many TV shows that were shooting in Toronto. I told my agent Gerry that I'd be willing and happy to read for anything he thought I might enjoy being a part of, although those roles came up only a few times a year. I stressed to Gerry that *Pi* came before anything else.

The school year was coming to a close, when Gerry called with an audition for a TV pilot called *Aliens in America*. I loved the script and the character I'd be trying out for—an Indian, immigrant, Muslim kid named Raja who participates in a student exchange program with a family in Wisconsin. There were elements of playing the stereotype in this show, but the whole premise was about breaking misconceptions, so I was okay with putting on an Indian accent and bobbling my head. Another perk was that the father figure in the show was already cast—an actor that I only knew about because of my sisters' obsession with *Gilmore Girls*. When I told my sisters that I was up for a part that would entail being in scenes with *Luke Danes*, they lost it.

A couple of weeks after submitting my taped audition, Gerry called and said that they wanted to see me in LA for a studio test. I was ecstatic.

My screen test dates could not have been timed more horribly—they wanted me there for two days, the same days that I had both a final art history exam at school and a mandatory yearly staff orientation at Black Creek. Wendy made her sour face when I told her I couldn't make it to the orientation, and I was ready to quit my job if she put up a fuss, but she conceded and let me take the day off. School proved to be the unexpected pain in the ass—the professor refused to grant me permission to miss the exam and told me I'd have to fill in paperwork *after* missing the exam, appealing to rewrite it. Some sort of board would either approve or deny my appeal, and if they denied it, I'd fail the course. *Whatever*, I thought, *fuck art history and fuck school*. It wasn't a difficult decision.

A few days later I got up super early to pack my bags, invigorated with the excitement of being invited to read at a cornerstone of the whole Hollywood picture business, the Universal Studios lot. I was slowed only by deciding between my black shoes or the brown boots. I settled on the black, rushed out of the house, and ran for the bus to Black Creek. On the bus, I noticed my shoes needed a shine and hoped that the Moneyworth's shoeshine stand at the airport would still be open when I arrived for my flight later that night.

I spent the day in a daze as I mindlessly kneaded bread dough and rolled out cookies in the Halfway House. I left work early, changed out of my costume, and headed to the main entrance building, where a driver in a suit was waiting by his black sedan to take me to the airport. I wondered whether this might possibly be the last time I would ever see Pioneer Village.

Seven hours later, I was excitedly peering out the tinted windows of another sedan, with classical music playing on the radio as the driver headed to a fancy hotel in Beverly Hills. I felt incredibly small, looking up at the palm trees, thin and so tall, dwarfing everything around them.

The next morning, crossing through the Universal Studios security gate and entering the lot seemed like genuine magic.

I met the director and the producers for a network test. There were two other Indian guys being considered for the part of Raja. One of them was there, and the other was someone named Jonathan. He was a kid my age, and Marcia had pointed him out as potential competition for *Life of Pi* when a movie named *House of Sand and Fog* came out. His name was Jonathan Ahdout, and I'd forgotten about him until then. When the casting director sat down and chatted with me, I casually asked her who else was reading for the role. She told me the names of the other two actors, and Jonathan Ahdout was indeed reading for the part of Raja. The other kid's name was Kamal. But the next day at the audition, only Kamal showed up, and when I asked the casting director where Jonathan was, she said that he had decided not to read for the part as he wasn't prepared to move away and miss a year of school. I suddenly wondered whether this might mean that he'd be free to read for *Life of Pi*, if it came up, while I might be stuck in the contract of this TV show.

But now I was only up against one other guy. In the waiting room, there were two of us brown guys trying out for Raja and two white guys trying out for the role of the other lead, a sixteen-year-old kid who would end up being Raja's best friend in the show. I was invited to read with one of the white guys, and it went well. Then they sent the white guy out and brought in the other white guy. Then they sent both of us out and asked Kamal to come in with one of the white guys. Then they sent out that white guy and brought in the other white guy. So it became clear that they wanted to see all possible combinations of the four.

Now the four of us sat silently in the waiting room, occasionally glancing over at the closed door, in which sat the makers of our fate.

Eventually, the casting director came out and pleasantly told Kamal he was, "free to go." *Yes! Score!* Then she asked me to come in with the first actor I read with. We did our thing once, the director gave us some minor notes, and then we did it again. Then they sent the white actor out and invited in the other white actor and we went through it all again.

It was still sunny and warm when I got back to the hotel, and the pool was completely empty so I went for a swim. Gerry called that evening and told me that I had "passed." Which meant that I'd stay overnight in LA again, and then go into the Universal Studios lot the next day to audition for the executive producers. "Tomorrow's the tough one, Rajiv," Gerry said, "there'll be about ten producers in the room and they will all have to unanimously agree that you're the one for this part."

Only one of the white boys was at the audition the next day. We hadn't talked much, outside of the actual audition, but it was strange to feel a connection to him while we were acting together. It was the revelation that *this* was the chemistry that the creators of the show were testing for . . . and I felt it. I liked this guy. His mom was with him. In the waiting room, the mom sat beside her son with her arm around his shoulder as he reviewed the lines of the scene. I was alone, and I couldn't help but think of Ma. She was probably home from work about now. I secretly wished she was here, too. Or just somebody else. I was alone and this was the first time since my arrival that I really felt it. The boy's mother looked over at me and gave me a smile. "Good luck," she mouthed.

"Thanks. You, too," I whispered back. "Well, Dan, I mean," I clarified, asking myself why I couldn't just shut up and then, "Well, I guess you, too."

Dan was great. I locked eyes with him when I needed to and I got lost in the world the two of us were creating. Our banter was punctuated with laughter from the producers, and the more they laughed the more we seemed to be able to give them. The final scene ended on a sad note, teary-eyed. And Dan and I nailed it. There was applause and then we were both briefly thanked. The producers looked to each other and after they agreed they needed nothing more from us, we were dismissed.

Back in Toronto, a few days later, Gerry called to tell me the studio had until the end of the week to decide whether or not they wanted me but they'd send us a preliminary contract to review while we waited. I started getting anxious.

It was a busy time for Gerry, as well, as he was flying off to England shortly to be married. I offered to write up the place cards for his reception in my calligraphy, and he gave me a list of the guests.

Details of the contract were reviewed. The deal was for six years. I was bound to the production for six years, if it got picked up every season. And that was a big if. Most pilots never see the light of day—never get picked up. It was a good deal—six years of work, thirteen episodes a year, and thirteen thousand dollars per episode. But I was bound to the studio for six years. They had exclusive rights over my performing while I was under contract with them. What if . . . I started to wonder . . . what if Pi actually comes up? Then what do I do?

Gerry left for England before we had an answer from the studio—

they had asked for a week's extension to make up their mind, but he assured me that his assistant would keep me posted. He loved the place cards I did for him; he said he'd be checking emails while he was away and told me not to hesitate to get in touch if I needed to.

There were just a few days left until the deadline for the studio to make its decision. Then one evening, while I was doing my periodic deep scouring of the Internet for any news on *Pi*, there was an official-looking notice posted on the Internet movie database about Jeunet moving forward and hiring a well-known casting director in London, Lucinda Syson, to find him the star of his next film.

At 6 a.m. the following morning, I picked up the phone and called London.

"Casting," a young woman's voice answered with a British accent.

"Hi, my name's Rajiv Surendra," I began. I asked about their office casting for *Life of Pi* and the girl elusively said that she couldn't really confirm that. I was desperate for anything she could tell me, so I pulled out all the stops, told her I was in *Mean Girls*, and then did my best to sum up, in a few sentences, how much effort I had put into this part already. As I stated my case, her silence suggested that I had at least made her think twice about brushing me off.

"My name's Clara," she said, with a tone that felt like she was throwing me a bone, "I'm Lucinda's assistant. Send a package to my attention, and I'll make sure she sees it."

I spun wool all morning and tried my best to remain focused while I talked about Daniel Stong. But when the house was empty, I was overcome with uneasiness. I had been working toward Pi for almost four years now, and just when there was some sign of hope on the horizon of it actually happening, sure enough, I could potentially be handcuffed to a six-year contract on a television show.

I wondered what might happen if—*if* I hear back from *Aliens in*

America, and the joyous news is that I have been cast in the show as Raja. Celebration as I pack my bags with my thirty-two cousins over at my house, who have come to wish me well and say goodbye before I relocate to Vancouver.

We're two months into shooting when Gerry calls and tells me that *Pi* is finally happening, and they want to see an audition tape from me. I go into a studio with a few pages of the official *Pi* script in my hand, which I've painstakingly analyzed, memorized, and internalized. I drop the recording of my audition into a Vancouver mailbox and then make a spitting noise with my mouth, three times, to ward off the evil eye.

I try my best to forget about the *Pi* audition as I continue to pour myself into this wonderful TV show that I've been employed to work on—the bird in the hand.

And then the inevitable happens. Jeunet wants to see me. In person. *Oh my God. It's happening.*

Gerry arranges a flight from Vancouver to Paris, with a layover in Toronto, on the few days off I have from work.

In Montmartre, at the preproduction office for *Life of Pi*, my walk to the little corner studio where Jeunet is waiting becomes my own personal march to the battle grounds. Every step feels like a million little paces that have made their way to this moment. I enter the room and there he is, sitting in a cheap plastic Ikea chair, wearing all black. "Bonjour," he says inquiringly.

And I go at it in French; I just dive right in. He can't believe it, "*Tu parles Français?*" he interrupts, incredulously.

"*Comme une vache espagnole,*" I say, apologetically.

He laughs a hearty French farmer-type laugh, claps his two large palms together as he leans back, teetering on the two rear legs of the chair, and turns to his casting director, raising his eyebrows at her, impressed. "*Bah, non!*" he contests turning back to face me, telling me that I shouldn't be so humble. He leans forward in his chair, rubs his hands together excitedly, and eagerly begins, "*Alors . . .*"

The next two hours flash by. I read for him as Pi, beginning with the calmer parts of the screenplay that have been chosen for the audition, and ending with the climactic gut-wrencher, the final scene of the entire film. He is moved to tears. He wipes them away and shakes his head in disbelief. He violently slaps the side of his face, to make sure he's "not dreaming," he says. He needs a moment to regain his composure before asking me to read again, with a few minor notes, a slightly different take on the same scene.

I am completely wiped as I board the plane back to Vancouver. I use the last bit of energy I can muster to lift my hand, politely turning down the stewardess who has approached me with a tray of bubbling champagne flutes.

I am back on set, at work on *Aliens* the following week. Gerry calls during lunch break with the news. I've landed the Pi part.

But wait, he says, we need to find out whether I can get permission from my current employer for a hiatus to shoot the movie.

Phone calls back and forth among Gerry, the studio, and me. Gerry has tried; he has pleaded and made suggestions; he has fought the battle with the sharpest weaponry of the wits. But it's no use. I am bound to my current, six-year contract, and I am not allowed to take time off to shoot Pi. They will just have to find another Indian boy. *Noooooooo oooooooooooooooooooooooooooooooooooooooooooooooooooooooooooooooooooo ooooooo!*

I scream, my cellphone dropping to the ground as I lose the feeling in my legs and fall to the floor, weeping.

"Rajiv? Rajeeeeeeveeee . . ." Gerry's voice can be heard through the abandoned cellphone, calling out for some response, but it's no use. I am inconsolable, and by now there is a small group of production assistants around my limp body, which is curled into the fetal position on the concrete ground of the studio. Someone yells out, "We need a doctor! Goddammit, somebody call a doctor!"

Clunk! The spinning wheel's whirring came to a halt, pulling me back to reality. My basket of fleece was empty.

Just a few weeks ago I had been begging the universe to send me an acting job, wishing with all my might that I could say goodbye to Pioneer Village and embark on a full-time gig in front of the camera. But was that really what I was asking for? Or was I just asking for proof that I was worthy of a part? There were countless actors out there who would give anything to be offered a lead role on a national US television show. Was I being completely foolish even contemplating my situation, assuming that I was in a dilemma? I wondered where Gerry was, wishing that I could call him, but I realized it was now the night before his wedding day. And tomorrow, as Gerry was tying the knot in some rural part of England, the studio would be calling the agency with news of my being a part of their show.

What do I do? It was the lone question that circled in my mind for the entire two-hour bus ride home that night.

Sleep was the quiet I needed to settle down and make a decision. I woke up refreshed, with a clear idea of what I needed to do. Before I left for work, I sifted through the paperwork I had been given for the *Aliens* contract and noted down the phone number of the executive vice president of business affairs at Universal Studios—the point person in LA whom Gerry had been corresponding with, Sharon Bell. It was too early to call her, LA being three hours behind us in Toronto. I would call her on my lunch break, I decided.

I was working in the Halfway House that day. I kept a fire going for two hours in the huge brick oven while I prepared the dough for two dozen loaves of bread, made with flour that was ground at the water-powered gristmill we had on site. I was braiding my twentieth loaf of bread, with no visitors in the huge kitchen, when two Orthodox Jewish men, about forty years old, slowly walked in. I looked to them and smiled, but said nothing. A long chain separated the kitchen into my area, where I worked, and the "viewing" area where visitors could observe safely away from the roaring fire in the brick oven behind me. The two men watched in silence for quite a while before one of them spoke up.

"What are ya doin' ovah there?"

"I'm baking bread," I said.

A lull as they continued to watch.

"What kinda' bread are ya makin'?"

I continued to look down at the floured wooden table as I braided the three strands of dough together. "Challah," I said clearly, making sure I accurately pronounced the *ch* sound at the back of my throat. I looked up and turned to the men—one had turned to face the other, eyebrows raised.

"Challah?" he asked, "You're makin' *challah*? You even know how to say that word?"

"Yeah, impressive, isn't it?" I asked. "I'm not just a little *schwarze goy* . . ." Kate and Eric had taught me the Yiddish words for "black" and "non-Jew." The two men laughed deeply. I braided the last few loaves and placed them into the iron pans.

One of the men piped up again, "Come ovah here a minute."

I wiped my hands on the towel hanging from my apron strings, and walked over to the chain where they stood. The men looked at me amusingly, smiling. They both wore black hats with big, wide brims. Two long curls framed each of their faces.

"Tell me somethin'," one of them asked softly, "how do you know all these things?" I couldn't help but laugh out loud. *All these things*, like I had discovered the meaning of life.

As I watched the men leave I started mixing up a batch of oatmeal cookies. *All these things* . . . the line echoed in my head again.

The cookies were in the oven while I took my lunch break. I asked Wendy for permission to use the phone to make an "important long-distance call that was time sensitive," and was relieved when she didn't ask any questions and gave me the special code needed to dial long distance. I walked down the steps to the basement. I could feel my heart thumping underneath my three layers of linen and cotton period clothing as I made my way through dialing the sequence of numbers to make the call to LA.

"Sharon Bell," a woman's voice answered. She didn't sound too pleased when she realized who I was; I was blatantly abandoning a well-adhered-to form of protocol, calling her myself instead of com-municating through my agent, but when I told her that I didn't want to disturb Gerry, knowing that she was aware he was out of the country, her response was a bit of a relief.

"No, let's allow Gerry to enjoy his wedding," she said.

I told her all about *Pi* and what it meant to me and that a break-down for the role had just come out. She asked about shooting details, locations, dates. She also said my timing was strange but good, as she had just opened my file and was going to a meeting to discuss it.

I basically told her, before we ended our conversation, that if they could not guarantee that I would be given permission to take time off to do the film, *if* it came up, and *if* I had been cast in it, then I un-fortunately had to pass on *Aliens*. She told me that she understood where I was coming from and would relay the info to the other deci-sion makers.

I hung up the phone and then picked it up again and dialed my agency. Gerry's assistant answered and I told her what I had just done.

"Wow," she said, "you really need to just take what's offered to you instead of speculating. Do you realize that this part could have opened the doors to a real career before you're too old?"

"I just had to do this, Cindy."

"You know, Rajiv, you're lucky Gerry's your agent. If you were my client, I would have dropped you for turning this down. It doesn't make sense to me . . ."

I returned to my brick oven without eating anything for lunch, just in time to pull out the four trays of cookies. I usually tasted one, for quality control, but my stomach was in knots. *What had I just done? Was it a huge mistake?*

There was a small slate chalkboard propped up on the pie safe that we used to advertise the baked goods we were selling. I went over to it and under "Fresh Bread" added, "Oatmeal Cookies, 75¢" with a nubby bit of chalk.

We never heard back from the studio about the part. After a few weeks, it was clear that I was out of the running. I wondered for a moment if I was crazy, boldly calling the studio myself with a "take it or leave it" approach. No, I concluded. I had no choice here. This was the clarity I needed—*Pi* was everything to me, and here on out, it was all or nothing.

From: yann_martel1963@yahoo.com

To: rajivsca@yahoo.ca

Subject: RE: Nuvo Magazine

Date: Wed, 25 Jun 2008 22:27:19

Hello, Rajiv.

Long time no hear. Summer is good here. I'd practically forgotten about the Nuvo interview.

Book still in the works, so it will be a while.

Jeunet will no longer be doing the movie, alas. Everything was in place—a studio backing it, a great director, a terrific script—except for the downward spiraling US dollar. Because of it, an already hefty budget ballooned by more than 25%. They couldn't agree on budget.

Another big name is being bandied about. Can't tell, but he's good. Things should firm up soonish, but who knows? When this is finally cast, you might be 52 years old.

Stay well,

Yann

12.

MAYBE I WAS JUST LOOKING for something to distract myself from the disappointment of learning that Jeunet was no longer attached to the film. Or maybe it was simply something to give me hope that there was yet another aspect of this book that could use my attention, that I had more work to do, and that further research would lead me closer to landing the role of Pi. Whatever it was, I listened. And I started asking myself what parts of Yann's novel were things I still couldn't relate to.

Odysseus was a big part of my third year at the University of Toronto. I had a bunch of mandatory course requirements in both classics and art history, and Homer's epic poem seemed to pop up in almost every class. The painted depiction of Odysseus strapped to the mast of a ship as he is tempted by the sirens appeared on a red-figure vase in my class on ancient Greek pottery. He played a starring role in my class on the classical literature of antiquity, and he even managed to appear in the one mandatory science course I needed to fulfill my degree requirements—Astronomy 101.

Tuesday was my busiest day of the week in my second semester. It was early January and I was still getting used to my new schedule, making my way from Greek Pottery to my swimming lesson for the day, Butterfly 101, where we were introduced to the dolphin kick.

My hair was still damp when I slipped into my next class, The Romantic Movement in French Art. The instructor, Ryan, a frazzled blond guy who seemed way too young to be teaching this course, apologized in advance for being "kind of out of it" that day, before admitting that he had taken a few muscle relaxants just before class. He tripped, fumbled with his notes, and the class laughed lightly, before he joined in to laugh at himself. The lights went out, the slide projector synced to his laptop, and the first image popped up—a painting of a dimly lit pile of severed human limbs, close-up and strikingly beautiful, despite the gore.

"We're talking about Géricault today," Ryan announced through a cough. "He was a commercial failure, and was labelled a madman, but to me, he was a forerunner of the French romantics." More coughing.

The next image came up. Naked and semiclothed figures entwined together in a pyramid-shaped pile, heaped on a wooden platform that is being tossed around the rough seas. As opposed to the prissy, flowery portraits of Marie Antoinette and King Louis that prefaced the works we were shown in this class, the slide on the screen evoked a dark sense of the tragic, the figures full of movement in a haunting tableau of desperation. This was *my kind of painting*.

"In 1816, a French ship called the *Medusa* sunk on its way to Senegal," Ryan read from his notes. "Of the hundred and fifty people that were able to climb onto a makeshift raft, only fifteen survived. The event was a huge scandal, and Géricault becomes obsessed with creating a depiction of what had actually happened. He tracks down one of the survivors and gets a firsthand account of the event. Then he spends the next year in complete isolation in his studio—making miniature wax models of the raft and its survivors, bringing home amputated body parts from the hospital and painting them in both daylight and lamplight, studying, obsessing, and completely engrossed in the beautiful horror of his confined world."

I've never been one to overthink why a strange coincidence played out in front of me; I usually take the hint and run with it.

Odysseus. *The Raft of the Medusa*. Castaways. Cast adrift. Lost at sea. Just like Pi.

Ryan had moved on to Delacroix and was picking apart a painting of a woman with her tits out, standing on a bunch of dead bodies as she waved the French flag. I gave myself permission to mentally opt out of class so I could made a checklist in my head of every imaginable element of the novel that could warrant being researched.

Living in a zoo, observing animals?

Check.

India, Pondicherry?

Check.

Religion? Hinduism, Christianity, and Islam?

Check. Wait, really? I hadn't done that much research on Islam. It wasn't a big deal, Pi practiced all three religions in the novel, but Islam only had a minor role. Yeah, right, good—check, yeah, check.

Swimming?

Check.

Being lost at sea? Hmmm . . . I guess I could imagine what it was like, Yann did a pretty good job of describing the mental and physical struggle in the novel. That was enough, right? *Check?* I thought about it for a while.

Was it really enough?

No, it wasn't. Because it was fiction. It still wasn't real to me. Sure, I could hope that when the time came to audition I'd have the acting skills to make that leap of faith and be immersed in the life of a kid stranded in the middle of the ocean . . . but the whole concept seemed fantastical, unreal, like a scene on an eighteenth-century oil painting or the engraved frieze on an ancient Greek amphora. Was it even possible,

I wondered, for a single person to survive actually being lost at sea for more than a few days . . . or weeks?

Was there someone out there who actually survived being cast adrift? It seemed like a newspaper headline from a bygone era—from the time of wooden ships with mermaid figureheads.

I quietly closed my notebook, grabbed my coat, and slipped out of class. Ryan seemed too dazed to even notice me leaving.

There were four large libraries on the U of T campus, and their computer system catalogued every book in their entire collection. Various combinations of "lost," "sea," "adrift," 'and "survivor" proved fruitless, so I abandoned the U of T library system and turned to good ol' faithful, never-let-you-down Yahoo.com. Yes, there were indeed modern shipwreck survivors. And yes, they had written about their ordeals. Most were out of print, but I tracked down and ordered three castaway sagas.

The first arrived two days later, *Survive the Savage Sea* by Dougal Roberston, and I devoured it completely within one night, ravenously licking up every single detail. 1972—Dougal, his wife, and their four kids are sailing in a remote part of the Pacific, when a group of killer whales attack, puncturing the walls of their schooner, *Lucette*. As the ocean rapidly gushes into their boat, the family frantically scurries into survival mode, inflating their emergency life raft and tethering it to their fiberglass dinghy while Dougal scrambles to salvage whatever he can get his hands on. He throws a bag of onions, a bag of oranges, and a small bag of lemons into the dinghy, and commands his eldest son to make his way over to the raft. Their nine-year-old is clutching his teddy bear when Dougal shouts to him to abandon ship! The boy plunges into the sea and—

"*Kanna*, come and eat!" Ma interrupted, calling me down to dinner, but I ignored her.

—he swims strongly and makes it to the raft. Dougal stands in the dinghy, now completely swamped with water, the oranges and lemons floating around in it. He tosses the precious fruit over to the raft, catching a last glimpse of *Lucette*, now only the tops of her sails visible. "Slowly she curtsied below the waves, a lady to the last: she was gone when I looked again."

This book was full of the real details I was craving that I had been introduced to in *Life of Pi*—but this time, they were real; dorado and flying fish the family caught and consumed, raw. A passing cargo ship causes overwhelming excitement with the possibility of being saved—rocket flares are lit and projected into the air—but it's no use, they go unnoticed and a haunting reality sets in, giving way to utter fear, despair, complete exhaustion, and then, in the end, salvation.

The following week, I eagerly checked the mailbox every day as I arrived home from school. When a little padded Kraft paper envelope showed up from a used bookseller in Indiana, I ripped it open right there on the porch, frantically unlocked the front door of the house, and ran up to my bedroom.

I grabbed the book and took in each minute detail of the dust jacket, turning it over in my hands, and reading every single word on its surface—the title: *117 Days Adrift*, below it, "Maurice & Maralyn Bailey," and at the very bottom of the cover, "foreword by Sir Peter Scott." On the back, in bold, white print sitting on a navy blue background: "For two people alone in a tiny life raft, rescue is at last at hand. Maurice and Maralyn Bailey's survival after almost four months of incredible hardship must stand as a feat of unparalleled fortitude. At this, the moment of rescue, a line thrown from the deck of a Korean fishing boat finally severs their utter dependence on the sea."

This book differs from the first one in that it was a couple, instead of a family, and their ordeal lasted much longer. More than just the physical trials they endured during their time adrift, it was the mental one that spoke to me the most. I finish the book, weary, and then realized that at the very least, Maurice and Maralyn had each other. Pi was alone. And what a huge difference it would be to not have anyone else to turn to, to talk to, to give you hope, in the face of such dire circumstances.

There was three feet of snow on the ground and more was falling as I walked home from the bus stop one evening. It was early January, but the package in the mailbox made it feel like Christmas morning. I sat down at my little 1820s writing table, opened the drawer, and pulled out my heavy pair of hand-forged scissors. Here was the book that I had longed for the most, I was happy it had arrived last. *Adrift: 76 Days Lost at Sea* by one Steven Callahan. Not as long a struggle as the Baileys endured, I thought, but the single feature I was seeking in this book was something that the other two didn't have. This was the struggle of one single, lonely survivor.

I didn't rush through this one; I savored it slowly. Ma called me to dinner just after I had started reading, so I put Mr. Callahan's book face-down on my bed before going downstairs. Ma had made one of her "quick" Tamil meals, one of my favorites—basmati rice served with curried lentils, tomato and onion salad, and two fried eggs on top, smothered in black pepper. As I ate, I thought about what I had just read.

"Finally," he had stated in his acknowledgments section at the opening of the book, "I would like to express my gratitude to the sea. It has taught me quite a lot in life. Although the sea was my greatest enemy, it was also my greatest ally. I know intellectually that the sea is indifferent, but her richness allowed me to survive."

Back upstairs, dinner was sitting comfortably in my belly while I read a little more and then thought about it as I showered that night. Seventy-six days in a raft on the Atlantic. Nine ships passed him and not one noticed his raft. Water, water everywhere . . . not a drop to drink. A few more pages and then bed.

I got up in the morning and Mr. Callahan accompanied me to the breakfast table.

"I find food in a couple of hours of fishing each day, and I seek shelter in a rubber tent. How unnecessarily complicated my past life seems. For the first time, I clearly see a vast difference between human needs and human wants."

More reading on the bus ride to school.

When I had leisurely finished the book, I read it over again. I came to the end for the second time, back on my bed, lying face up with the book propped up on my chest.

"The accident has left me with a sense of loss and a lingering fear," read the epilogue on the last page of the book, "but I have chosen to learn from the crisis rather than let it overcome me."

Being lost at sea? A voice in my head asked meekly, *check?* There was a long moment of internal silence.

"No," another voice answered deeply, ominously—as if it were a grand and ancient oracle.

"What?!" shouted the first voice. "Why the hell not?"

"*Patience, peasant!*" the oracle bellowed. "We must pause to contemplate our present situation."

Snow continued to fall outside my window. I turned the final page of the book, revealing the rear flap of the dust jacket. There was a little black-and-white picture of the author, with tousled, shoulder-length hair. He was squinting from the sunshine. "Steven Callahan, a naval architect, lives in Lamoine, Maine" it stated underneath the photo. That was all, nothing else.

"It just doesn't feel real to me," the other voice said, back in its normal, colloquial tone.

"What are you talking about?" the first voice snapped, "it's a true story, dummy."

"Yeah, but it's still just a book. It may be nonfiction, but it's a book. A story in a book."

Steven Callahan, I read again, contemplating the little black-and-white picture. Teeny, weeny text above his picture gave credit to the photographer with a copyright symbol appearing beside it: ©1986. *How old was this Steven Callahan?* I wondered. I flipped through the book—he was thirty years old when his boat sank in 1982. He spent his thirtieth birthday on a life raft on the Atlantic. *Was he still alive?* I wondered. He would be fifty-seven years old if he were still alive. *Not old*, I thought. *Maybe he is still alive.*

The winter light was pink with the sun starting to set. I propped myself up in bed and leaned over to glance at the old clock on my wall that I hand-wound every night—almost four thirty. *Steven Callahan. Lamoine, Maine.*

I ran down to the basement where the computer was, passing my sisters lounging on the couch, watching a rerun of *Gilmore Girls*. My older sister had a hand-held mirror in front of her, and was plucking tiny hairs out of her chin with a pair of tweezers.

I hit the power button on the computer and as it warmed up I realized that my sisters were completely unaware of my Pi quest. *I bet they have no idea what I'm doing*, I thought. Wait, but I really had no idea what they're up to . . . nor did I care. Things at home were great without my dad, and my sisters and I no longer had the need to band together against our common enemy. Maybe the trauma between Ma and my dad had left my sisters and me with the need to fend for ourselves out there in the real world, without support from each other . . . I don't know. I realized I wasn't close to them, and it didn't bother me.

The computer screen came to life, jolting me out of my daze. I started typing, in a frenzy. Yahoo.com gave me exactly what I was looking for. I grabbed the cordless phone and ran back up to my room, shut the door, and dialed the eleven-digit American phone number I had scribbled down on a Post-it.

Ringing. This *is real*, I thought. One ring, two rings—

"Lamoine Town Office," a gruff male voice answered.

"Hi, there . . . uh . . . this may be a long shot, but do you by any chance know a man named Steven Callahan?"

There was quite a long moment of silence on the other side before he cleared his throat and replied, "I do, actually."

I thought he might go on, so I waited, but when the silence continued, I spoke up, "Steven Callahan, a sailor? He wrote a book about being cast adrift."

"Yup," the man chirped with a bit of intrigue in his voice. I had the feeling he was smiling. "That's the one."

"Would you be able to give me his number, please?" I asked.

"No. But I can give him your number."

Surprised that he didn't question me further, I was all aflutter as I gave him my number.

"And one last thing," I added for good measure, "please tell Mr. Callahan that it's *very* important."

From: yann_martel1963@yahoo.com

To: rajivsca@yahoo.ca

Subject: RE: Happy New Year!

Date: Fri, 16 Jan 2009 06:32:18

Dear Rajiv,

Happy New Year to you too. Hope 2009 keeps you busy
in front of the camera.

I see you're doing your homework. Excellent book,
Robertson's. Understated and powerful.

There's some progress on finding a new director, but
I have to keep mum about it. Fingers crossed.

Yann

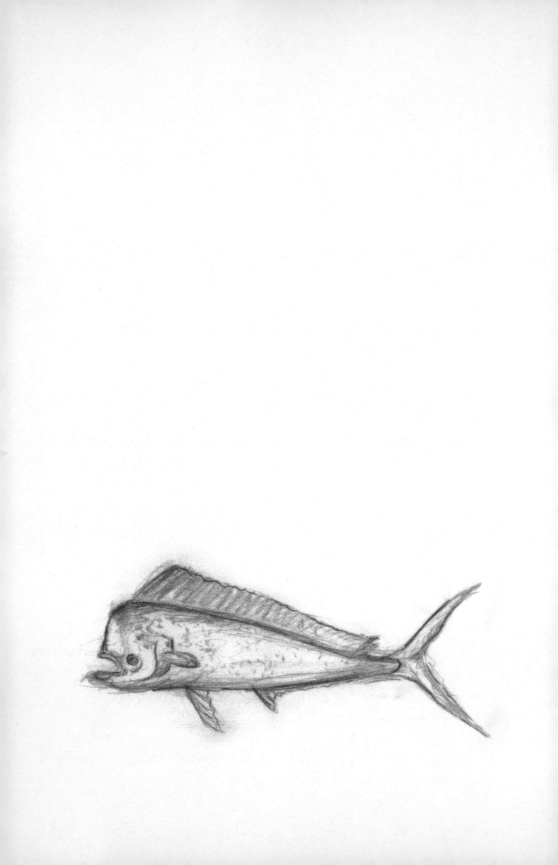

13.

IT WAS FREEZING IN MY window seat. My ass itself was the only thing that was warm, but for that reason alone I was reminded of Audrey once warning me about sitting on cold surfaces, telling me that I'd get hemorrhoids if my bum hole was cold. *Phew*, close call.

"Steven Callahan, a naval architect, lives in Lamoine, Maine." Bangor was the closest airport. I had finished the book for the third time, having begun it just before leaving Toronto and reading the entire time during my layover in New York, waiting for my connecting flight to Maine. It seemed counterintuitive to be flying south in order to go back north but there were no direct flights from Toronto and the easiest route ended up taking me an entire day of traveling.

It was now almost 9 p.m., and I peered out of the window at the concentrated mass of orange lights below indicating the city of Bangor. The plane was quiet but I was bursting with a sense of adventure. I was going to Maine to make Steven Callahan's story *real* to me. It was, essentially, the last piece of the puzzle, the final thing I needed to fully become Pi.

Steven told me that he would be waiting for me when the plane landed, and not to worry, the tiny airport terminal was just one big room, so it would be easy to find him. I wondered what he looked like now, and whether I'd be able to recognize him. In his dust jacket photo, he was shirtless, but cropped only down to his collarbone, which jutted out deeply. He was thin, but maybe that was because he was still recovering from starving, almost to death. But it was now over twenty years later, and perhaps he had gained weight. Maybe he had succumbed to the American Dream and had become a huge Gargantua. Maybe he was a four-hundred-pound sailor missing his front teeth, and wore a ratty, sweat-stained undershirt, smoked a pipe, chewed tobacco, had to spit every three minutes, and was too fat to even walk, so he was in an electric wheelchair that he maneuvered with his fat pinky—and he had a nickname for his fat little finger: "Pinkus the Almighty."

I walked through the gate into the outdated 1970s interior of the airport, with carpeting underfoot, and I realized I was holding my breath, and had to tell myself to relax.

I recognized him as soon as I entered the terminal—a man in a baseball cap wearing a red Eddie Bauer jacket and blue jeans. He was thin and about five foot ten. He still had the same mustache and beard from twenty years before, except it was now graying here and there. And as I was the only brown guy on the plane, there was surely no reason for any kind of mix-up on his part. He smiled and walked toward me.

"Hi, Steven," I said, shaking his hand and looking up at him.

"Hi, nice to meet you." Steven replied. "Raaa-jeeve, is that right? Am I saying it properly?" he asked casually.

"Yeah, that's it. There are lots of ways to say it, and *I* don't even say it properly, so however you say it is fine with me," I said easily.

"I'll carry your bag," Steven offered, as we made our way out of the terminal.

"No, it's fine, thanks. I've got it."

His face was made up of the features that I had imagined a weatherworn sailor to possess—freckles, skin that was aged by the sun, almost like fine leather, and crow's-feet at the edges of his eyes, with grooves that deepened with the widening of his smile. I was forcing myself to act casually and hide my overwhelming feeling of awe, walking side by side with this modern-day Odysseus. Lost at sea for over two months, pushing away sharks and dying of thirst, being lured by the deadly sirens and incurring the wrath of Poseidon.

The night air was blisteringly cold as we walked through a set of sliding doors and headed to Steven's car. The snowbanks on the side of the road were waist-high. I had debated wearing my snow boots, but they seemed too adolescent and clunky, so I wore my leather penny loafers instead and in the place of my heavy down jacket, I chose a thin brown, woolen, tweed coat from Brooks Brothers. Shivering in the cold, I chastised myself for stupidly dressing to impress instead of being practical. I was glad I had decided to wear long johns underneath my corduroy pants.

"So, how was the flight?"

"Fine, no problems." I said. "But it wasn't easy getting here, there weren't any direct flights from Toronto, so it meant I had to leave the house early this morning."

"There's actually a line that the local old-timers use, 'Ya can't get there from here!' they say."

We both laughed.

It was almost 11 p.m. when we arrived at Jasper's Restaurant and Motel, a tiny little place off the main road. I had expected my room to be something from a Hitchcock movie, but it was far from that—clean, with shiny new furniture; a single bed with a Queen Anne–style headboard; and a framed print of a sailboat on the wall.

"Jeez, it's freezing in here," Steven exclaimed, heading for the thermostat. He seemed worried about not being a good host and leaving me there in this refrigerator of a room, so I insisted that it wasn't that bad, that I actually preferred to sleep in rooms that were on the colder side.

"I can't thank you enough for letting me come down here . . ."

"Well, technically it's 'up'—'up' here to Maine. Maine is north of Toronto, ya know," Steven said with a cheeky grin.

"Soooooo," he started, looking down at the generic gray motel carpeting, "I'm not exactly sure of what it is you're looking for from me . . ." he said slowly, doing his best to not sound discouraging. "You have my book. There really isn't any more information I can offer you than what's already in there . . ." All he knew about me was that I was an actor chasing a role.

"Do you have time to sit down for a bit?" I asked, motioning to the small round table and two chairs near the door. "I *know* you actually experienced all this . . . but it's just . . . kinda tough connecting to it."

"Well . . . ." he said, stretching out the vowel of the word, "the book is about survival. And while I am actually talking about what happened to me on that life raft in the middle of the Atlantic, survival isn't just something that people have to deal with when they're lost at sea or stranded in the woods . . . in a way, every single person's day-to-day existence is about survival—you're doing it right now; you're here because you're doing your best to survive."

I nodded.

"Your story is amazing, though. And what you endured, how you managed to survive . . . it's incredible. I kind of can't believe I'm actually here, sitting with you . . ." I admitted.

"My experience on the raft is often idolized as a heroic accomplishment, but it's not," he said, raising his hands in a gesture of surrendering. "In fact, I see it as the opposite. Too many people want to play hero because they have a notion of glorification by the media." He wasn't reprimanding, just full of passion, waving his hands as he spoke.

I had an impulse to argue. To me he *was* a sort of hero, a mythical figure who had survived an epic journey and I *did* very much idolize him. *That's why I came here, dammit.* He survived against incredible odds and it was his wit, internal strength, and unique makeup that contributed to making this possible—why wasn't I allowed to glorify that? I was a little disheartened, but decided it was too soon (and too late at night) to begin a debate about his identity.

"The part of your book that floored me the most was when you finally saw land. After all those days at sea, when you describe seeing the faint outline of land on the horizon, I lost it."

He leaned back in his chair, put his glasses back on, and cocked his head, keeping the same pleasant smile on his face.

"Stepping out of the boat and onto land was like having my senses plugged into an electrical outlet. It was like what it must have felt like when we were first born. Seeing all that color again, after being at sea for so long, was like seeing it for the first time . . . the smells, the faces of other people, all new again." There was a calming, stoic quality to Steven that made him very easy to talk to.

"*That's* what brought me here," I proclaimed, almost as if I was articulating it to myself for the first time, "Pi being lost at sea, for so long . . . it's still a story, it's romanticized—and just hearing you tell me that it *isn't* heroic is exactly what I came here for. I may not personally agree with it, but I wanted to hear it from the horse's mouth. You're the horse."

Steven sat up in his chair and cleared his throat. I sensed it was getting late and had a feeling he was going to look at his watch, but he didn't, so I pushed ahead. "I have a list of questions I've made—from reading your book. Things that weren't quite answered in there. Is it okay if I asked you some of them now?"

"Sure," he said.

I got up and ran over to the armchair where I had put my bag. There was a bedbug scare going around, and I knew better than to put anything on the floor (where there were also probably traces of pee/period juice/semen). I pulled a small notebook out of my bag, one that I was saving for something special—I had bought it at the school store in Petit Séminaire, a small, blue, square notebook with thin lined paper in it. The school crest appeared on the cover, a small torch with a ribbon banner around it encasing the Latin motto, *Nil magnum, nisi bonum* (No greatness without goodness).

I excitedly opened the book to the page with the questions I had noted down and asked the first question. "What do you think was your most valuable trait that allowed you to survive, aside from luck, chance, and that stuff?"

Steven thought about it only for a few seconds. "Well, my ability to survive was most likely a product of my previous experience—a mariner is often alone, and deals with problems that may arise at a moment's notice. Doctors, policemen, and guys in the army usually do better and react more quickly in these situations of distress than people who haven't been trained to do so."

I was going to ask my next question, but I decided to wait in case he had more to say, which he did. "Those first two weeks on the raft were a period of shock, adjusting to the environment—mentally, physically. Then another period starts, of routine, or acceptance, maybe. Acceptance of the situation. You know, my greatest enemy wasn't the water, the weather, or the sharks . . . it was my mind. If I thought about my chances of surviving and dwelled only on that, I would have given up completely. But I realized that in order to stay alive, I had to focus on what I needed to do just in the present moment—collect rain water, catch the dorado fish that was swimming under the raft, protect myself from the sun."

I had a pen and was frantically taking notes.

"Your sex drive completely shuts down after a few days," he added as an afterthought.

I moved to my next question. "I would think that surviving something like this would make you appreciate life so much more than anyone else . . . that you'd return to land and be so grateful for being alive that . . . Do you get what I mean?" I tried to articulate the question I had written down, which was simply, Lucky to be alive/No more complaining. "I don't know, like you wouldn't sweat the small stuff anymore . . . almost like you see life through new eyes? Does that make sense?"

"Yeeeeeah, I get what you're asking," he said, taking a deep breath, crossing his arms and looking to the ceiling. The room was still freezing, and I hadn't even taken my coat off. He didn't seem to be too bothered by the temperature. "You know, the experience is not a salvation. Life goes on; I continue to make mistakes. The fact that I survived doesn't change the fact that I'm a human and have human qualities. It did make me more patient, initially, but later, especially nowadays, I've become a lot more impatient with the world. I have faults and flaws—I still get in silly arguments and fights with Kathy, and still have to admit that I was being a jackass . . . and apologize. None of that ever goes away completely."

Hmmm. I like this man. I like his answers. This is fun. Next question: "At the end of *Life of Pi*, his own personal salvation is how he looks back at his journey. He spent all this time drifting, waiting, hoping, and eventually surviving . . . but when he finally landed, although he had lost everything he had in the world, the way he mentally recovered was by looking back at his journey and crafting it into a story. Do you feel like that was what helped you recover from the ordeal?"

He was nodding slowly as he started with his response. "Choosing a story to tell, after the fact, is actually very cathartic and maybe it is what enabled me to go on. You know, there's case after case of army officers from Vietnam or even Iraq who fly home then kill themselves because even though they are safe now . . . they haven't found a healthy way of dealing with the trauma. Officers from World War Two spent a month in Europe after it was over, another month on a boat coming home, and then another month on a base here before returning to their families. They were together with other officers and had a chance to process and construct a story."

I was scribbling furiously, wishing I'd brought along a tape recorder.

Then, he subtly lifted his wrist and glanced at his watch. He looked back at me and smiled again, not moving in his seat. *He's being polite*, I thought. "What time is it?" I asked.

"Almost two," he said calmly.

"Oh, shit, I'm so sorry," I winced, getting up from the table and closing my notebook.

He asked me if I'd be okay in the room, pointing out again that it seemed a little too cold, but I reassured him that I'd be fine, and then we made plans to meet in the morning, at the local greasy spoon across the street. His wife, Kathy, was looking forward to meeting me, he said, and there was no rush to get up early—they had cleared the day just for me.

Steven left, and I changed into a T-shirt and my favorite pair of plaid, flannel pajama pants, threadbare at the knees. I pulled back the quilted polyester coverlet on the bed, got in, and then jumped right out and ran for another pair of socks and the sweater I was wearing when I arrived.

I was shivering for a couple of minutes while my body heat filled the cocoon formed by tightly pulling the coverlet over my head and around my body. But although I was cold, there was a warmth to knowing that I was missing school for the week, playing hooky for a very worthy cause.

From: yann_martel1963@yahoo.com

To: rajivsca@yahoo.ca

Subject: RE: New Director?

Date: Thu, 19 Feb 2009 18:41:11

Dear Rajiv,

Yes, it sounds like it's going to be Ang Lee. The studio flew me to New York to meet him. I spent five hours with him. And now he's committed himself to helping develop the screenplay. Don't know why he'd do that if he wasn't keen on directing. But who knows, Hollywood moves in mysterious ways.

We're in Bristol. But we should be heading to warmer climes in a few weeks, when I've actually, truly finished my next book.

Stay well.

Yann

14.

I WAS BLEARY-EYED WHEN I woke up the following morning. It was still absolutely freezing in the hotel room, even the baseboard heaters were ice cold. I called the front office and asked if they'd send someone over to check, and then headed into the bathroom to brush my teeth, only to realize that I had no toothpaste. I had packed a tube but it was confiscated at the airport.

"Iss too big, you can't take dis on da plane," the sassy officer at the security scan stated flatly. Her name tag read "Laverneesha."

"That makes no sense; I was able to take it through airport security in Toronto," I said, annoyed. "Why can't I take it through here?"

"I dunno what dey's doin' in Toronto, butchew ain' gonna take dis on da plane here." She held the full tube of toothpaste with her latex-gloved hand up in the air, her hip cocked to one side and her lips pursed.

"It's brand new!" I argued.

"Iss not about bein' new or not; iss too big," she said in a monotone voice, turning her head and looking blankly to her side, impatiently. "I already said dat . . . *shoooot*."

"Fine," I conceded reluctantly—and with that, she just opened her fingers to release the tube, allowing it to fall from eye-level, going straight into the garbage bin with a deadening thud.

Fucking liquid restrictions, I thought to myself, shivering in the bathroom.

I remembered spotting a supermarket across the street as Steven pulled into the parking lot the night before, so I put on all my skimpy layers and ventured out into the cold. It was snowing again, and I had to walk carefully in my penny loafers to make sure my feet didn't get soaked.

Everyone at the supermarket seemed to be giving me sideward glances. I guessed that Ellsworth was small enough for people to be familiar with most of their fellow townsfolk, and I assumed that the locals were probably all white.

I found my toothpaste and picked up a can of hair mousse—it had been confiscated, too, and without it, I'd end up with an Afro after showering.

Martha's Diner was packed. Waitresses ranging from twenty to sixty years old were dexterously weaving around the tables with plates full of food and carafes of black coffee. Hearty laughs shot out randomly, regularly, and people were chowing down on their meals with fervor.

Heads turned in unison as I made my way along the black-and-white checkerboard floor tiles, through the rows of tables to a booth at the back where I had spotted Steven. He didn't have his baseball hat on, and I could now see that the full head of waving hair in his dust jacket picture was no more—he was bald up top, with thick dark brown hair around the sides and back. I slipped into the red faux-leather booth, opposite him.

"Here's Kathy," Steven announced, his gaze focused over my head at the crowded front door of the diner. Kathy walked over and I stood up, towering above her. I didn't think there was any other woman in North America as short as Ma (four foot ten), but Kathy almost made the cut. She was dressed for the cold, in a knee-length parka, with heavy-duty winter boots and a knitted hat, which she pulled off, revealing her shoulder-length, salt-and-pepper hair. On her face was an incredibly genuine (and huge) smile.

"Raaa-jeeve? Am I saying it properly?" Then she pulled off her gloves and cupped my face in her hands, "It's so nice to meet you," she exclaimed in almost a whisper, beaming. "Oh, jeez, Steven," she said, still holding my face as she turned to her seated husband, "he'd make a perfect Pi, wouldn't he?" I loved her instantly. Steven nodded nonchalantly as he took another sip of coffee.

"I thought about what you asked me last night, what it was that I wanted from you," I said as I pierced my poached egg with the tip of my knife, the dark yolk spilling out onto my buttered toast. "As cheesy as it might sound, I realized that all I'd really like is . . . for me to be able to get to know you and, hopefully, for us to become friends." When I had actually said it out loud I was reminded of how childlike the thought had been and I laughed at myself. But still, it was exactly what I was looking for, and I figured I'd just say it with no frills.

"Awww, jeez, isn't that wonderful, Steven?" Kathy placed her hand on mine and gave it a rub.

"Oh, I don't knooow . . ." Steven jested, tilting his head and looking to one side with his eyes widened, in an exaggerated gesture of cautioning me, "I'm not so sure you want that—I'm kind of an asshole once you get to know me!"

A woman in her fifties, wearing an apron and holding a coffee pot, walked over to refill our mugs. Kathy proudly informed me that this was Martha.

"*The* Martha?" I asked.

"Yup, this is her place. Martha, this is our *friend*, Rajiv," Kathy cooed.

The following few days and nights played out like a seamless montage set to Mama Maybelle and the Carter Sisters' vintage recording of "The Waves on the Sea."

Steven and Kathy's place is the back of an old 1830s house in town, very eclectically decorated with cracking walls, tin ceilings, a wood-burning stove, and paneled shutters.

Kathy shakes her head and looks disapprovingly at my penny loafers. I try on a pair of her boots, Ugg style. They fit perfectly. Kathy glows.

Meryl Streep and Alec Baldwin light up the big screen at a funky movie house in Bar Harbor where Kathy, Steven, and I are seated on a worn-out sofa, laughing as we chow down on a pizza.

The full moon shines over the Atlantic as we drive along the coast.

Kathy and I sing hymns at Catholic Mass. We roll our eyes as the priest drones on, and on, and on.

Steven rummages through his files, and pulls out his original pencil drawings for his boat that sank in the Atlantic, beautifully rendered. I am blown away.

Snow falls outside the red clapboard antique mall that Kathy takes me to. I spot a captivating old painting of a seascape, surrounded by a beautiful gilded frame. I pull out my credit card.

A big feast is prepared by them—potato salad, corn on the cob, mussels, kale salad, asparagus with salmon, and huge local lobsters, the stars of the show. I have no idea how to take apart a lobster—but flanked by Steven and Kathy, I learn the ground rules. After dinner, we play darts (I win!). We cozy up by the fire with tea, coffee, and cookies. I look over at Steve and it hits me—life goes on. Life doesn't stay the same. Ups and downs. Loud and quiet. There he is, sitting by the fire, having his coffee and smiling, when about thirty years ago he had been in the middle of the ocean, all alone.

Steven drives me back to Jasper's afterward, my last night in Maine.

"You may find these interesting. A little bedtime reading," he says, handing me a couple of booklets, and then wishes me good night as I step out of the car.

I keep my sweater on and climb into bed, reading through a section from one of the small survival pamphlets which reminded me of the lifeboat manual that Yann describes in *Life of Pi*. The intro from the pamphlet I held ended with a paragraph titled "The Will to Survive":

> *The tools for survival are furnished by you—your survival equipment, your attitude and by the natural environment— but the tools and training are not enough; none is effective without the "will to survive." The records prove that will alone has often been the only deciding factor in many survival case histories . . . they show that stubborn, strong will- power can conquer many obstacles.*

The next morning Steven and I walked along the red granite coast that looked out over the Atlantic. I wasn't used to seeing it in the flesh— the ocean was something that always felt so far away from Toronto. The white-capped waves in the distance were rough, and the frigid winter air was filled with a refreshing briny, sulfury scent. Below us was a perfect example of nature's astonishing color-coordinating ability; the contrast of the teal water wildly lapping up against the face of soft pink rockery.

"We're friends, right?" I asked Steven cheekily.

"I guess you could say that, yeah. Kathy just loves you to bits, " he admitted in his serious tone, shaking his head and turning to me. "Did you get everything you needed, though? Did I answer all the questions in your little notebook?"

"Yeah, you answered all those questions. Thank you." I hesitated before going on. "But, I had just one more—one that I thought of last night at Jasper's. It may be asking too much, so if you're not comfortable with answering, just tell me—"

"To fuck off?" he teased, finishing my thought. "Yeah, don't worry, I will."

"Well," I started, "you faced death every day on that life raft. But . . ." my voice trailed off and I struggled to finish my question, but forced myself to continue, " . . . do you ever think about the day you actually *will* die? How do you think you'll face it?"

The waves crashed onto the rockery below us, spraying up dramatically. I felt the mist on my cheeks and almost stepped away from its advances, unaccustomed to such personal interactions with the ocean.

"In all the interviews I've done over the past thirty years," Steven began, "I've been asked many of the same questions over and over." He turned to me again and gave me a little smirk. "No one's ever asked me that one." He returned to staring straight ahead. "You know," he continued, "you really are Pi."

My heart leaped.

"I have thought about it," he admitted, "and the truth is, I really don't know. I'd like to think that when that time comes, I'll be able to accept it gracefully, with dignity."

I looked up at him but he had his eyes down at the granite below his feet as we continued to make our way along the craggy outcrop. I turned my gaze out over the Atlantic—the sheer massiveness of endless water that wrapped itself around the entire globe never ceased to amaze me. These very waters had brought this man back home to safety, to Kathy . . . to me. I squinted, peering out to the horizon, as far as my eyes could see, the undulating water continuing until it met the bottom of the morning sky.

Being lost at sea . . .
Check.

From: yann_martel1963@yahoo.com

To: rajivsca@yahoo.ca

Subject: Mr. Lee

Date: Mon, 29 Jun 2009 18:48:05

Hi Rajiv,

Yann is in Peru for the next two weeks, trekking in
the Andes, and he has no internet access at all.
He'll be back and attending to email after July
11th.

Warmest wishes,

Ali

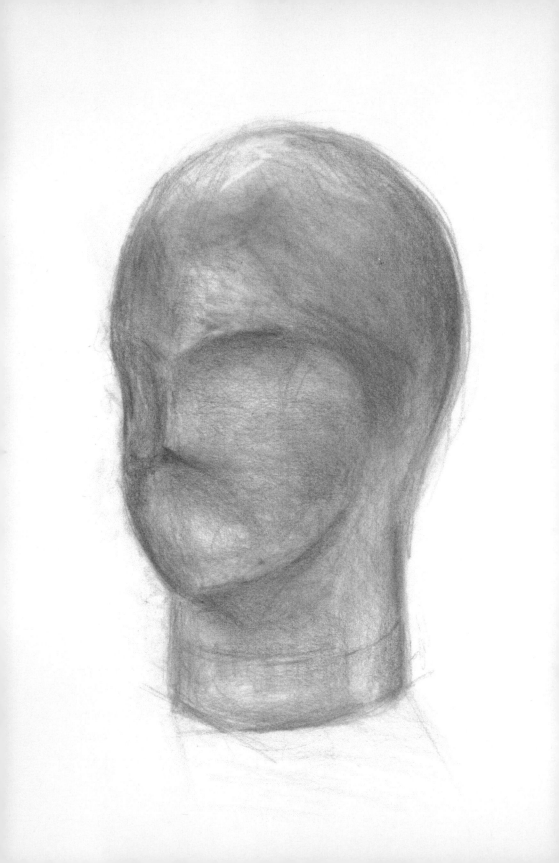

15.

THE SHAPE OF MY BODY HAD changed in the years since I had begun swimming. My back and shoulders were growing larger and I was developing the V-shaped torso that was characteristic of a swimmer's build. I still only weighed 118 pounds, which raised no concern about being too big to play Pi.

I was stronger now than when I had initially set out on this quest, both physically and mentally, and it felt really good. I was once filled with the hope and excitement of someone else changing the fate of my life by making a decision to cast me in their movie, but now I took pride in knowing that I had worked hard to take my fate into my hands. Both body and mind seemed to be solidly ready for what seemed like it was just around the corner. My face was another story.

The skin that covered my cheeks, jawline, and neck wasn't the greatest. It was bumpy, inflamed, and darkened to an almost purple color—a problem I had been struggling with as a teenager. Aunts and uncles weren't shy about pointing out the issue, repeatedly asking, "What happened to your cheeks?" year after year, always forgetting my curt response of, "It's just a rash, the doctors don't know how to fix it." Numerous visits to various dermatologists had resulted in cortisone creams, regimens involving sunscreen, face masks, exfoliants, and even moisturizers containing horse urine, but although there were occasional signs of subtle relief, nothing eradicated the problem entirely.

"Can you just please tell me what I can do to get rid of this completely, Dr. Curtis?" I asked my dermatologist in frustration one afternoon, wondering whether there was any way I could ever possess the smooth and blemish-free skin that would certainly contribute to helping me look like I was a healthy, fresh-faced sixteen-year-old.

"Hmmmm . . ." the doctor pondered, squinting as she hunched over, inspecting my skin with her face about one inch away from my cheek. She took her index finger and ran it slowly down my cheek, applying quite a bit of pressure.

Dr. Curtis's office was on Bloor Street, in a high-end building in the heart of the city. Although her fashion choices were a bit bewildering (she had long, flowing brown hair down to her bum, and always wore billowing, floor-length, floral-patterned skirts with granny blouses), she came highly recommended by a photographer who had once taken my headshots—a beautiful brunette who was a former model. I was ensured that this dermatologist was one of the best in the city, and if there was anyone who knew how to help me, it was she.

Dr. Curtis stood upright, put her glasses back on, and took some notes on my medical chart. "The problem's coming from the hair follicles," she declared authoritatively. "Have you ever had a beard or mustache?"

I admitted that I couldn't really grow one. The hair would grow in patches randomly, but there was always the problem of ingrown hair that made the effort horribly itchy and irritating.

She nodded rapidly, birdlike. "It's a common condition known as keratosis pilaris. Can you take off your coat—I'd like to see the backs of your arms."

One of the classics courses I had taken at U of T was a language course, Latin and Greek in Scientific Terminology. The professor, a comical Einstein-like, sweater-vest-wearing linguist, proclaimed during that first class that we students might assume that these words would be forgotten once the course had ended, but he assured us that somehow these prefixes, suffixes, and Latin and Greek roots would miraculously etch themselves into our minds and would stay there, to be recalled randomly, for the rest of our lives.

He was right. Dermatology was an example he had used in class—*dermatos*, Greek for "skin," and *logia*—the Greek suffix for "the study of." But now I was doing it on my own; *keratosis*, I thought, sifting through my mental file folder containing ancient vocabulary . . . *keratin*—Latin for "horn" or "cone-shaped," *osis*, the suffix meaning "condition of" . . . and *pilaris*—*pilos*, Greek for "hair," and *aris* . . . the Greek suffix for "pertaining to." Hornlike condition pertaining to the hair. It made sense to me, just as Dr. Curtis began to explain further while examining the skin on the back of my arms as she lifted the sleeve of my white T-shirt. "See, it's here, too, commonly on the back of the arms and legs—the hair's trying to grow, but the skin is blocking it from breaking through the surface, causing it to become ingrown, and then irritating the surface further, resulting in these small, dark bumps."

"What can I do?" I asked with determination in my voice.

"Well, not much, really. I can prescribe a cream that may lighten the skin a bit."

No, thank you. No more creams, I had decided. She didn't seem too empathetic and even though I knew it wasn't her job to pat my back and comfort me, it was somewhat upsetting that there might not be a solution to this issue that I had been dealing with for over a decade. I started putting my coat back on and was going to slip off the examining bed, when I reminded myself chidingly that I had waited for four months to get an appointment with this doctor and it was with the goal of leaving her office with a final solution to my problem. *Speak up*, I told myself, *and make it happen.*

"The cream isn't going to get rid of this entirely, is it?"

"Probably not. It'll lighten the appearance of the bumps, but they'll still be there," she said, looking down at her clipboard again, and writing quickly.

"What exactly is the root of the problem here?" I asked, deciding to be a bit more forceful and play detective if she wasn't going to offer more suggestions from her end.

"It's the hair—literally . . . the roots of the hair."

"What if the hair was gone, completely?" I asked.

"Well, I think the skin would calm down if it didn't have to deal with the hair follicles."

"Is *that* an option?" I asked, pointing to a poster on the wall behind the doctor—an advertisement with a woman sensually caressing her bare legs.

"Laser hair removal?" She continued scribbling and nodded her head. "Yeah. I think that would get rid of the problem, but you know the hair would be gone forever," she said, looking up from her clipboard and making eye contact. "You'd never be able to grow a beard or mustache again."

"I can't grow one as it is," I responded. "Are there any risks?" I asked.

"No side effects, but the skin can be burned if it's not done properly. Our nurses are experts, though, so if you want to do it, I'll make sure that you're in good hands."

I sensed that her concern was more an issue of playing with my manhood than anything else. She seemed to want to make sure I understood that there was no turning back. Once the hair was gone, it was gone for good. I did pause and ask myself if this was going too far. *Was*

I crazy? Was this going overboard, for the sake of this potential movie role? No. No, it was not. My skin would hopefully forever remain more healthy than it was now, so regardless of whether I landed the Pi role or not, this was a valuable investment.

I almost backed out of it when I saw the price list for laser hair removal. Back, shoulders, legs, arms, bikini, chest, and then . . . ah, there it was, face—$600 per session. And Dr. Curtis had mentioned that I'd require a total of four to six sessions before the hair would be completely gone.

A couple of weeks later, my nerves were in full panic mode as I tried to put on the space-age-looking metal goggles that the nurse handed me. I lay down on the examining table in the treatment room and she placed two pieces of cotton gauze over my eyes before helping me pull down the goggles, which were like titanium swimming goggles. With my eyes closed and protected, Lori called out, "Okay, ready?"

"Yup," I lied.

I heard a tap, which I assumed was her pressing a button on the touch screen of the large machine that the wand of the laser was attached to and then I heard a chime from the machine, indicating it was ready for shooting—it reminded me of the one-up sound from a video game.

"I'm going to press some ice to your face first, and then I'll start the lasering," Lori explained.

The ice was uncomfortably cold—I could feel the skin on my face going numb before my jawbone started hurting from the towel-covered icepack pressing onto it—and I wanted so badly to pull away, but I took deep breaths and focused on accepting the situation, instead of trying to fight it. And then the lasering began. With every shot of the laser I heard a tiny *blip, blip, blip, blip,* simultaneous with a sizzling sound that intensified the searing pain on my face. *Ow, ow, ow,* my mind would echo. *This is pain,* I told myself, *and you have to endure it.* I could feel the roots of the hair under the skin literally frying and then I smelled that horrible smell of burnt hair, as if it had caught fire. More ice and freezing pain. *Blip, blip, blip,* sizzle, and the stench. There were numerous moments during the session where I had to fight really hard to not shout out and ask her to take a break from the infliction of this torture I was subjecting myself to . . . *paying for,* in fact.

An hour later, I removed my goggles and stretched my eyes, my vision blurry for a few seconds, before everything came into focus. My face felt swollen and sunburned.

"You did really well!" Lori said reassuringly. "I've had big, burly body builders run out of here crying that it was too painful for them . . ."

Whether she was exaggerating or not, it was comforting to hear.

"Your skin is going to blister over the next few days. Don't scrub or rub it with anything, especially in the shower. The scabs will fall off on their own and then the hair will start coming out—it'll seem as though it's growing, but just leave it alone—it's the remaining root under the surface of the skin, and it'll push itself to the surface and fall out naturally in about two weeks. And then it'll slowly grow back, finer, in patches. So you'll keep coming back until it stops growing entirely."

It ended up taking more than six sessions. It took about ten, in total. Lori and I became fast friends. We would talk as she fired away at my skin—she would tell me about the goings-on in her life, and I would usually update her on my Pi progress. By round three, she was up to date on the story thus far. She was forty, but looked like she was twenty, and when I asked, she shared her opinions about cosmetic procedures—administering them, but even more fascinating to me, going under the knife herself. She'd had a nose job and a boob job. I asked her if I could feel for myself (her nose, her *nose,* okay? . . .) and she obliged without hesitating. I wiggled around the tip of her nose and felt through the skin, guessing and correctly identifying the portion of cartilage that the plastic surgeon had scraped down. I was in awe of her line of work—injecting Botox and Restylane, in addition to laser hair removal. I once asked what her worst body part to laser was—*back*? I wondered. *No, probably armpits.* As she zapped my face, she responded without even thinking, "Anus and testicles."

Just as Lori said it would, my skin scabbed up after every session, noticeably visible early on, but lessening in its intensity with every subsequent session of lasering. Then I'd go through the phase of feeling somewhat reptilian as my face shed the scabs and hair roots to reveal healthy, smooth, and blemish-free skin underneath.

I kept my procedure a secret, but it was tricky hiding my scarred face. After one particularly intense session early on, I had scabs all over my cheeks and neck as my sisters and I helped Ma plant the flowerbeds of our new house with perennials. The morning sun was shining on my face as I pushed a wheelbarrow full of compost over to my older sister. Dad used to do all the gardening at the old house—and while he mowed the lawn or pruned the hedges, he always had a glass of whiskey on the go, tucked behind some foliage.

"What the hell is wrong with your face?" my sister asked, squinting up at me with a small lavender plant in her hand.

"Oh, it's just my rash," I fibbed, "it flares up when I'm hot."

The procedure worked. *Keratosis no-more-is.* I got rid of it, entirely. It was a subtle transformation, but it helped me feel good about looking in the mirror, and truly believing that I was one step closer to playing Pi.

Ang Lee was now attached to *Life of Pi*, and I had a strange feeling that it was going to happen this time. When, exactly, I had no idea.

I focused on Ang Lee and worked on becoming familiar with his style and what he sought from actors. I ordered DVDs of all of his films and watched them with Ma and my sisters while we ate our dinner. His early Chinese films weren't as elaborate or polished as the movies that later had studio backing, but the stories were solid and entertaining.

There were a couple of books I tracked down that were published about him and his directing style. One of the obscure things I found was the published screenplay of *Sense and Sensibility* by Emma Thompson, which contained excerpts from the diary she kept while shooting the movie, which she also starred in. It was Ang's first major directorial debut in Hollywood, and Emma Thompson detailed the process of working with him. She sat in on a casting session and noted down some of Ang's particularities. "Physiognomy matters a great deal to him," she wrote—I could just hear her saying this aloud, beautifully articulate in her British accent— "not whether a person is good-looking, but the spaces between their lower lip and chin, and between the bridge of the nose and forehead. Praxitelean proportions, virtually."

I was familiar with her reference—an entire month of one of my Greek sculpture courses was devoted to Praxiteles. Ancient Greek sculptors developed an ideal version of the human body based on proportions of one body part in relation to all the rest; the size of a figure's pinky, for example, was used to scale the exact (ideal) size of its bicep, wrist, neck, and penis. This was the world of Anteater Willy's glory.

Further Internet excavating around "Ang Lee" revealed articles and interviews with the one casting director he seemed to use for his American films, Avy Kaufman, based out of New York. In one interview, when asked what it was she looked for in actors she auditioned, she said,

> *Someone that is honestly in a character. Someone who you really believe is that person.*

I looked away from the screen, savoring this moment of discovery and reassurance as my heart beat faster.

The best auditions happen when actors don't push the performance . . . I feel that most casting directors understand how difficult it is for an actor to walk into an office, pour out their emotions, and be judged by that. I actually prefer to take meetings with people, rather than have readings with them.

I was giddy; this lady might be the one who would stand behind me, championing my efforts.

Near the end of the interview, she was asked, "When actors come in, do you have an immediate sense that they are right?"

"They may not know that but, yes, that does happen. I'm not going to discourage anyone or give them any false hope, but I let them know if I'm enthusiastic about what they've done."

Perhaps the long, drawn-out process of adapting *Life of Pi* to screen was a good thing; maybe Ang Lee was, in the end, the best person to make this happen, and maybe six long years of research were exactly what I needed in order to land this role.

From: yann_martel1963@yahoo.com

To: rajivsca@yahoo.ca

Subject: Mr. Lee

Date: Tue, 7 Jul 2009 18:48:05

Hello, Rajiv.

News from Mr. Lee? Well, let's see; he was in India recently—may even be still there—doing some scouting with David Magee, the screenwriter (Finding Neverland). Lee was heading for a family holiday in Indonesia and decided to stop in India and check Pi places out there.

I presume Magee will work on the screenplay this summer. Don't know when filming will start, or anything else. I'm just the writer.

Greetings from the Amazonian Peru.

Yann

16.

THREE LARGE CLOUDS SHAPED like sheep slowly made their way eastward across the blue summer sky. Maybe they only looked like sheep to me because I was lying on my back in Central Park's Sheep Meadow. The school year was over and I had taken a week off work.

New York City was insanely hot in July, but I loved it here. There was an energy in the air. I always seemed to feel jolted into overdrive mode the instant I stepped foot onto the island of Manhattan.

"180 Varick Street, sixteenth floor, this afternoon at two thirty. Now, I've gotta warn you, Rajiv," Gerry instructed, as I spoke to him on my cellphone while staring up at the sky, "she's not the warm and cuddly type. Don't expect her to fall in love with you, okay? But remember, this is a good thing—she wouldn't have agreed to meet with you if she didn't think that you would be right for the part of Pi."

I was ready. I was pumped. I was nervous, but in a good way. I had a meeting with Avy Kaufman, Ang Lee's casting director.

I had sent her a beautiful, hand-written letter a month before, using my most cherished French paper. I took my time and wrote out her name and address with insanely ornate calligraphy—and I had sifted through dozens of postage stamps at the post office, choosing an oversized pale blue one of a native chief that matched the blue envelope it would be stuck to.

Now, Avy Kaufman would be meeting with me, and while the bustle and chaos of New York City whirred around me, I felt incredibly still inside. I had been drifting for so long now. Although faint, I could make out land on the horizon. Land ho!

For the many thousands of other people whom I crossed paths with that day, perhaps this was just another day, like the ones that had come before and those that would follow after. For the balding man who jogged past me as I made my way out of the park, sweat soaking his yellow T-shirt, this was another day of burning calories along Central Park West. For the thirty-something lady I brushed shoulders with on Seventy-second Street, in her oversized sunglasses, speedily chattering away while she walked her giddy golden retriever, this was maybe just another lunch break filled with errands. But to me, this was a day in which every second was to be savored, this was the day in which my dreams, hopes, and efforts over the past six years could finally all be laid out on the table. This was the city that millions of others had flocked to in the hopes of bringing meaning and fulfillment to their lives. This was the little island where huddled masses of immigrants had arrived with pennies in their pockets knowing that hard work, perseverance, dedication, and just plain luck could lift them up to rise above the humdrum into a world where their dreams could be turned into a tangible reality. I felt a comfort in knowing that I was here, finally, to realize my own dream.

Although this was just a meeting and not an audition (there wasn't even a script for the movie yet), I wanted to walk in with the appearance of a sixteen-year-old. I spent the morning on the seventh floor of Macy's in the boys' section, rapidly combing through racks of skater attire and finally settling on a cream-colored V-neck T-shirt with a print of a crazy monkey on a motorcycle—and an overpriced sky blue-and-black–striped hoodie. But I left the price tag on the hoodie, so I could take it back the next day, anticipating the huge Visa bill that I had racked up on this jaunt to New York. I estimated it would take about thirteen days of spinning wool to pay for it all.

There was the thrill of seeking out a destination on a treasure map as I made my way downtown to SoHo and emerged from the subway onto Varick Street, with giant brass numerals embedded into the sidewalk in front of me: 180. Two American flags flanked the entrance of this impressive art deco building, and I pushed through the fancy bronze-and-glass revolving door into the lobby, where I signed in with the security desk.

The elevator doors closed. I shut my eyes, quiet and alone.

Ding. The elevator doors parted. In Avy's suite, a young brunette greeted me and told me to take a seat in the small waiting room. I chose one of the six black chairs, and looked around at posters of the movies framed on the walls—*Brokeback Mountain, The Sixth Sense, The Ice Storm*—all films that Avy had cast. *Would I be up on these walls one day*, I wondered, *in a lifeboat with a tiger on the poster for Life of Pi?*

A tiny woman with a dainty frame emerged from around the corner, and I knew instantly that it was Avy. But despite her diminutive size, she had the air of Athena to her—the goddess of wisdom, courage, justice, and war—a goddess who was known for her calm temperament but could be moved quickly to anger, fighting only for the worthiest of causes.

"Hi," she offered, "come in."

I hopped out of my chair and followed Avy into her office. The thin, white, sleeveless blouse she wore was tucked into high-waisted beige pants. Her brown hair went just down to her neck and she wore large, amber-framed glasses. On her feet were flats, and she walked with confidence. This woman had the power to completely shape my future and

I had something that she needed—I had to make sure she'd see how valuable I could be to her.

"Have a seat," she said, inviting me to sit in the chair that was across from her desk, as she went around to take her seat opposite me.

"I have to take a call in a few minutes, so I don't have a lot of time." Then she just leaned forward, rested her chin on her palm and stared at me with furrowed brows, shooting off questions.

"Where are you from?"

"Toronto."

"Oh, Toronto," she echoed, nodding her chin, still resting on her hand. "Where are your parents from?"

"Sri Lanka."

"Have you ever been?"

"No." Dammit! Yes, I actually *had* been there once, as a kid . . . but it was too late to backtrack—I was flustered and decided not to correct myself. "But I've been to India . . ." I offered, hoping to segue into my Pi research.

"Funny, you don't have a Canadian accent."

"Yeah, I got rid of that a long time ago." I tried to make it sound like a joke.

"But what do your parents sound like?"

"They have a Tamil accent."

"What does that sound like?" she asked, slowly swiveling side to side in her chair.

"Well, it sounds like this," I started, mimicking Ma's accent. "The consonants are verrry hard. They rrrrroll the R sound. It is verrrry choppy." *Smile, dammit,* I scolded myself. *Smile, for God's sake*—I could feel a bead of sweat dripping down the hollow of my back and I knew I was nervous, but I had to work hard not to show it. *Just have fun with her, smile*—I kept telling myself.

She had stopped swiveling and continued to scrutinize me with her eyes, which subtly darted back and forth, across my face.

Gerry was right. This woman's tough. I couldn't read what she was thinking, or where she was going with this, so I decided to go on. "It's different than the North Indian accent," I offered, in my normal way of speaking.

"What does *that* sound like?" She was now hunched forward, with her elbows propped on the desk, her fingers entwined together, acting like a relaxed hammock for her chin.

"Well, it's a lot mooore fluid-sounding," I started up without hesitating, putting on the air of the Bollywood movie stars I despised, always sounding so arrogant yet disgustingly pretending to be self-effacing. "You see, it's very aspirated, the vowels are a lot longer and the consonants are only briefly touched upon . . . it can also be sometimes slightly British, depending on the speaker's education . . ."

"Wow . . ." still with furrowed brows.

I broke out of the pattern we were in, of her questioning and me responding, like this was an interrogation. The phone call she mentioned hadn't arrived yet and I was tensing up, guessing I might only have a short window to convince her that I was actually the only guy for this part.

"Do you cast all of Ang's films?" I asked assertively.

"Not the Chinese ones, but I've cast the last five or six."

"So . . . are you casting *Life of Pi*?"

She didn't answer right away. For a moment, I wondered whether I was pushing my luck and being too forward. Maybe this wasn't the approach I should be taking if I really wanted her to believe I could convincingly play sixteen.

"It's not official yet," she admitted finally. "We're still waiting for a green light from the studio. But when that happens, yes, I'll be the one casting it."

"I'm the guy for the lead role." Wow, it just came out. I hadn't planned on saying it like this, right then, but there it was, fast and dirty. "I want this more than anything I have ever wanted, and I've worked so hard for it . . ." I said, staying calm and collected, and doing my best to not sound like I was begging or pleading, but more like I was stating a fact that she could possibly benefit from.

"I know . . ." she said, straight-faced. I wished that she would just give me one little smile. It would have put me at ease and cleared the air a bit.

"Avy, I *am* this character. It started with me just reading about him in the book, but over the last six years I have given every bit of myself to becoming him entirely. I went to India and spent time in Pondicherry, going to the same school that's mentioned in the book, Petit Séminaire. I tracked down a sailor who wrote a book about being cast adrift for seventy-six days. I learned how to swim from scratch."

"Can you do me a favor? Can you write all of this down and send me a letter?" she asked.

"I did send you a letter," I retorted, shocked. I thought that was why I was here.

"You *did*?"

"Yeah, and it would have been the most beautiful letter you've ever received—I even put a big red wax seal on the back! You didn't get it, did you?" I pretended to sound reprimanding, using a sarcastic, joking tone. "They sort through your mail and throw stuff out, don't they?"

She shuffled around a few things in front of her, looking under binders and magazines, and then grabbed the edge of her desk, pushed back her chair, and quickly got up. "Come with me," she instructed.

Shadowing closely behind her, I felt a rush of excitement as we scampered out of the room, feeling as though I had crossed a boundary of sorts, and was now on the same team as her. Together, we darted into the room across the hall, where three interns were busy typing on computers and sorting through folders.

"Did a letter come through here? Describe it to them," she snapped, turning to me.

"Small, about five-by-seven inches. Blue envelope, *very* fancy writing on it, wax seal on the back."

"I want that letter," Avy spat, as if she were speaking to herself.

No one seemed to recall such a letter. I guess Gerry had single-handedly managed to convince her to see me, without my initial request on paper. Avy flew out of the room without saying anything, and I followed her back into her office. She shut the door behind me and went to her desk, picking up a blue Post-it pad and a pen.

"This is my home address. Write down everything you've told me and send me another letter."

She handed me the Post-it as she took a seat on the sofa by her desk and I tucked it preciously into the front pocket of my jeans.

I asked if I could show her a few things that I had brought along, and she seemed intrigued. I kneeled on the ground as I went through my backpack and pulled out some photos of Pondicherry. She was flipping through them slowly as I gave her a short commentary on each one.

"That's me with the other boys in my class—my friends at Petit Séminaire," I said proudly.

"Wow," she exclaimed, looking down at Akash, Deepak, Nosey, and Karthik. She was quiet for a beat and then her face changed, as if she had suddenly realized something.

"How old are you?" The question I had been dreading. I had suspected that she'd ask it, so I came prepared.

Avy had cast a few movies that Rachel McAdams had starred in. She was twenty-seven when she played sixteen-year-old Regina George in *Mean Girls*, so I asked her what I should do if Avy wanted to know my age.

I didn't fully expect to hear back from Rachel—she was a huge star now, and it had been years since we had bonded on set, sneaking off during lunch breaks to thrift stores or historic sites near our shooting locations. But there was a response from her in my inbox the following day. She prefaced her answer by raving about Avy being one of the best in her field, and went on to say that she would probably want to hire someone a bit older and soulful anyway. Then she admitted that if she were in my shoes, she just wouldn't tell her, and would advise my agent not to do so, either.

"How old do you think I am?" I asked, looking up at Avy from my position on the carpeted floor.

"I don't know," she admitted, brows furrowed once again, "I'm looking at you and you could play anywhere from . . . seventeen to . . . twenty-eight."

"Can I convincingly play the part of Pi?" I asked boldly.

"Absolutely."

"Then that's all that matters, right?"

"Right. Fair enough," she conceded, turning back to the pictures on her lap. Phew.

"And this is something from another era," I explained, as I handed her an old sepia photograph from Ma's photo album. "This is my mom, at twenty-five, playing the veena. This is the world that my parents grew up in, Avy. It's the same world that acts as a setting for *Life of Pi*. I know that world."

"Your mother is stunning," she gasped, turning away from the photograph and looking me in the eyes through her large, amber-framed glasses. "She's beautiful."

She looked back down at Ma, in her lap, and shook her head.

"That was just before she left Ceylon and moved to Toronto," I added.

"Why'd she move to Canada?" she asked, still studying the picture.

"Her father died. They didn't have a real future there, and her two oldest brothers were living in Toronto, working, so they decided to bring the rest of the family over." I handed her the next old photograph, a tiny sepia portrait of my grandfather.

"That's a funny mustache," she noted quietly, almost as if it were a question. *Jesus, fuck,* I thought, realizing Ma's dad had a Hitler mustache—it was "a thing" at the time in Ceylon, Ma once told me, but I guess I hadn't even thought twice about bringing it along and showing it to Avy. I had just handed this powerful Jewish lady a picture of my grandfather with a Hitler mustache.

"Oh, yeah, weird, huh?" I tried to brush it off and move on, quickly handing her a picture of me with Steven Callahan, breaking apart our lobsters. She chuckled slightly and I breathed a sigh of relief.

Avy looked up from the picture of me and Steven and closed her eyes as she delicately pulled her glasses off from the bridge of her nose. She turned to me, still kneeling on the floor, beside the sofa. Again, she looked me in the eyes. And then she said it. "You're wonderful. I love you. And you'll definitely be seeing me again."

Wait a minute, did you hear that? Let me just give you some space to let it sink in.

"I love you."

She said it! Waaaaaaaaaaaaaaaa-yeaaaaaaaaaah-yaaaaaaaaaay!
I sat at her feet, reeling from the euphoria of this moment.

The doors of the uptown subway train were closing just as I went down the stairs into the station at Houston Street. But I didn't care. "Delay" appeared on the LED screen that listed the subsequent trains, but it didn't matter to me as I pulled off the striped hoodie and put it into my backpack. I was completely content to just linger on the subway platform, because even though my feet were planted on the cement floor, I was somewhere else entirely. I was floating, and I couldn't help myself—drifting away, up over the high buildings that lined these city streets, soaring with the clouds on that hot summer's day.

When the train finally arrived, packed, I eased in and was pushed and squished to ensure the doors would close, but it didn't bother me that hundreds of other sweaty commuters were dripping all around me. At Thirty-fourth Street, I remained languid as I was thrust out of the subway car by the flood of the others exiting, and I mindlessly took the elevator to the seventh floor of Macy's, where I returned the striped hoodie and fifty-six US dollars was credited back to my Visa.

The hum and whirr of the city continued around me as I leisurely made my way up to Columbus Circle and walked along the western edge of Central Park, where people filled the grassy expanses, sitting or lying in both the bright sun and the shady groves, provided by the huge old trees.

"She was testing you," a voice in my head began, "when she asked you what your parents sound like."

"Hmmm . . ." the other voice responded, lackadaisically.

"You didn't even realize what she was doing. She wanted to hear your Indian accent, and you showed her your stuff. Maybe she didn't even realize there was a difference between the North Indian Accent and the South Indian one . . ."

"Uh-huh . . ." the other voice said, obligingly.

"Maybe she was trying to see whether you have what it takes to be a star—to be put on the spot, asked a bunch of questions, tested. Maybe she was trying to see whether you'd break."

"Yeah, maybe . . ." the other voice responded. "Look, can we stop and just be quiet for a bit?" it asked, as I spotted a space on a bench in the shade.

There was a breeze that ran through the warm, humid air as I slipped the backpack off my shoulders and slouched into the dark green park bench. I stretched out my legs and balanced my heels on the pavement path. I lifted my face to the sky and closed my eyes.

Land, there, on the horizon.

"*I love you,*" she had said, "*and you'll definitely be seeing me again.*"

From: yann_martel1963@yahoo.com

To: rajivsca@yahoo.ca

Subject: RE: Beatrice and Virgil

Date: Sat, 03 Jul 2010 16:03:38

Hello, Rajiv.

Yes, the touring is finally over, thank god. I've been back in Saskatoon for the last four days, settling in for the summer. Book got very mixed reviews in the US and UK, some positive, but many very negative. The way it goes.

About *Pi* the movie, I've heard, and it's not good news for you, I'm afraid. They've found a 17 year old boy in India who is, according to the producer, amazing. He's one of the reasons the gods that be at Fox have opened their wallets. So the project is going ahead, with shooting starting in India in December and then moving to Taiwan six weeks later. So Pi is cast and the die is cast.

Sorry to be the bearer of bad news. It's not something I had any control over.

We will think of you on Theo's birthday.

Stay well,

Yann

17.

MY CHEST FELT WEIGHTED down as it rose and fell with every deep breath I took, audibly, reading Yann's email once again—to make sure this was actually happening.

No, I hadn't missed anything. They gave the role to someone else. Some unknown Indian kid.

Meesha was whining at my feet, telling me she needed to pee. I placed my fingers on the edge of the laptop screen and slowly pulled it down toward the keyboard, until I heard the gentle click as it closed.

Meesha scurried behind me as I walked downstairs. I knelt down and pulled the harness and leash over the dog's head and shoulders as she panted and wiggled around impatiently. Then we headed out of the house.

18.

S CHOOL WAS FINALLY OVER for good. Done, finished, and I would never, ever have to go back. Audrey sent me a little "congratulations" card in the mail, and had slipped in a crisp, red, fifty-dollar bill— it arrived just two days before commencement.

Ma and my two sisters took the subway downtown—this was my whole family now, and without my dad, it finally felt complete. Summer was officially in full swing as I joined a thousand other kids in their black caps and gowns to cross the giant lawn of King's College Circle to Convocation Hall, the impressive round Classical Revival–style building surrounded by Ionic columns. It was a landmark on campus and held a special place in my heart. In my four years of classes, I'd had only one of them in that building, Astronomy 101, and I sat in the cavernous round space with its domed ceiling, along with fifteen hundred other students, looking down at the tiny professor on the stage, with scenes of the universe blown up on the giant screen behind him.

That screen was the same one that had once featured a math problem of limits on it, and that stage was the same one that I had stood on during my first month of classes at U of T, with Lindsay Lohan, as Tina Fey sat in the front row and looked up at us while we shot our famous mathletes scene for *Mean Girls*. It seemed fitting that I ceremoniously walk across that stage on my last official day as a University of Toronto student, but the moment was bittersweet—this was where my Pi quest had begun and now it was over, with nothing to show for it.

My name was called out through the loud speakers, filling the cavernous space. I shook the dean's hand and made my way down a ramp, where I was photographed with my scroll in front of a neutral backdrop. As I turned and walked away from the photographer's setup, making way for the next sucker to have his turn, I let out a giant sigh of relief. I now had my little piece of paper, fulfilling the one thing that Ma had ever really asked of me, that I "complete my studies." She and my sisters were waiting outside, on the front steps. Ma wiped away a few tears and gave me a hug. I leaned down so she could kiss my forehead with her eyes closed, as she had done every night before going to bed, and every morning when we woke up. As Ma, my sisters, and I walked toward the restaurant where we had a reservation for lunch, I took one final look over my shoulder at Convocation Hall and said a few words of thanks in my head. I knew I was lucky to have had the opportunity to be a student here, and I was grateful.

I was no longer working at Black Creek and was now spending every weekday in rural fields east of the city, wearing a beekeeper's suit and assisting Russian Mike, the small, soft-spoken, and good-natured beekeeper who needed my help only from July until the end of September. I had always wanted to work with bees as a kid, but once I was actually doing it full-time, I realized that the charm and romance associated with hives and honey lasted for about ten minutes, on the first day—after that, it was brutal, backbreaking hard work. The summer sun beat down on us all day and the cotton suits that covered us, from neck to ankles, were like pristine white body ovens. On my head, I wore a bee veil, and my hands were covered in long, thick leather gloves. Within twenty minutes of working, I could feel the seams of my underwear sopping with sweat. Sweat dripped from my chin, sweat pooled at the corners of my eyes, there was even sweat inside my ears. By noon, both Russian Mike and I reeked of body odor, so we both silently excused each other of the stench. He never seemed to get stung, but I did. Every day, despite my determined efforts of tucking my suit legs into my socks or making sure my veil was all the way down to my neck, somehow a bee would find a way to access the tiniest bit of exposed flesh and sting me, giving its own life in an effort to protect the hive.

I was uneasy, Russian Mike said, and the bees sensed it—that's why they were stinging me; they felt the nervousness of a predator. I found it hard to believe, but the fact that he was able to handle the hives without wearing gloves, and often even without a veil, made me accept that maybe he was right.

I would either grow immune to the stinging, Mike said, or develop an allergy and be forced to stay away from bees for good. The stings during the first couple of weeks swelled up and throbbed with pain for days, but the intensity of my symptoms lessened with every subsequent sting.

It was quiet work. Russian Mike wasn't a big talker, and his English was horrible, so he'd mumble a few instructions to me, and then we were good to go for a few hours until the task changed, and another couple of words dictated our next move. The only noise that surrounded us was the constant humming, the buzz from the many thousands of bees, and it was so foreign to me early on that I continued to hear it when I'd return home at the end of the day, thrumming in my ears.

I didn't think about the Pi movie. I just went to work every day and lifted hives or opened them up and checked on the health of the worker bees. Or I replaced full frames of honey with empty frames that the bees would fill up. Or I'd pull out every frame until I found the queen, checking to make sure she was present, alive, and healthy. It all entailed detailed observation, but didn't require too much thinking, so I just let my mind sit there silently and listen to the hum. And still, almost every day, I'd get stung.

Like the bees, focusing on their one assigned task and carrying it out without complaining, I worked quietly all summer. Every so often, I'd catch a glimpse of myself in the rearview mirror of Mike's beekeeping truck, all covered up, and I'd imagine how anyone could be under that suit. It was a strange way of seeing myself.

With the arrival of the fall, Russian Mike and I moved our work into the honey house, where we brought in the bounty that the bees had worked hard to collect all summer—contained in the white supers that were full of honey and beeswax. The color of the honey was determined by what blossoms the bees were collecting pollen from—clover and dandelion yielding pale golden yellow, whereas buckwheat provided a distinctly dark, almost molasseslike honey.

In the honey house we'd remove the capping of beeswax from every frame using an electrically heated knife and then we'd insert the frames into the spinner, which extracted the honey through centrifugal force. One of us would fill up the jars with this liquid gold while the other screwed on a lid and slapped on a label.

The crispness in the air as I left the honey house one night in early September reminded me that I should begin bringing a jacket to work. I had been stung earlier that day while loading the extractor, yet again by a dreary bee that I hadn't noticed on the edge of a frame of honey.

I couldn't bend my thumb as I tried to press down the latch of the front door at home.

Ma had rice and seven different vegetable curries on the table for dinner when I got back.

"It's good, darling?" she asked with concern as I chewed on the first mouthful of food and mixed together the next little mound of rice and curries with my fingertips, awkwardly trying to maneuver my swollen thumb. She was seeking the approval that we customarily offered up without solicitation.

"Yeah," I replied dully, looking down at my plate.

"Good," she said, mixing the food together on her own plate while craning her neck to make sure I had served myself a bit of each of the curries that she had laid out.

The TV was on in the adjacent room, tuned in to Sun TV, the Tamil channel that Ma streamed in from South India. An old black-and-white Tamil movie was on, and the characters had broken into song—one that I recognized. Ma hummed along as the two actresses on the screen danced around in saris.

"Ma?"

"Yeah, darling?"

"Remember that part I was trying to get—*Life of Pi*?" I began, solemnly. I hadn't told anyone about my failure. In fact, I hadn't really relayed to any of my friends or family how much I was investing in this goal.

"Yeah, darling."

"Well . . . they gave it to someone else."

"Awwww . . . I'm sorry, darling. That's too bad." Ma continued eating and momentarily turned her face to the TV screen.

My confiding in her didn't give me the consolation I was expecting.

"Something else will come up," she said, putting her hand on mine. "Don't worry, darling."

I finished my last morsel of food and got up from the table, heading to the sink to wash my hands.

"There's a job at the bank," Ma said, "in the call center, *kanna*."

The call center at the bank was the entry point into a potential lifelong career behind a melamine desk, dealing with numbers on a computer screen. Many of my cousins worked at "the bank"—my older sister was majoring in fine art at the university when she panicked after her first year, wondering how she'd ever make any money with art, before switching majors to computer science. She worked at the call center during the summers that I spent spinning wool and baking bread, and immediately after graduating had a job in the IT department, one floor above where Ma worked.

"Shall I . . ." Ma began hesitatingly, "give the manager your résumé?"

Ma knew my beekeeping job was coming to an end. We hadn't really discussed what I planned to do afterward. In fact, I hadn't given it much thought myself, numbly making my way through one day at a time.

"Yeah, sure," I said, rinsing off my plate and putting it into the dishwasher.

I followed the manager of the call center department along a narrow walkway that divided a vast field of cubicles in a huge, windowless, warehouselike space, lit entirely with tubes of fluorescent lightbulbs. The manager was a tall and slender graying man in his early sixties. Each cubicle housed a worker wearing a headset, and as I took in the expression of face after face, soulless and dead, I felt as though I was following Hades himself right up to his throne, where he sat as Lord of the Underworld.

He held the door of his office open, and closed it behind me as I took a seat in front of his desk.

"So, you're Lozani's son!" he boomed, grinning widely.

"Yup," I confirmed, trying to muster up a bit of enthusiasm, so I could just meet him halfway.

We exchanged mild pleasantries before getting to the matter at hand. He outlined the details of the job—I would work from either 8 a.m. to 4 p.m., or 4 p.m. to midnight, and I'd answer calls, dealing with customers who were primarily phoning in with complaints or debit card issues.

"Tell me a bit about your customer service skills," he began, leaning back in his chair.

"Well, I spent five summers dealing with the public at Black Creek Pioneer Village. I learned to connect and communicate with people of all ages. A lot of those people couldn't speak English very well . . ." As I continued to babble on, I felt as though a part of me had climbed out of my body and walked to the corner of the room, marveling at the situation from a distance.

What are you doing here? I wondered, as I made a case for myself to this man.

"Can you see yourself working in this kind of environment?" he asked.

"I'm not going to lie to you," I admitted. "I'm used to working in places with at least a window in it. And usually I can hear sheep bleating or birds singing while I work."

He raised his eyebrows, caught off guard.

"But I will say that I am a hard worker, and if I were given this job," I sighed, "I'd do my best."

He didn't respond, but put down the paper he was holding and picked up my résumé, scanning it briefly.

"You play the violin?" he asked.

It took me by surprise that he had noticed a part of my résumé that I had filled with fluff. Under "hobbies," alongside "pottery," "painting," and "beekeeping," I had added "violin" to give myself a bit of variety— the truth was that I had played the violin for only a couple of years, beginning when I was ten.

"Yeah, a bit."

"I used to play the English horn for the symphony," he said in a nostalgic tone, and although his eyes were still on my résumé, I could see that he was somewhere far away.

"Wow, really?" I asked excitedly, sitting upright in my seat, impressed that this man was actually a classically trained musician, good enough to play for one of the city's few official ensembles. "Do you still play?"

"No, no," he shook his head, looking back up at me. "No . . . I realized I couldn't rely on music to bring in a sustainable income, so I got a job at the bank thirty years ago and . . . well, here I am."

Yes, here he was. And here I was. As I sat across from this man, I witnessed the spark in his eye rekindle a period of warmth from his past—a flame that was instantly extinguished when he brought himself back to the reality of his present situation.

You don't want to work here, a voice in my head pleaded.

"Well, thank you for coming in today," the manager said as he got up from his seat, moving to the door and opening it for me. "You'll be okay finding your way out?"

Run, I thought.

"Yes," I confirmed, "and thanks for seeing me."

I walked out of the manager's office and once again treaded through the soulless field of cubicles, heading back to the world of the living. *Leave this place. Keep your eyes straight ahead, and whatever you do, don't look back.*

19.

I RAN. I RAN FAR AWAY FROM HOME. Far, far away, to a world that seemed like it had sprouted from the pages of a children's storybook—cobblestone streets, church bells ringing on the hour, and feathers—huge, long feathers adorning the hats of the women shopping in the outdoor market at the center of town. This was the home I had always wanted but never actually knew existed.

It didn't take long for me to fall head over heels in love with Munich. Small things about this city made me smile, like men and women routinely carrying bouquets of flowers home—flowers on the table were a staple part of every apartment, it seemed.

The beautiful, old gothic, baroque, and neoclassical architecture took my breath away on a daily basis—stone façades with fruit, flowers, and gargoyles protruding from the eaves seemed like vignettes that were once alive and breathing, but were frozen in time. Cathedral spires, turrets, and towers capped with copper or bronze onion domes pierced through the skyline.

After my bank interview, I found a website for au pairs (fancy talk for a youthful nanny) and created a profile, listing all my credentials and artistic skills—drawing, painting, and pottery. "I'm an excellent cook, and I'd be the greatest caregiver for your kids . . ." I typed confidently.

I posted a few pictures of myself and in the bracket stipulating salary expectations, I clicked on the highest option. Within a few days, I had a message in my inbox. Anna and Joel, a British couple, had recently moved to Munich for work and were looking for an English-speaking male to take care of their two sons, Sebastian and Alexander, nine and ten, respectively.

I hesitated briefly—*did I really want to take care of two (potentially bratty) kids? And what happened to their previous nanny? Was this going to be like The Sound of Music—and was I the latest in a long line of governesses who had come before me?*

No, I decided, I would not be fazed by fear of the unknown. Just like Fräulein Maria, I would have confidence in myself. I turned back to the email.

The parents needed someone to pick their kids up from school, make them snacks, and do homework with them on weekday evenings. Preferably someone who could cook dinner and also play soccer with the kids. During the day, when the boys were at school, the au pair would pick up the dry cleaning, and do the laundry and grocery shopping. And they had a separate apartment in their building for the au pair.

A month later, I was perched on the back of an old 1920s bicycle, a big, old honker I had found on German eBay, complete with a worn leather seat, a wicker carrying case, and a dynamo lamp powered by the wheels, riding with reckless abandon over the cobbles as I made my way down the shopping list that Anna had written out for me—English on the left with the German equivalents on the right.

The *Viktualienmarkt* in the middle of town was full of stalls selling fruit and vegetables imported from Italy, Spain, or North Africa, as well as a luscious selection of cheeses, breads, fish, and meat. I was the only darkie in a population that seemed entirely white, and the market vendors were now familiar with me. It was here that I began pushing myself to learn German. On that particular morning, after buying the household staples of milk, eggs, bread, and fruit, I wandered around, brainstorming ideas for what to make for dinner that night. I settled on chicken curry, and it was only when I was standing before the short, stout German butcher, bald with round glasses perched on his button nose, that I realized I had no idea of how to say "boneless, skinless chicken thighs" in German.

The one line I used only as a last resort was pulled out, "*Sprechen Sie Englisch?*" I asked. (Do you speak English?)

"*Nein, leider nicht,*" he apologized, grinning and placing his chubby hands on his hips. (No, unfortunately not.)

I stood there for a moment, refusing to be defeated. Then I searched around in my head for something, anything that I had learned in German by then that could help me.

"*Ich brauche . . .*" (I need) I said, my eyes to the blue sky overhead as I continued to brainstorm. I looked at him, tucked my fists under my armpits and flapped my elbows.

"Huhn?" he asked, pointing to a picture of a chicken behind him that I hadn't noticed.

"*Ja!*" I shouted. "*Genau!*" (exactly). Then I patted my upper thighs.

"*Schenkeln?*" he asked.

I had no idea what the word for "thigh" was, so I decided to take a chance. At least it would be some part of a chicken, hopefully.

"*Ja,*" I said, then added, "*aber . . .*" (but). I searched for another word. "*Ohne*" (without), and then I pinched and pulled up the skin on my arm.

"*Ohne Haut, ja,*" he said, nodding.

"*Ja, ohne Haut, und auch, ohne . . .*" then I pointed to the bones in my finger joints.

"*Knochen?*" he asked.

Sure, whatever. Sounds like it could mean bones. "*Ja,*" I confirmed.

"*Hähnchenschenkel, ohne Haut und Knochen!*" he bellowed jovially as he turned away from me and headed out of sight into the back of the shop.

I was beaming—somehow I had figured it out. An older lady stepped up beside me, dressed in traditional Bavarian clothing, a dirndl dress that cinched her waist tight and pushed her breasts up to her chin, with a full skirt gathered into pleats. She had a hat on with a feather in it that was two feet long. We looked at each other and nodded slightly.

"*Hallo,*" I said to her quietly, amazed with the characters that filled my new world.

"*Grüß Gott,*" she offered back formally—the very local salutation that literally translated to "greetings in the name of the Lord."

I wasn't only taken by the incredible history of this medieval city, where every street and building went back hundreds of years—it was the people, too. I got the Germans and they got me. Their way of life just seemed to make so much sense to me. There wasn't the false lathering on of niceness that was typical of American customer service, in which an overly saccharine greeting would often be followed by incompetence.

At the *Viktualienmarkt*, I was usually greeted with a simple, "*Der Herr?*" (literally, The Sir?). And I loved it. No bullshit. Within a few months, the fruit and vegetable lady and I were on a first-name basis—a true sign of closeness here in Bavaria. She'd laugh or smile while we conversed, and her reactions were real.

It took some time to get to know my charges, Sebastian and Alexander, but I started developing a trust with them that was formed through a bit of struggling early on. They'd rebel and throw tantrums every now and then—once, at Nonnberg Abbey, in Salzburg (the actual abbey where Maria Von Trapp was a postulate, dating back to the year

740!) I took the boys on a "field trip'" one weekend and we happened to enter the chapel, only to be greeted with the haunting sound of the nuns singing evening vespers, out of sight in the choir loft behind a huge stained-glass window. It was pouring rain outside, and I warned the boys that when we entered, we had to be completely quiet. We had the place all to ourselves, and carefully sat down on one of the old oak pews. Alexander began fidgeting, kicking the pew in front of him. I gave him a warning glance—Anna cautioned me that they would test their boundaries, and that I had to show them that I was on their side but also the authority figure in the relationship. I mouthed, "Stop it" to Alexander as the beautiful chanting filled the stone chapel, but he defied me, continuing with a steady *thump*, *thump*, *thump*. Burning with fury, I took both boys outside and reprimanded Alexander—and he blew up instantly, crying, screaming, and stomping his feet in front of the ancient tombstones that sat crookedly in the graveyard.

When he had stopped crying, I crouched down to him on the ground beside a completely weathered tombstone.

"We can go home, if you want. You wanna get back on the train and go back to Munich? 'Cause I'll do it. Or," I patted his head, teasing, "you can be a *big* boy; you can say sorry to your brother and me, and we can move on—and go have some schnitzel at the place we passed on the way up here."

"I'll be good," Alexander whispered in his British accent. "So-rry."

I was surprised at myself about six months in, when I realized that I really did love these kids. I always knew, solidly, that I never wanted kids of my own, but there I was taking care of them like they were mine—and I couldn't help but put their safety, comfort, and happiness before my own.

I gradually became a friendly taskmaster, enforcing rules that had an effect on the boys. Their eating habits became tidier, they started saying *"bitte"* and *"danke"* more often, and their attention spans grew longer and more patient during our weekly watercolor painting lessons by the edge of the Isar River.

Between the laundry, grocery shopping, ironing, and activities with the boys, my days began at 8 a.m. and only finished at around nine or ten at night. One day, as I was pulling the laundry out of the dryer and folding it piece by piece, I picked out something that took a moment to identify—a thong. *Do I fold this?* I wondered, looking down at this undergarment that seemed to be just a few strands of narrow fancy ribbon . . . *If I do have to fold this, how do I do it?* I was so far away from the direction in which I thought my life was heading.

I tried to find things to laugh about during the day—whether it was something related to my work, or my bold attempts at learning to speak German and failing horribly, early on. I think that laughing during the day helped me to lie in bed, all alone on the third floor at night, and begin to look back at what I had run away from. The rusty floodgates slowly creaked open. And that's when the tears came.

I lay in bed, looking up at the ceiling and feeling so very alone. And I was sobbing. *You weren't good enough,* I heard myself say. *You thought they'd want you, but they didn't.*

I felt worthless, useless, only good for washing other people's underwear and buying their groceries. But night after night, I gave myself permission to weep—and I started feeling as though I was mourning the loss of not something, but *someone.*

"Why are you crying?" I asked, reprimanding myself, "Pi wasn't even real."

I think I had to force myself to look back and realize that unlike the many auditions I had had over the years, where I'd have just a few days to develop a character, Pi had built up inside me, gradually and slowly, over the course of six long years. And eventually, he *was* real. He was a solid, tangible part of me. And he left me so unceremoniously, without even saying goodbye. It hurt, and I began to allow myself to mourn that loss.

Recognizing my tragic condition, I made an effort to do things that would help me recover. I had recently christened my bike "Herr Gritzner" (Mr. Gritzner), inspired by the tiny, semirusted plaque below the handlebars that read "Gritzner," indicating the make of the huge steel-framed beast. He quickly became my trusted sidekick, my faithful companion on my ventures around the city. I'd get out on Friday nights, or on the weekends. One of my favorite things to do was to put on my black suit and ride to the opera house in the middle of town. I still had my student card from the University of Toronto, and I used it to wait in the stand-by line for last-minute tickets that were sold to youths under thirty years old for ten euros.

I knew this music—works by Puccini, Verdi, Bizet, and Dvořák. My iPod was full of the classics and they served as the sound track that accompanied the many art projects I'd worked on in our basement— gilding picture frames, oil painting, or making historically accurate clothing to wear at the village.

One night, at the season's premiere of *La Traviata*, I wiggled into my rose-colored velvet seat in the opera house as the lights went down. The place was full—even the standing room tickets were sold out. I looked around me and relished the gilded spectacle. I was surrounded by; Munich's locals dressed to the nines, the women dripping in jewels, the men in their closely cut suit jackets and high-polished shoes. The energy in the room was palpable, pouring down from the terraced sweep of seats, five stories high.

The conductor appeared under a spotlight and applause erupted. Then quiet. Then a string quartet pulled out the first few, long notes of the overture. A pause. More strings, sad and melancholic, rising to a crescendo as more of the string section joined in, bass notes anchoring the melody. A pause again. Horns, quietly, playfully . . . *um paa paa BOM, um paa paa BOM* . . . and then the strings swept back in. My lips quivered. I tried to keep it together. *Um paa paa BOM* . . . and more strings. *He's alive,* I thought. *Giuseppe Verdi is floating around here, filling up this space . . . this was something in his head, two hundred years ago . . . and right now, in some way, he's right here, in this room.*

By the time the first signs of snow arrived, Munich was everything to me, and I couldn't imagine ever leaving.

Anna, Joel, and the boys would be spending a few weeks in Oman over the holidays at a resort and they asked me to come along but I wanted to stay put and soak up an authentic German Christmas. Before they left, Anna had enthusiastically insisted that I spend some of my leisure time at the Roman Baths that were not too far from our apartment. The huge art nouveau building was the project of the emperor of Bavaria in 1903, and inside was a spectacular pair of swimming pools, along with a huge stone-sauna facility, rooms of varying temperatures, and a Roman steam bath.

The ceiling of the pool rooms was incredible, a mosaic masterpiece. Water was fed into the pool by two huge stone lion heads at either end of the pool. I swam laps and then waded around in the shallow end along with a few locals. It wasn't crowded on this weekday afternoon.

After swimming I made my way over to the giant set of double doors that led to the steam rooms. A little German lady was mopping the tile floor, and from the corner where she stood she called out, "*Nein!*" causing me to halt in my tracks.

She muttered something else that I couldn't understand so I asked her to clarify. "*Entschuldigung?*" (Excuse me?)

"Ohne die Badehosen!" she stated firmly, standing upright and leaning on her mop.

I picked apart the words in my head.

Ohne . . . without . . .

die . . . the . . .

Badehosen . . . Hmmm . . .

Bade . . . bath or *pool,*

Hosen . . . like *Hose, pants . . .*

Oh, no! I gasped.

I can't wear my swim trunks in here!

I stood there, frozen to the spot, the German lady standing in the corner, acting as the gatekeeper to the sauna, ensuring that all who entered did so with their bare bottoms. I didn't know what to do! Anteater Willy had never been forced to be displayed in all of his unassuming glory!

"Fuck it," I said to myself, feeling defeated but also surprisingly daring. I stood in the corridor, held my breath, pulled down my trunks, and then, one foot before the other, took them off. I could feel Anteater Willy recoiling from the chill in the air, and wished he would just man up and not retreat into hiding. I had no idea of what the German lady was looking at; I had turned away from her and put my hand on the brass handle of the steam room door, pulling it open.

A huge billowing cloud of hot white steam gushed out of the door as I stepped into the blinding fog. It was dark in the steam room, but as the moisture evened out and my eyes adjusted to the darkness, I spotted an ornate iron rack of hooks where a bunch of swimming trunks and bikini tops hung. I obligingly hung mine up as if it had been some form of ritualistic initiation. To my right was the door to the first sauna room—turning the dark corner and entering the room, I was greeted by the light of the full afternoon sun, streaming through the narrow windows that ran along the top perimeter of the walls. Tiered stone seating projected out from the walls and there were about a dozen other men and women sitting on various levels, buck naked. I nervously found a space on a lower tier and took a seat. Everyone else seemed relaxed and I noticed a couple of men and women glance at me and smile welcomingly.

Completely overwhelmed, I wondered whether I should cross my legs, keep them together, or slightly apart. All around me were bodies of varying ages, sitting in various states of both tautness and droopiness. Penises, breasts, nipples, pubic hair in every imaginable frame of vision . . . I closed my eyes to calm down. When I opened them again, nothing had changed. I wondered whether anyone was looking at me, and then, startlingly, after about four minutes, everything was fine. Penises, breasts, nipples, and pubic hair. *So what?* a voice in my head asked. *Yeah, so what?* another voice asked. I relaxed, and closed my eyes, but this time it wasn't to escape—this time, it was simply to take in the warm and soothing feeling of the steam permeating my skin, muscles, and bones.

I made my way over to the next room, even hotter than the first, and again was surrounded by naked Germans. And now, I wasn't scared, embarrassed, or concerned. I was proud of myself for shedding my inhibitions. With my eyes closed, I breathed deeply and fought the urge to be overwhelmed by the heat of the room.

I moved on to the third and final part of the sauna—a huge round room with a vaulted stone ceiling, and in its center a round pool full of ice-cold water. The naked Germans were jumping right in, wading around for a few minutes, and then climbing out. It looked like a scene from some ancient Roman ritual. I made my way to the edge of the pool—I was ready to become completely part of this culture, this city. Anteater Willy was also ready. I jumped in, the ice-cold water hitting me to the core. I shivered spastically for a few seconds, and then laughed, feeling completely awake, rejuvenated.

I probably could have survived in Munich without learning German. But I wanted to assimilate. I wanted to reach out and make friends, but only with Germans. I wanted to learn the language, and I wanted to feel like I belonged here.

It started with my neighbors in the building—the chic young couple that lived next door to me on the third floor, two architects, Nicola and Claus. We'd make small talk whenever we'd meet in the hallway or happened to be taking the elevator up together.

Then they invited me over for dinner one night—Claus made risotto—and eventually it became a regular thing. When the weather was warm enough, we'd sit out on their little balcony and get tipsy at the end of the day, overlooking the courtyard. Nicola was stunningly beautiful. She had long, brown hair, bright blue eyes, a sharp nose, and delicate pink lips. She'd go out of her way to speak to me slowly, constantly double-checking that I understood what she said in German. She was an avid reader and we often talked about books—one night I surprised her with a copy of *Schiffbruch mit Tiger* (the German translation of *Life of Pi*). She loved it, and after reading it, she joined me in mourning the loss of the movie role one night over a bottle of wine. "You would have been peeerfect," she said, shaking her head and looking down into her glass.

"Yeah," I sighed. "I know."

Whenever we got together, I insisted that we speak German so I could practice, and she obliged. It suited Claus, who absolutely refused to speak English and would occasionally chuckle to himself when I said something incorrectly. I'd turn to him and ask what the mistake was, and he'd continue to laugh, waving it off with a light *"Nein, nein,"* insisting that all was fine. Nicola would chime in, "He is taking great pleasure in hearing your attempts in German . . . don't pay any attention to him, Ra-sheeve." I loved the way she would say my name; it sounded German. The loneliness I had felt for the first few months after I arrived started to fade away.

Munich opened up to me. I had my favorite coffee shop, which I'd frequent between my weekday errands. Every Friday, I'd treat myself to a breakfast of *Weisswurst* with a pretzel. Herr Gritzner had his regular tunings at Meister Hoppe, the bike guy that had proven his skills when I broke a pedal once. And my haircuts took place at Vidal Sassoon, right in the heart of the old part of town—I had been getting my hair cut at Vidal Sassoon in Toronto for years, and it had proven to be the one place that wouldn't butcher my wild mane; they had a specific way of cutting hair that was the same in every country. On the day of my first Munich haircut, I was assigned to the assistant manager, a twenty-eight-year-old named Anne (pronounced *Ann-eh*). I was surprised with how well she spoke English.

"I spent a year on an exchange program in the US," she explained, running a fine-toothed comb through my wet curls, "In a tiny town in Utah, with a Mormon family."

We laughed about the ignorance of the Americans she was surrounded by, who, upon learning she was German, sprouted questions like, "Are you related to Hitler?" or "If you're German, why aren't you fat and blonde?"

Anne wasn't even halfway through the haircut before I had learned quite a bit about her. She was engaged and would be married at the end of the summer. She was a vegetarian, and this too was a sore spot with her Mormon host family, who used to bring the Bible up to her and cite passages where it stated that it was wrong to abstain from consuming flesh.

"Funny," I said, "in my religion, being a vegetarian is kind of essential."

I asked her if, being vegetarian, she had ever eaten Tamil food, which was, essentially, vegan. She didn't even know what "Tamil" was, so as she neared the end of the haircut and after I had filled her in about the details of the cooking I had grown up with, I made a bold choice and asked if she and her fiancé would like to come over for dinner one night.

A couple weeks later, when Anna, Joel, and the boys were away for the weekend, Claus, Nicola, Anne, and her beau, Florian, were over on the family's swanky rooftop patio overlooking the city for a traditional Tamil dinner. I persuaded them to eat with their hands and everyone seemed to be enjoying the new experience and food, except Claus, who, when I asked what he thought, responded with a smile-filled, "Ver-ry in-ter-esting . . ." in English.

Anne got married to Florian at the end of the summer, and I was invited to the reception—a small, understated evening in a cool, little bar at the center of town. I got dressed up in my black, three-piece suit and pedaled Herr Gritzner through the market as the bells clamored and the vendors were closing up shop, waving to me as I whizzed by.

The early evening sky was pink and orange, and I heard the cheerful sounds of a celebratory crowd as I turned the corner onto the cobbled street. Everyone was impeccably dressed, and I made it just in time to join the others in welcoming the new bride and groom. Anne was wearing a knee-length lace cocktail dress, simple and classy, and winked to me as she made her way through the crowd.

Servers walked around with Aperol spritzers and Hugos—Munich's two signature cocktails. I reached out for my favorite—the Hugo, a refreshing concoction of fresh mint leaves, Prosecco, elderflower syrup, and a dash of soda water served over ice with a lime wedge. A group of friends whom I didn't know gathered around the piano and boisterously belted out some traditional Bavarian songs. Two girls in black dresses had their arms around each other, and swayed side to side as a young guy in a blue suit, with waves of golden blond hair, sat at the piano and effortlessly played along to everything they sang, without any sheet music in front of him. I couldn't take my eyes off his fingers dancing over the keys.

I knew about half the people in the room, and the evening was spent dipping in and out of lively conversations in both German and English.

I was sitting by myself after the cake was cut, enjoying being the silent observer for a moment, when Anne came over and sat beside me on the caramel-colored leather bench.

"*Der Herr.*"

"*Die Dame.*"

"Your hair looks nice," she teased, looking up at my coiffed mane of black curls—it had been a while since I had gone in for a haircut, but one of the things she said regularly about her work was that her cuts had incredible longevity—they grew out well.

"*Danke.* It's all because of you."

"*Ich sage auch danke,*" Anne said in a phony formal tone—she knew I loved when the Germans said this, literally meaning, "I say also, thanks."

Anne was radiant—it was her night—and I told her how much it meant to me to be included.

"I am really happy you live here, Rajivski," she said, her head tilted to one side, looking me deep in the eyes. My German friends now unanimously used the name that Kate and Eric had ordained me with, many years before. It felt like a secret password, code for my inner circle of like-minded compatriots.

The music had transitioned from the old-world sound of the live trio at the piano to the speakers overhead, blaring out current pop tunes, administered by a hipster-type DJ spinning records in the corner.

It was loud and people were grooving to Lady Gaga. I pulled Anne onto the dance floor and we threw up our arms, busting out some moves as the Champagne flowed. People on the periphery were cheering us on and joining in and soon there was hardly any room to move. I wiggled around in place with both the familiar and new faces. Eventually, my surroundings became too hot for my three-piece suit.

In the quiet street, the night air was a relief. Herr Gritzner was lit up under the streetlamp where I'd parked him. I took my jacket off, loosened my tie, and then opened up the collar of my shirt in an effort to cool down.

I heard the door open behind me but didn't turn around to look.

"Anne tells me you are from Canada." It was the blond pianist, now standing beside me with a glass of Champagne in his hand.

"Yes, Toronto," I said, looking up at him. He was a little over six feet tall and his pale blue eyes were captivating, even before they lit up to my response.

"Ah, Toronto! I spent one year in Canada, for an exchange program— it's my favorite place in the world."

"Funny—*this* is my favorite place in the world," I countered.

"It is a great city," he admitted, nodding before extending his hand. "Anton." I shook it and couldn't help but feel slightly intimidated by what was, essentially, a flawless specimen of a face looking down at me, like one of those Norse gods from the locker room at U of T. A lock of his golden hair had just fallen to touch the side of his Anglo-Saxon nose, slender, with a bridge that resembled the finest of ski slopes. His chin looked like it had been chiseled out of marble by Michelangelo. The slightest hint of pale blond stubble was emerging from his jawline and his upper lip protruded out just slightly over the lower one.

"Rajiv. *Freut mich*," I said as I shook his hand, forcing myself to break away from staring into his eyes.

"*Rasheeve*," he echoed with his German accent, sweeping up the fallen lock of blond hair. "*Schön*. Does it mean something in . . . Indian?"

I tried not to laugh, but it just came out. *Indian*—there's no such language, but I wasn't about to correct him. "Well," I offered, "it's Sanskrit for 'king of life.'"

"Ah!" he exclaimed, "Then I am standing with royalty. It's an honor."

Everyone was jamming to Beyoncé when we rejoined the party, and as things calmed down, the waiters brought around shots of schnapps, signaling the end of the night. I gave Anne and Florian a huge hug and headed out to Herr Gritzner.

The blond pianist appeared in the pool of light where the bike and I were standing and asked what direction I was headed in. He was going my way, he said, so we'd walk together.

He was doing his master's in business administration at the University of Munich. The piano was a hobby of his. He had two sisters who lived with his parents in a small town about three hours north of the city. He played soccer on a small local team.

It was just past midnight—the streetlamps cast a warm glow over people sitting out on restaurant patios, or strolling around under the chestnut trees in pairs, and the lack of a breeze created a surreal stillness that made me feel like I was on the soundstage of some grand movie set. We passed through Odeonsplatz, the huge impressive open square that was surrounded on three sides by gigantic neo-classical buildings that looked out onto Ludwigstraße, the long straight avenue that featured a large, white triumphal arch. This was historically a site for parades and marches (one of Hitler's routes during the Third Reich). As I wheeled Herr Gritzner along, Anton walked beside me, looking down at the cobbles as I told him about my job as an au pair and briefly mentioned my endeavors as an actor.

Our conversation turned to Munich's past and somehow I was

getting a very intriguing history lesson from him about the city's line of Bavarian kings.

We were walking across an old stone bridge, over the Isar River, as the blond boy filled me in on the monarch who was primarily responsible for Munich's current beauty—"Crazy King Ludwig," as he was known, who was criticized in his day for frivolously blowing away his personal assets to build the squares, monuments, palaces, and castles that now draw millions of tourists to Bavaria every year. "He loved stories. He spent much time daydreaming.

"Your Walt Disney World," Anton said with a smirk, flitting his hand around as he searched for the right words. "This . . . Sleeping Beauty's castle . . . it is modeled directly after Ludwig's Neuschwanstein. Have you been there?" he asked, looking over at me as we walked.

"Last week, actually. It was incredible." I had taken Alexander and Sebastian out there on the train. "Didn't he die tragically?"

"*Ja*, he was found floating in the Starnberger Lake. They declared it was a suicide, but many believe he was murdered."

I looked over the bridge at the calm flow of the Isar below us. On the hottest days of the summer, I joined other locals and found relief swimming in the frigid water of the river, which flowed from the Alps.

"These *fairy tales*, they all have some darkness," the blond boy was looking up at the starry sky above us. "I would like to imagine that in his last moments, at least Ludwig was glad he did what he wanted during his lifetime."

A softly dinging bell warned us of a bike approaching from behind, and we moved out of its way as it sped by in a blur.

"You know what?" I asked.

"What?"

"I think it's time for another king."

"What?"

"Yes. *I* will become the next king of Munich. I mean, the triumphal arches, the squares, the palaces—they're all still here, aren't they? And the Germans unfortunately still have this stigma with the rest of the world. It's time we try to change all of that," I heard myself saying, unable to control myself, the words just falling out of my mouth. I went on, "And what better way to say to the world, '*Look, that's not who we are!*' than to have a little, brown King of Bavaria?"

"I like this idea," he said, nodding, then chuckling.

"Yes. I don't need any power; I'll just be a sort of figurehead. I was at the Nymphenburger Schloss just last week with the kids, and everything's in perfect condition, you know. They'll dust off all the carriages and crowns and bring them out for my coronation. And I'll walk along Ludwigstraße with a huge crowd behind me—"

"Yes," he interrupted, "and you must be accompanied by two real lions—the symbol of Bavaria!"

"Yeah!" I shouted, enthusiastically turning to him and grabbing his arm, envisioning myself robed in ermine as we concocted this scheme together. "And I'll have the perfect name." I stopped walking with the bike and stood in my tracks, lifting my chin up into the air, signaling my announcement, "*König Rajivski*," and as an afterthought, added, "*Der Dunkel.*" King Rajivski. The Dark One.

He burst out laughing loudly, keeling over with his forearm across his stomach. "*Wie lustig!*" How fun!

We continued to concoct the plan, adding bits of important detail.

"*Du spinnst* . . ." Anton muttered, smirking again (you're crazy). "You just might have what it takes to become the king."

We had reached the other side of the bridge, and as I headed straight ahead and Anton made a move to turn right; we discovered this was the point where our paths separated to our respective apartments.

"*Ihre Hoheit*," he softly declared (*Your Highness*), "It was really fun . . . to meet you."

The blond boy was looking down at me once again, and once more I was locked into the gaze of his pale blue eyes. And this time, I didn't want to look away.

I leaned in, and he leaned down to me, and as we closed our eyes, our lips met.

Fireworks. Trumpets. Confetti.

If there was ever a single moment in my life where the world seemed to stand completely still, just for me, it was now, and in that moment I had no future and no past, only the present.

"I don't want to say 'bye to you," I said.

"I don't want you to say goodbye," he whispered down to me.

I could feel my heart thumping around in my chest, going a mile a minute as we walked in silence, he leading the way back to his apartment.

This wasn't a surprise to me—I always knew I liked guys, but I just wasn't allowed to. And now, as I walked with the blond boy, I asked myself who wasn't allowing it—Ma? Hollywood? Yann Martel, Ang Lee, or Avy Kaufman? No. No one had ever said no, and even if they had, when had I ever listened to anyone else anyway? No, it was *I* who had not allowed it. I had tried so hard to become something I thought I wanted to be, and it didn't work. Kissing this boy, without thinking at all, broke the spell.

We passed church after church while we walked; it seemed like there was one on every street corner, and if it wasn't a church it was a random crucifix tucked into a corner or anchored to a wall. And then it dawned on me, and I understood why Munich had helped me. It had become the place of my redemption—not at all religiously, looking up to something else and praying I would be forgiven; this was an internal redemption that only I could grant myself. I think, inherently, I had wondered whether I had been burned so badly that I'd never take a chance again, never gamble, never dive right in without thinking. But here, unexpectedly, I had learned that my quest had the opposite effect. At the end of my year of mourning the loss of Pi, I had moved on, and I had realized that I could do anything, try anything, and not be afraid of falling flat on my face, because I now knew how important it was to have simply tried. That realization was my salvation.

With one hand, the beautiful blond boy took over steering Herr Gritzner, and with the other he took my hand. We reached his tiny apartment, on a little side street, beside an old metalworking studio in a building with a giant copper crown on the top of it, green with verdigris.

I had never allowed myself to touch, or be touched. But now, the blond boy was leading me up the six flights of steps to his little place. He unbuttoned my vest, pulled off my tie, and then gently took off my shirt, letting it fall to the ground.

I closed my eyes as his fingers slowly ran over my shoulders and down my back. I took off his shirt, revealing his pale, smooth, alabaster skin. We lay down on the bed, facing each other, and now I was at peace. It was okay to follow my heart; it was okay to let go.

From: yann_martel1963@yahoo.com
To: rajivsca@yahoo.ca
Subject: Today
Date: Tue, 19 Jul 2011 23:52:30

Hello, Rajiv.

Happy Birthday to you too. Theo has had a good birthday, not that he quite understands the concept of time and its arbitrary divisions. He certainly enjoyed the party and the presents.

Your books arrived. We knew of them but didn't have copies, so they're perfect gifts. Theo will love them. Thank you very much for sending them, and wrapped in such lovely gift wrap paper—and for the lovely note.

Glad to hear that you've made the best of the Pi saga.

Hope Munich continues to treat you well.

Cheers,

Yann

20.

B Y THE END OF MY YEAR in Munich, I was back to my old self; scheming up plans to celebrate my coronation as the unexpected, yet highly glorified new King of Bavaria was a sign that things had returned to the way they once were. It was hard saying goodbye to Anna, Joel, and the boys, to my German friends, to the smiling faces of the market vendors who had patiently taught me to speak their native tongue, but even harder was saying goodbye to my storybook world of cobblestone streets and church spires. I couldn't bear to take Herr Gritzner away from his homeland, so Anne and Florian offered to store him in their cellar with the promise that he would wait there for me, as they were certain that I would one day return.

I moved back to Toronto and fell in with a group of bohemian types—sculptors, painters, and musicians who whizzed around the city on skateboards or doubled on one bike. One of them was looking for a roommate and together we rented a crumbling, dingy two-bedroom apartment in The Annex, just north of the downtown core. It was an old building from the twenties and despite the cracked bathtub, the leaky toilet, and the splintering floorboards, there was a charm to the place, a Peter Parker type of roughing it out.

I had no idea of what I was going to do to make money, but

somehow things came together. The one thing I knew was that I was only going to do something that made me happy.

I was picking up some of my calligraphy supplies from The Paper Place, on Queen Street West, when I noticed a "hiring" sign by the cash register. I began my shifts there later that week, making minimum wage. The manager and I were restocking the shelves one morning, and when she found out I did calligraphy, she came up with an idea for an in-store event—customers could buy cards in the store and I would customize greetings on them with my script. It was a big success, a giant line of people waiting outside the store as I wrote on card after card.

A high-end wedding planner in super high heels happened to swing by for the event—she gushed over my work and then chastised me for wasting my time selling paper when I could be running my own calligraphy business. Then she insisted that I set up a table at the ritzy wedding show she put on once a year, sweetening the deal by offering it to me free of charge.

So I set up a small business, which I named Letters In Ink, and my little booth at the wedding show was crammed with people all day.

Work came in slowly at first—brides and event planners would hire me to address the envelopes of their invitations by hand, and I'd sit at my desk for hours, under my old framed painting from Maine, quietly transcribing hundreds of names and addresses with pen and ink. I managed to make enough money to get by, meekly.

My heavily tattooed friend, Christian, and I were riding our bikes around one summer afternoon and we stopped into Café Pamenar, in Kensington Market, for a coffee. We were sitting out on the patio, soaking up the sun, and Christian began brainstorming how I could further capitalize on my artistic abilities. We started bouncing around ideas. The first few weren't great, but then he spotted the A-frame chalkboard on the sidewalk, advertising the specials at the café.

"Look at how bad that writing is. You *knoooow* . . ." his eyes widened as he sat upright, "—you should rewrite that shitty board. Heck, do it all over the city, and put your website on the bottom . . . I bet people would start hiring you for calligraphy work."

It was a good idea. "Go over and do it right now," Christian whispered, "that guy behind he counter is the owner."

"How much?" the soft-spoken young Persian guy asked.

"How about another round of coffees . . ." I proposed, happy to just try it out.

He handed me some chalk and then headed off to the espresso machine to make our lattes. I spent about half an hour on his chalkboard, kneeling on the sidewalk as I carefully laid down various fonts to spell out the message he wanted. People stopped occasionally and watched what I was doing, and every so often someone would shout out, "Nice work, man . . ."

I spent the following few weeks on the prowl, riding my bike around the city all day in the scorching summer sun—and every chalkboard I spotted would be a target for advertising my wares. I stuck to plain white chalk, staying away from color; I loved how the simple black-and-white pairing showcased my skills in design and composition in an elegant and classic way.

I always offered to do those sidewalk chalkboards for free initially, and the owners or managers wouldn't hesitate at all to grant me permission. I'd leave my card behind as they stood in front of the boards, thankful for what they hadn't expected. Then, as I rode away, I would pray to the Blessed Virgin for rain. And when that happened, they'd call me back, telling me that they had noticed an actual influx of business after the chalkboard was fancified. And this time, they'd pay me for the work.

By the end of July, a popular city blog had reached out for an interview and published a post entitled "Who's Writing All Those Fancy Restaurant Chalkboards?" I was thrilled—being featured on blog.to was akin to being endorsed by Toronto itself.

The jobs started trickling in. Restaurants wanted me to come inside and do the large boards that featured their wine lists or weekly specials. Following close behind came commissions from advertising agencies, whose employees had spotted my work in the bars, cafés, and restaurants they frequented for lunch or dinner. And this was where the real money was.

My cellphone rang one afternoon—I wasn't familiar with the number. The woman introduced herself as the executive art buyer at a major advertising firm.

"We've seen your chalkboards all over the city," she explained, "and we'd love to see what you'd come up with for this project." My chalk work would be photographed and then printed to make posters and spreads that would appear on billboards, bus stops, and subway trains. It was a big job, and I was to submit a quote to them, outlining my fee for the entire project. I was thrilled when I got a call from the head of the agency saying I had the job. She told me I'd hear from the art director shortly—and when he called, we went over the details.

"So I'm thinking you'll do the artwork in green and white chalk, maybe some red . . ." the art director said over the phone.

"I only work in white chalk," I noted, reminding him that I had stated that early on, in the quote I had submitted.

They were adamant about using color and I was certain that I wouldn't be happy with the result if I gave in. So I stood my ground and they curtly told me this would mean we couldn't work together.

That was fine with me. I lost out on seven thousand dollars, but I really, truly wasn't disappointed. I was almost completely broke, gathering twenty-dollar bills one at a time from my sidewalk boards, and collecting them in my sock drawer to save up for rent, but I had told myself when I decided to turn my beloved childhood hobby into a business that I was never going to do any work that might compromise my passion for my craft. Saying no to that job reassured me that I would not be swayed by money.

Two weeks later, another big job request came in—a huge chalk wall in the headquarters of a big food company. The art director asked for a quote, and I sent one off to her along with a rough sketch of what I proposed for their wall. We had a conversation on the phone and she mentioned some elements she wanted in color. I didn't hesitate at all to tell her I'd only work in white chalk and then there was a brief moment of silence before she said, "Well, I've looked through your website, and I love everything I see, so that's fine. If you want to do it all in white, I trust you."

Seven days of hard work climbing ladders and drawing all over their walls ended with a check in the mail for more money than I had ever made in a week. I thought my wild dreams had covered every possible scheme and scenario that my potential career paths could lead to, but this? This was above and beyond anything I had ever imagined—being paid so much to lay out lettering on a wall with a stick of ordinary white chalk.

I met up with a group of friends to celebrate—a place that I had done some elaborate chalk work in. The owner, very happy with my work, generously sent out a bunch of plates we hadn't ordered and gave us a complimentary bottle of wine. We topped that off with a few rounds of cocktails and by the time we headed out onto King Street, we were laughing and slurring our words.

It was a swelteringly hot summer night as our motley crew made our way uptown on our bikes at about 2 a.m.

We were riding along a side street, when I noticed the high fence that protected a huge outdoor swimming pool.

"Let's go swimming!" I yelled out, and without any discussion or negotiations, our entire group veered off the road and quietly took our bikes around to a dark side of the fence, looking all around, making sure there were no cop cars heading down Dundas Street. Then we stumbled up and over the fence, safely landing on the cement paving that surrounded the pool.

Then the lot of us stripped off all our clothes and cannonballed into the water. Another group of people appeared on the other side of the fence, drunk and cheerful, watching us with wonder.

"What's happenin'?!" one of the guys asked.

"We're swimming!" I yelled back. Christian shushed me, and I told him not to shush me.

I was free. I could swim. The cold, blue water was now liquid light—and I basked in it. I opened my eyes under the surface and could just make out another body in the water, illuminated in a blue-green hue from a streetlamp nearby. I bobbed up and Christian's head was out of the water, too.

"We-have-comp-aneeeee!" Christian said in a singsongy way, grinning.

The group of four had climbed over and were standing at the edge of the pool, ripping off their clothes and jumping in.

"Woooooooo!" one of them shouted, making a loud splash.

I went back under the water, closed my eyes, and pulled a large breast stroke, propelling myself forward, then allowing myself to just glide slowly, loving the comfort in this world of water. I kicked to the surface, flipped over onto my back, and looked up at the city sky, floating.

❦

It was Christmas. Ma had asked me to come home, but that day I just felt like being alone. I had a big calligraphy commission that I was working on at my desk, and decided to spend the day in my apartment, taking advantage of the rarity of having it all to myself. The daylight streamed in through the plate-glass window of my bedroom, and I silently wrote one name and address after another in brown ink on thick ivory-colored stock, making my way through the pile of three hundred envelopes.

Snow started falling around 4 p.m., and the light was fading. My eyes felt strained, so after reheating some leftovers and eating my dinner alone in my tiny kitchen, I wondered what I should do next.

Then it hit me—the perfect thing to do this Christmas night, alone. I pulled on the long woolen Bavarian hunting cloak I had bought just before leaving Munich, and eased my bike out into the snow, still falling lightly on this quiet winter night.

I rode down through the Annex, going slow, gliding over potential patches of ice covered in snow, safely arriving at my destination—the Varsity Cinemas in the Manulife Centre on Bloor Street.

"One ticket, please, for *Life of Pi*," I said to the scrawny Jewish kid working the register.

The theater was almost completely full, but I squeezed into a row at the back.

As the house lights went down, the hair on my arms stood up, then the iconic sound of marching drums and trumpets blared out the fanfare accompanying the golden 20th Century Fox logo lighting up the screen.

A blank, black screen. Silence. A few coughs from the audience.

The black screen fades into full color, a giraffe nestles into lush greenery and blooming flowers.

"*Kanné . . .*" a woman's voice sings out in Tamil—"precious one"— and like a blow straight to my heart, my mouth contorted and tears quickly fell from my eyes.

"*Kannmanniyé* (the jewel of my eye) . . . *kannurangai* (close your eyes) . . . *poové* . . . (little flower) . . ."

Could anyone in the room understand the words of this Tamil lullaby? To everyone else, it was just music, but I knew the meaning of every single word. *Was she singing just for me?*

The opening credits unfolded as zoo animals flew in and out of the frame, and the lady continued her song.

"*Mayilo . . . thooghai mayilo?*" (Is it a peacock, or the fan of the peacock's plumage?)

"An Ang Lee film" fades in and out of focus over the scene.

"*Kuyilo . . . koovum kuyilo?*" (Is it a bird, or the song from the bird?)

"Casting by Avy Kaufman, CSA"

"*Imaiyo . . . Imaiyin kanavo?*" (Are they the eyelids? Or the dream within the eyelids?)

"Based on the novel by Yann Martel"

Pondicherry appears on screen in all its glory: bullock carts, whitewashed French colonial buildings, and ladies selling flower garlands on the roadside. A woman lays out an intricate *kolam* on the ground in front of her house with rice flour.

Then, a Tamil boy sits among his peers—dozens of uniformed schoolboys with coffee-colored skin and jet-black hair, surrounded by the plastered walls of Petit Séminaire. Within these walls, the boy's name takes on a new meaning.

On a whim, by chance, the young boy finds himself in a quiet church where he is first introduced to a man on a cross. Compelled by the story, he thanks Vishnu, for introducing him to Jesus.

Later, with no warning, the boy is thrown into the deep end of a swimming pool, gasping and struggling before eventually becoming one with the water.

Life continues in peaceful, repetitive sequence.

Curious, eager, and his body trembling with anxiousness, in the dark and confined backrooms of a zoo pavilion, the boy comes face to face with a huge, live tiger.

The spectacle of Hindu ritual lights up the screen, Vishnu swathed in jewels and flowers as Brahmin priests chant sacred Sanskrit prayers, their eyes rolling back into their heads in a trancelike state.

An unexpected turn in events and the boy is cast adrift.

Tragedy. Loss. Despair.

All alone, he struggles; he waits; he hopes; with little control over the world around him.

He survives, and looking back at his journey, shaping it into a story, enables him to go on.

It was nearly midnight and the roads were empty as I stepped out onto the street, where snow continued to fall lightly. I turned up the collar of the wool cloak and lifted the hood onto my head, before getting back onto my bike and making my way westward. Riding along Bloor, I passed the Royal Ontario Museum and a few U of T buildings, before making a right turn onto Huron Street—the 1920s brick houses and huge maple trees that lined this quiet residential side street always made for a peaceful bike ride back to my apartment. Twinkling Christmas lights coupled with the streetlamps overhead casting a warm glow onto the freshly fallen snow blanketing the asphalt. All that disturbed the perfect sheet of white was the single track that my bike left behind.

A gust of wind laden with snow blew toward me, sending my cape billowing behind the bike as I rode. All around me, people were tucked away in their houses on Christmas night and I, alone, would make my way home, put my bike away, take off my snow-covered cloak, and, happily, go to bed.

Hello, Rajiv.

I thought I'd get a few ideas down on the page, so
to speak.

Life of Pi is a story about the choices we make
in life. One set of tragic facts—the sinking of a
ship and the dying of a boy's entire family—yields,
to the reader, two stories, one with animals, one
without. The reader is invited to choose between
those stories; that is, to choose how to make sense
of what happened to Pi. In your story, the tragedy
at its heart is that an aspiring actor did not get
the role he yearned with all his heart to play. That
thwarted artistic aspiration has symbolic resonance,
because nearly everyone has artistic aspirations.
Everyone at one point or another in their lives,
aspired to be an actor/novelist/poet/singer/etc. Or,
at the very least, everyone has had aspirations that
have been thwarted, whether to get a promotion, get
a girl/boy, and so on. What to make of failure will
speak to everyone, because it's what life is about.
We learn through failure and defeat; we discover
who we are through failure and defeat. In that
sense, victory comes through defeat. That's what
Christianity is about, as an aside: victory through

defeat. Christ enters Jerusalem as the Messiah who will free the Jewish people, and then he is strung up on a cross like a common criminal. What kind of Messiah is that? Well, as the apostle Paul figured it, it was part of the plan. Christ would win—our hearts, our souls, our faith—through his crucifixion. I would suggest that you make your book about an actor who discovers who he is through his quest to play a role and his failure to get it. There's a quote from Joyce that I will paraphrase poorly here but it goes along the lines of: whatever the roles we play in our lives—son, father, brother, employer, lover, student, teacher, and so on—we are always aspiring to play ourselves. That might be the theme of your book, of someone finding out who he is in trying to play someone else.

I'm sorry for being so general, but I hope you get my drift. You have, I believe, a very good, original, touching story at hand. It just needs work. And by the way, I have no problems with you using (and abusing) Life of Pi all you want. You're just using my novel to tell your own story, and I'm fine with that.

Talk/write/keep in touch.

Om shanti.

Yann

From: steve@stevencallahan.net

To: rajivsca@yahoo.ca

Subject: Peach Pie

Date: Wed, 15 Jun 2015 11:55:34

Rajiv,

Always a joy to have you around. Thanks for making
the effort to come up and inspire us and bring so
much energy into our lives, not to mention the meals
you made and that peach pie. You didn't oversell
that. It was fantastic. I found it very interesting
when you were talking about your chalkboard biz and
how you would never accept working in color. I was
thinking of how we approach work very differently.
I'm much more of a slut, but it seems that our
opposite approaches have served each of us well.
I've done so many things in my life that I would
have rather not done, but if I wanted to eat . . .
if I was a chalkboard artist and somebody had
asked me to work in color, I might have been very
uncomfortable undertaking it, but generally, I
have always tried to accept a client's desires and
tried then to get into it by looking at it as a
learning opportunity, a way to push myself into a
new direction. Since I was a kid, I wanted to taste
a wide variety of experiences, become conversant
in as wide a range of subjects as possible, try to
take a Renaissance approach to work, and I have
been very fortunate to have "been around," done
everything from working in a chemical plant and a
shipyard, to books and film. It's allowed me/us to
meet a lot of people, been a lot of places, see a

lot more of life than I could have imagined. And since I was always piecing together a "career," and basically struggling to make ends meet for much of my adult life, I just would accept whatever task walked in the door. What's been nice in more recent years is that I have been able to actually turn more stuff down, but I don't regret most of what I did. I did have some rather unproductive, in fact anti-productive associations and projects, and it would be nice to be able to recoup all that time and investment, but I guess waste is a substantive part of life, and from compost, gardens grow.

I guess, the bottom line is, you can't do it wrong. As we have discussed so often, you try to be captain of your own ship, but even captains know that they must work with the wind and waves, and we do not control our path but only guide it. And every so often, someone is cast upon the rocks or finds himself in a strange, sometimes hostile, land. It really doesn't matter. It's what you do with it, how you face it, where you go from there that matters, that defines who you are.

Anyway, enough drivel for now.

Take care,

S

List of Illustrations:

1. Araucana Hen

2. The King Edward Hotel, Toronto

3. Padakam Necklace

4. Nataraja (The Dancing Shiva)

5. Crucifix, Petit Seminaire

6. Nepenthes, Tropical Pitcher Plant

7. Antique Spinning Wheel, 1838

8. Antique Stoneware Butter Churn

9. Sarcophagus of Djedmaatesankh, Toronto

10. Clawfoot Bathtub

11. Border Leicester Ewe

12. Red Figure Vase - Eurykleia washes Odysseus' feet

13. Dorado Fish

14. Crustaceans

15. Antique Wooden Hat Maker's head form

16. 72nd Street Subway Entrance, New York City

17.

18. Apis Mellifera (Honey Bee)

19. Coat of Arms, King Ludwig II of Bavaria

20. Gritzner Bicycle, German, 1920s

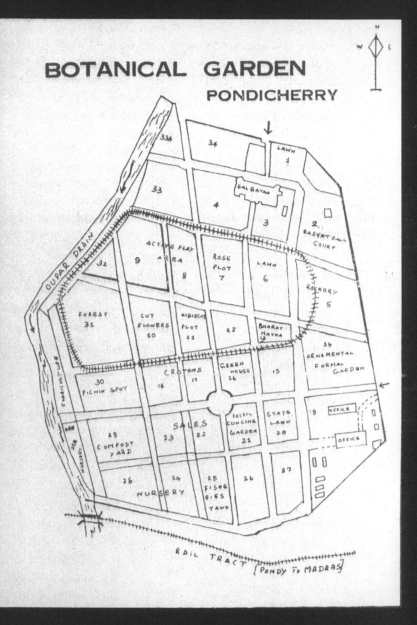

you young devil —

Sassy broad. eh ?!
OLD broad. + yeah sassy @ times.
Right! Yeah. I noticed everything — Audrey, my lavender
sachet — hand made. my tape. your
pic. Thank you. thank you! I will
treasure all. Sachet will go st.
away into my scarf drawer.

Thought you might get a
kick out of hearing the police giving
condolences to my swimming kids
for Audrey's passing — 2 days
after fine. "The rumours of my
death are grossley exaggerated!"
                Groseley
                Grosley
                SHIT

Thank you!!!
                Love. hugs + x's
                Audrey.

9 February 2009

Dear Rajiv Pi,

I'm sorry that you couldn't take all of this on the plane with you, and we've tried to wrap each item with delicacy and care; however, if any bottle is broken, please let us know and I'll order you another from NYC.

I can't tell you how much I enjoyed our weekend with you. I also can't believe that I've found a friend who loves much of the films, operas, and books that speak to me. Babette's Feast was beautifully filmed in Sweden. What Babette did to show her appreciation and love to the sisters who gave her a meaningful new life touched me deeply. Babette gave them something that all her money could buy, but no money in the world could buy what she gave and received in return. The gifts that she and the sisters gave were divine, which made the food and the meal divine.

I am so happy and overjoyed that you have come into our lives and graced us with your beauty and creations.

I've asked our great universe to help Ang produce the Life of Pi and choose the only person we know who is heart and soul Piscine Molitor Patel.

Love & Blessings,

Kathy

What can I say but to repeat K's sentiments? "... this is the beginning of a beautiful friendship." (is that close to the end of Casa Blanca?)

Joy & fulfillment on all your voyages

ANG LEE

1992 - Tui Shou ✓ (Pushing Hands)
1993 - Xi Yan ✓ (Wedding Banquet) ✓
94 ✓ Yin shi nan nu (Eat Drink Man Woman) ✓ Media Commons
                                              DVD 751 511
95 - Sense + Sensibility ✓
97 - The Ice Storm ✓   Media Commons
                               DVD   752 433
99 - Ride with the Devil
2000 - Crouching Tiger / Hidden Dragon   Media Commons
                                         DVD 752 142
2001 - Chosen
2003 - Hulk
2005 ✓ Brokeback Mountain ✓
2007 ✓ Se, jie (Lust, Caution)
2009 - Taking Woodstock (Post-production)
2009 - A Little Game (announced)

Watch ✓ "The Virgin Spring" by Ingmar Bergman! ✓
        St. Miller - Due Feb 26. DVD GR 225
                                          585.

524

Wednesday:
Taxi to NY   35.
(Photo for Dr. Baker) (314)
Taxi to Eves   7.
Metro Card $8
Utrecht Art Store $46
Lunch   3
Coffee   2
Cream   2
Nax Arms   30
Groceries   17.50
                      $150.50

Thursday:
Quicksilver Tshirt - $26
Metrocard $8.05
Lunch (Taco) $3
Top Shop man - Shirt jacket $144
Groceries $20 $29
                      $212

Friday
Groceries at Fairstand 15.80
Ice Cream   9.50
                      24.00

May 4th, 2009

Dear Avy: *my name's* ~~Rajiv Smith~~ [handwritten]

A few years ago, while filming 'Mean Girls', I was told by a
producer that I "was Pi" after he'd finished reading 'Life of Pi'.

I hadn't yet read the book but picked it up one day after lunch
and read it on set.

It was almost scary reading about what was, essentially, an uncanny
description of myself! The main character was not only South Indian
like me, but ethnically Tamil, as I am. He was, "small, slim, no
more than 5'5 with a pleasing coffee-coloured complexion" ~~&~~ dead on.
He ended up moving to Scarborough - a suburb of Toronto - the same
one that I live in. He grew up in a zoo where his father was the
manager and I, believe it or not, live right behind the Metro Toronto
Zoo, one of the leading zoos in the world. I hear elephants, lions
and peacocks on most summer evenings and grew up frequenting the zoo.
But the strangest similarity between us was something that gave me
goosebumps; When I was a little boy I was fascinated with religion.
Not only did I freakishly love going to the temple with my parents
to take part in whatever Hindu festival was going on but I also felt
completely at home in the Catholic church that I accompanied my Irish
Aunt-Brigid to.

I didn't really know what to make of the book when I'd
finished it, so I read it again, in 2 days. And then I fell completely in love with it. I was so excited to learn, shortly after-
wards that it was being made into a movie.

THAT is what brings me to this letter. I realize that Ang
Lee is still working on his latest movie and that 'Pi' is ~~still~~
~~being developed~~, but after speaking to Robin Cook last week (who
cast me in 'Mean Girls' and suggested I contact you personally), I
am writing to ask if you would take a meeting with me this summer. I
will be in New York for a few days in July and would love to tell you
in person why I think I'm so right for this role.

I have been tracking this project for the past few years and while
waiting with anticipation for it to get off the ground I've done
a whole load of research. I spent a month in India, in Pondicherry-
the little town ~~where~~ the story takes place - at the boy's school,
'Petit Seminaire' observing how the local kids walked, spoke, played,
etc. I've read ~~a bunch~~ of books by survivors of shipwrecks who ~~were~~
lost at sea ~~and have~~ spent quite a bit of time with the tiger at the
zoo here (with ~~it's~~ handler right beside me!!).

I've asked my agent to send down a pic and res and will have
my manager contact your office to inquire about a meeting, closer to
July. I look forward to, hopefully, meeting you, and remain, most sincerely, *Rajiv.*

[handwritten margin notes: "Dad discovered so many subtle metaphors, symbols and" / "just down the road" / "re word this" / "behind the scenes, with keepers at the zoo too." / "This movie & has become so close to my heart and I hope you'll give me the opportunity to..." / "will wait in anticipation"]

D	E	
Citronen	Lemons	(10)
Limonen	Limes	(10)
Avocados	Avocados	(4)
Apfeln	Apples	(Gala - 3kg)
Ananas	Pineapple	(3)
Ghurken	Cucumbers	(3)
Carotten	Carrots	(1 bund)
Stangenseleri	Celery	(1 bund)
Broccoli (Rota Bait)	Brocolli	(1 piece/stück)
Rote Beet	Beetroot	(3)
Zucchini	Zuchini	(1)
Ingwer	Ginger	(1 stück)
Brunnenkress	Watercress	(1 bund)
Spinat	Spinach	(500g)
Peterseli	Parsley	(1 bund)
alfalfa	alfalfa	
Fenchel	Fennel	(1 stück)
Minz	Mint	(1 bund)
Gelb paprika	Yellow pepper	(1)
Brombeeren	Blackberries	(2)
Blaubeeren	Blueberries	(2)
Himbeeren	Raspberries	(2)
Orangen	Oranges	

Master fruit + veg list

München

Munich 11-19-2011

Dear Raj,
in den letzten Monaten bist
du für mich ein ganz toller Freund
geworden mit einer beeindruckenden
Persöolichkeit und warmherzigen
Charakter. Ich bin sehr froh, dass
wir uns kennen gelernt haben damals
mit den lustigen Musikanten in den
Fünf Höfen (Remember? They looked
scary, eh?). Ich habe unsere
Treffen immer sehr genossen an
der Isar, bei dir oder am
Viktualienmarkt. Ich hoffe, wir wollen
uns nächstes Jahr wieder sehen
und wieder so tolle und
tiefgründige Gespräche haben wie
in 2011.

© BOKELBERG

For you personally,
I wish you all the best
from the bottom of my
heart and that all your
wishes and dreams become
your fascinating future!

To Raj Surendra

Toronto, Ontario, Canada

München, Bayern, Deutschland

Tour Anton

Rajiv Surendra in his favorite article of clothing, a gansey knitted for him by Marion Brocklehurst of the Flamborough Marine knitting collective in North England.

A gansey is a distinctive British woolen sweater originally designed to provide protection for fishermen from wind and water, with origins dating back some three hundred years.

Using a tightly spun worsted wool, the intricately patterned gansey is knitted in one piece on five steel needles. The patterning to back and front and, in some cases, the upper part of the sleeve provides an extra layer of protection, while the combination of seamless construction, fine wool, and tight knitting produces a garment that is both wind- and waterproof.

Many of the stitch motifs used to decorate the ganseys were inspired by the everyday objects in the lives of fishing families. Some of the best-known designs represent ropes, nets, anchors, and herringbone. Other patterns are based on the weather, echoing the shapes made by waves, hail, or flashes of lightning.

At a time when the loss of a boat was a frequent occurrence, the patterning of a gansey made it possible for fishing families to recognize which fishing village, or even which family, the wearer came from. Deliberate mistakes or the wearer's initials were often incorporated into the design in order to help to identify a body recovered from the sea. As the gansey was traditionally worn tight-fitting and close to the skin, and with no seams to come apart, it could not be washed off in the water.

By tradition, the sweaters worn by all kinds of seafarers, whether they be fishermen, naval, or retired sea salts, are navy blue—a color reflecting the sea and sky. Before the advent of synthetic dyes in the late nineteenth century, blue was obtained by using natural indigo, a plant extract imported from India.